D1860268

A Wife from the Forbidden Land

A Wife from the Forbidden Land

The scene of this Story is laid in the Tibetan Capital during the lifetime of the predecessor of the present Dalai Lama

Archer Philip Crouch

GYAN

Published by

Gyan Publishing House
5, Ansari Road
Daryaganj, New Delhi-110002
Phone: 011-47034999, 9811692060
E-mail: books@gyanbooks.com

Distribution Network
gyanbooks.com
India, USA, Canada, UK, Australia, France

© Publisher

All rights reserved. No part of this work may be reproduced, stored, adapted, or transmitted in any form or by any means, electronic, mechanical, photocopying, micro-filming, recording or otherwise, or translated in any language, without the prior written permission of the copyright owner and the publisher.

ISBN : 978-81-212-9650-2 (PB)
First Published, 1907

2nd Impression 2023

Printed at: Gyan Press, Delhi.

The book is sold subject to the condition that it shall not, by way of trade or otherwise, be lent, resold, hired out, or otherwise circulated without the prior publisher's written consent.

A WIFE FROM THE FORBIDDEN LAND
Author: Archer Philip Crouch

A Wife from the Forbidden Land

(The scene of this story is laid in the Tibetan Capital during the lifetime of the predecessor of the present Dalai Lama)

By

Archer Philip Crouch

A WIFE FROM THE FORBIDDEN LAND

CHAPTER I

THE setting sun shone in Philip Harwood's face, as he rode through the eastern gate of Ta-chien-lu, a town in the Chinese province of Se-chuan, lying on the borders of Tibet. Though mounted on a sorry mule, and followed on foot by two ragged coolies, who stumbled wearily along with his baggage on their backs, the rider bore himself as proudly as if he were the governor of the province, attended by a brilliant suite. His Chinese costume and pigtail secured him from the annoyance to which a European in European clothes is subjected in an inland Chinese town. Indeed, the dark eyes, in conjunction with a complexion deeply tanned by travel, might have caused the casual observer to take him for an Asiatic.

The young man rode at a walk along the main street, looking with interest at the scene before him. For here met and commingled two very different nations, the frail offspring of the effete Chinese civilization rubbing shoulders with the robust, uncultured children of Tibet. Philip Harwood paid no attention to the long line of Chinese coolies forming a tea caravan, which he had overtaken at the gate. Man is the cheapest beast of burden in China, and for several weeks past during Philip's journey through the country he had been familiarized with the fragile figures of the coolies, emaciated by constant opium smoking, carrying, for the magnificent sum of three-halfpence a day, a framework supporting from three to four hundred pounds of brick tea. What excited his curiosity was the stream that met him coming from the western gate of the town—Tibetans with their fearless bearing and hearty laughter, the richer class attired in gorgeous silks, and mounted on gaily caparisoned horses, the poorer driving that shaggy, uncouth, grunting transport animal of Tibet, the yak.

The contrast between the Chinese and Tibetan women was still more striking than between the men. It seemed almost incredible that these handsome women with their fine figures and graceful carriage should belong to the same racial stock as their crippled and sickly Chinese sisters. After the timid and oppressed air of the latter, it was refreshing to see the frank smiling countenances of the Tibetan women, and to listen to their musical laughter. Even the style of the buildings attested the dissimilarity between the two nations—an insignificant Chinese tea-house made of wood being overshadowed by a massive Tibetan structure two or three stories high, and built of brick or stone.

But the fading light warned Philip Harwood that he must be seeking shelter for the night, and reining in his mule, he inquired of a Chinaman who stood at the door of a small store which was the best inn in the town. The man pointed to a Chinese building a little further down on the opposite side of the street. It proved to be a fairly large structure, with a courtyard full of mules and yaks. Philip leapt lightly off his animal, and giving the bridle to his coolies, who had already deposited their burdens on the ground, marched towards the door, calling loudly for the landlord.

A Wife from the Forbidden Land

A typical Chinese innkeeper made his appearance, and asked querulously what the traveller wanted.

"I require accommodation for myself and stabling for my mule," he replied curtly.

The innkeeper's manner changed at once. With his travel-stained clothes, jaded mule, and meagre retinue he had taken Philip for a customer to whom there was no occasion to be more than ordinarily civil. But the young man's words—he spoke excellent Chinese—and the authoritative tones in which he uttered them, produced an immediate effect.

"My house and stables are very full, Your Excellency," said the innkeeper, bowing obsequiously, "but a room shall be made ready for you, and your animal shall find a stall."

"That is well," replied Philip, appeased by the man's deferential attitude. "The next question is, what can you give me to eat? The air of Ta-chien-lu is very appetizing, and I am ready for my dinner. Is that your eating-room?"

Philip advanced towards the open door of an apartment from which the welcome odour of savoury viands came, but the innkeeper quickly placed himself in front of him. "The meal is not yet prepared, Your Excellency!" he exclaimed.

"Then my sense of smell deceives me!" answered Philip. "At any rate, you can empty the room of these noisy fellows whom I hear within it, and I will wait there till the dinner is cooked."

The innkeeper could not conceal his agitation. "If there were none but Chinese in the room, the heaven-born would only have to show himself at the door for each of them to make his obeisance and withdraw. But there are several braggart Tibetans within, who, having no acquaintance with the usages of civilized society, might refuse to leave the room."

Philip turned and took the mule's reins from his coolie's hands. "If you were the only innkeeper in Ta-chien-lu," he said, "I should make short work of your objections. As it is, there are plenty of houses for me to choose from, where I shall doubtless be better served."

During the course of this conversation a small crowd had collected at the entrance to the inn. When they saw that the traveller who had spoken so dictatorially intended to depart, they looked at the landlord to see what he would do, the Tibetans laughing at his predicament, while the Chinese wondered that he had shown so bold a front. The innkeeper himself was fully aware of the danger of inconveniencing a person of such evident authority, and had recourse to abject entreaty.

"If the father of the poor," he said, "would only have a little patience, I will cause the room to be emptied for him, and he shall dine alone as becomes his rank. But I must first find some apartment where the present occupants may take their food. Will that suit His Excellency?"

But Philip would not submit to any compromise, and without replying to the innkeeper was on the point of remounting his mule when some one stepped out of the crowd and laid his hand upon the young man's arm. Although attired in Chinese costume like himself, Philip recognized a European in the tall middle-aged man who stood before him.

"Do not seek another inn," he said in English. "I can offer you a plain bed and simple fare, if you will be content with that?"

"It is very kind of you, sir," replied Philip, "and your offer is too tempting to refuse. But may I ask whom I have the pleasure of addressing?"

"John Ransome, of the English mission here."

A Wife from the Forbidden Land

A smile of pleasure lit up the young man's face, and he held out his hand.

" I might have guessed that you were Mr. Ransome," he said. " Your brother missionaries in the districts I have traversed gave me your name, but I was ashamed to impose myself upon you till I had at any rate tried to get quarters elsewhere. I am an Englishman, as you no doubt saw at once, and my name is Harwood—Philip Harwood."

Mr. Ransome had already given the reins of Philip's mule to an attendant, and was leading the way down a side street in the direction of his house. He seemed to be on the best of terms with both Chinese and Tibetans, the latter being especially cordial in their manner towards him. As for the children, they ran up and struggled with each other for the possession of his hand, walking along at his side in supreme content when they had secured the coveted prize.

But the English mission was soon reached, and Mr. Ransome led his guest into a spacious courtyard. Here the mule was stabled, and Philip paid off his coolies with a liberality which left them speechless. The missionary then conducted him into the house. Philip had spent the last eight or ten nights in small wayside Chinese inns, and only those who are acquainted with them can realize his satisfaction in entering once more a European's home.

" I will take you to your room," said Mr. Ransome. " By the time you have washed and changed, supper will be ready."

The bedroom, though scantily furnished, delighted Philip's heart, the narrow bed with its spotless sheets, the clean floor, and the trim washstand in one corner. But he was too hungry to spend any time inspecting his new quarters, and in twenty minutes he descended again to the room to which he had been first conducted. He found Mr. Ransome awaiting him, the table laid for two.

A Wife from the Forbidden Land

"I live by myself, you see!" the missionary said, motioning Philip to a seat. "It is now nearly three years since I had a fellow-worker here."

"You must find it lonely," observed Philip, as a Chinese servant entered with an appetizing soup.

"I missed my late companion at first, of course, but I have so much to occupy my thoughts that there is no time to be lonely."

If Philip could judge of the extent of Mr. Ransome's acquaintances by the numbers whom he greeted in the short journey from the inn to the mission, it was evident that the missionary would have few opportunities for loneliness. The young man did full justice to the plain but well-cooked food which was set before him, and then they drew their chairs up to the fire, for the thermometer, which had been over 70° in the sun that day, now stood at freezing-point. To Philip's delight, his host produced a box of cheroots.

"It is one of the few luxuries I allow myself," said Mr. Ransome, taking one of them himself. "A cheroot is company for a solitary man. As I smoke it I go over again my day's work, or make projects for the future."

"Your cheroots are in good condition, considering they have gone a sea voyage," said Philip.

"On the contrary, they have never been afloat!" Mr. Ransome answered.

"You do not mean to say that they are of Chinese growth and manufacture?"

"No; they are Indian, and come to me overland through Bhamo. Some friends in India send them to me regularly."

"Have you lived in India then?" inquired Philip.

"I was for several years chaplain to an English regiment there."

"You do not see many Englishmen here, I suppose?"

"No Englishman but myself lives in Ta-chien-lu, but one

occasionally passes through the town. Tibet possesses a great attraction for explorers, and the majority of them are English. A man called Grigson was here a few months ago."

"I do not remember having heard the name," said Philip.

Mr. Ransome smiled. "The world does not hear of every one who tries to explore Tibet. Some men have sense enough not to make their failures public."

"Was Grigson's attempt a failure then?" asked Philip.

"It was. I saw him before he entered Tibet, and I hardly recognized him on his return. He had talked to me of his plans. Travellers had hitherto failed to reach Lhasa for two reasons, he said; the huge caravans of the rich excited the suspicion of the Lamas; the funds of the poor gave out before half the journey was accomplished. Grigson had plenty of money, but he intended to take only one attendant, and his caravan would be restricted to the wants of two persons."

"And his plan did not succeed?"

"He forgot to reckon with the brigands, or 'Chukpas,' as they are called. One of their number, who offered his services as a guide, led him into a narrow defile, both sides of which swarmed with his fellows. A single repeating rifle was useless against such odds. Grigson's attendant was shot through the heart, and he himself, stunned by a stone, was left for dead, while all his property was stolen. It is wonderful how he ever got back alive. One evening after dark a wretched being in rags and half dead through want of food knocked at the mission gate, and I found that Grigson had returned."

Philip was silent, pulling hard at his cheroot, and gazing into the glowing embers of the wood fire in front of him. Then he looked up and said—

"Well, I hope to have better luck than Grigson."

This observation did not take Mr. Ransome by surprise. He had already taken stock of his visitor, and divined the object of his journey. In fact, so certain did he feel of the truth of his conjecture, that he related the story of Grigson for the young man's special benefit. He now laid his hand on Philip's arm and said—

"I can tell you how to make certain, my young friend, of having better luck than Grigson."

"How?" asked Philip.

"By not making the attempt at all."

Philip smiled.

"I do not wish to insure against failure in that way," he answered. "I would sooner fail than not make the attempt at all. I have been working for the last five years in my uncle's office in Shanghai, but the occupation was distasteful to me. I lost my father when a child, and my mother has just died, leaving me a little money. As my only sister is married, I am free from all ties, and nobody would be any the worse if my venture ended fatally."

"Heaven forbid!" exclaimed Mr. Ransome. "But are you specially qualified for the task you wish to undertake?"

"In Shanghai I made the acquaintance of a Tibetan Lama. He gave me lessons in his native language, and I can speak it very fairly."

"You will find it useful in your travels. As to the customs and manners of the inhabitants, if you know them as well as you know the Chinese, you will do well. I could not help overhearing your conversation with the innkeeper this afternoon," he added, smiling.

"I suppose you thought I took matters with a high hand," said Philip, in some embarrassment at Mr. Ransome's avowal.

"If you had been a special envoy from the Emperor himself you could hardly have demanded more. Not that you were wrong in doing so. In fact, it is the only way to deal with the Chinese. The reverse of the scriptural text holds good with them. 'He that exalteth himself' obtains the first place, while 'he that humbleth himself' is still further degraded by them. But I must warn you that the same rule is not applicable in Tibet, or at any rate amongst the eastern population."

"Do you know Eastern Tibet?" asked Philip.

"I spent some time in the English mission at Batang, but we were driven out of the country many years ago. Though it has always been my dream to go back there, I am afraid its realization is as far off now as on the day of our expulsion. The opposition to us came not from the laity, but from the Lamas."

"I can understand that neither the Tibetans nor the Chinese approve of Europeans settling in Tibet. They point to India, where state after state has been absorbed by us when once it has given free entry to Englishmen. But that is no reason why travellers should not be allowed to pass through Tibet. I should be content if I could visit Lhasa for a couple of weeks, or even a couple of days."

"That has been the object of scores of travellers since Huc and Gabet were driven from the city in 1845. Yet not a single man has succeeded, though many capable and experienced explorers have made the attempt."

"Their failure only strengthens my resolve to try my luck. At the worst I shall but meet with the same rebuff which fell to the lot of my betters."

Mr. Ransome regarded the young man with an approving gaze.

"Now that I have said all I can, though without effect, to dissuade you from your project, I cannot help letting you know that I admire your determination. Youth, after all, is half the battle. If I were young again, and did not have this mission in my charge, I should be inclined to join you, In any case, you may be sure that I will do all I can to help you in your venture."

CHAPTER II

IN spite of the unaccustomed luxury of a European bed, Philip Harwood rose with the sun on the following morning. He found Mr. Ransome already about, and they sat down to breakfast together. In connexion with the young man's approaching expedition, the question as to the most suitable beast of burden with which to cross the barren and storm-swept regions of Tibet came under discussion. In Western Tibet sheep are much in favour for purposes of transport. They carry twenty-eight pounds each, and are docile and easily managed. Their chief recommendation lies in the fact that fodder need not be taken for them, as they pick up sufficient sustenance from the scanty patches of withered grass to be found by the roadside. Not only can they do without supplies of carried food, but they form a walking larder for their master, from which he can supply himself with meat whenever he requires it. In Western Tibet caravans of two or even three thousand sheep are not at all uncommon. The chief objection to this animal is its slow rate of progress, eight miles per day being a usual average.

Horses are seldom used for transport purposes on account of their initial cost, and because they break down more readily under the scanty food and other hardships incidental to travelling in Tibet. The camel makes a useful beast of burden in districts like the Tsaidam, where fresh water is scarce. This cumbersome animal, however, is apt to get footsore on stony ground, and its great bulk and weight are unsuitable to the narrow paths cut in the face of cliffs, of which the main roads in Tibet very often consist. Mules and donkeys prove very good baggage carriers, but the best animal for the work is the indigenous yak. The yak seems positively to revel in the cold of its native country, picks up its sustenance along the track it travels, and can carry two hundredweight of baggage. No animal can equal it in rocky and precipitous paths, and the only thing that can be said against it is its inability to cover level ground as quickly as a mule or donkey.

The question of transport was fully discussed by Mr. Ransome and Philip, and it was eventually decided that the caravan should consist of mules alone for the first part of the journey. Mules were plentiful in Ta-chien-lu, while the yaks were comparatively scarce and dear. The town stands only eight thousand feet above the sea, whereas in a natural state the yak is seldom found below twelve thousand feet. The climate of Ta-chien-lu, in consequence, does not agree with these animals, and they are seldom to be found there in large quantities.

The next question Philip had to consider was the hire of muleteers, as well as a personal attendant for himself. This last matter proved to be a difficult one. Mr. Ransome knew several Chinese who would make good servants, but were not strong enough to withstand the rigours of the Tibetan climate. Nor could their courage be relied upon. They had before them the fear of punishment at the hands of the Chinese Amban in Lhasa for accompanying a European in a forbidden journey in Tibet. Thus a Tibetan servant was regarded as almost indispensable, and Mr. Ransome promised to do his best to procure one.

Meanwhile Philip Harwood set out by himself for a walk through the town. The bright sun and the crisp morning air seemed to enliven even that most patient of drudges, the Chinese tea coolie, while the Tibetan mule drivers were full of merry laughter. The young man made his way to the market, as he would soon have to get in a stock of provisions for the journey, and he wished to gain an idea of the price of articles, and the best places for purchasing them. Here he was once more struck by the contrast between the two races, which meet in Ta-chien-lu—the weakly Chinaman, with his stall full of useless trinkets, side by side with the burly Tibetan, who confined his stock of goods to tea, parched barley, and other necessaries of existence.

Philip Harwood was returning along the main street in the direction of the English mission, when loud cries and the cracking of whips assailed his ears. A person unacquainted with the customs of the country might have thought that a street riot had broken out, and that the sharp cracks were the reports of the firearms used by the combatants. Philip, however, knew better, and stepped into a doorway to avoid the hustling of the foot passengers, which takes place when a mandarin of high rank passes through the streets.

On came the procession, a group of attendants in front carrying long whips, which they cracked incessantly and used upon any one who failed to get out of their way in time. Philip had often witnessed in the native quarters of Shanghai this evidence of the despotic tyranny of the governing over the governed classes. But what he had not seen was the effect of such a display upon a partially alien population, and he looked round to observe the bearing of the Tibetans in its presence.

It so happened that a small Tibetan caravan of perhaps a dozen pack mules had been brought to a standstill by the approaching procession close to where Philip stood. The drivers were for the most part typical specimens of the muleteer class, with long, unkempt hair, sheepskin garments looped up by a belt at the waist, and cloth top-boots soled with untanned hide. This was, apparently, the first visit of some of them to a Chinese town, and as they drew their animals as close as possible to the sides of the street, so as to leave plenty of room for the approaching mandarin, their gaze was fixed in boundless admiration on the imposing retinue which preceded him. Their leader, the head muleteer, a fine fellow with a good-humoured expression of countenance, had evidently been in Ta-chien-lu before, and acted as cicerone to his fellows.

"See what fine clothes these Chinese servants have," Philip heard him saying to them. "And what splendid horses! It would be hard to equal them even in Lhasa. Here comes the mandarin's litter. Look! Even the Grand Lama's palanquin is not more gorgeous!"

Philip was amused at the man's language, and glanced at the cause of all the hubbub. Leaning back amongst the cushions with a scowl upon his face sat the mandarin, who was the central figure in this royal progress. The plain red button in his cap told Philip that he belonged to the highest order of mandarins, while the peacock's feather which he wore showed that he had received a special token of the Emperor's regard. Yet his face made it plain enough that his high position had not been won by merit. The dull, heavy eyes, the puffy cheeks, and sensuous mouth pointed to the probability that his promotion, as is too frequently the case in China, had been bought step by step with money and not with honest work.

Philip was turning away with disgust from the contemplation of the mandarin's repulsive features, when the lash of a whip aimed at a small child, who was obtruding too far into the street, missed its object and fell with full force on the flanks of the mule which was held by the leader of the Tibetan caravan. In an instant the animal, a powerful, ill-tempered beast, began to plunge and kick, and, backing out into the centre of the street in spite of all the efforts of its driver, rattled its heels against the palanquin of the mighty mandarin himself. This high official, his face becoming pale with fear, half rose in his seat, and seemed about to get out on the further side, when his attendants dragged away the offending mule, while the holders of the whips lashed the driver unmercifully.

As soon as the mandarin felt sure that he was safe, he stopped his bearers, in order to witness the beating of the muleteer, by whose negligence the accident was supposed to have happened.

" Flog him well," he exclaimed, leaning out of his palanquin, and watching the operation with evident enjoyment. But the muleteer was so taken by surprise that he did not utter a protest against the blows which were rained upon him. Indeed, considering the thick sheepskin coat he wore, it was doubtful if he felt them. The mandarin, suspecting this to be the case, grew angry and cried out—

" Strip him bare to the back, and beat him with the split bamboo. I will teach these clumsy Tibetans to show more respect to those who are in authority over them ! "

The man's sheepskin was instantly torn off his shoulders, and bare to the waist he was thrown face foremost on the ground, being held in that position till a man came up with the split bamboo. The first stroke on the muleteer's bare flesh laid open two parallel cuts across his shoulders, and the second added another pair. But the third stroke never took effect, for while the bamboo was still in mid-air the striker was hurled backwards by a blow between the eyes from Philip's fist.

For a brief space there fell upon the crowd an awed hush at this public flouting of the mandarin's authority, and then the Tibetan muleteers, realizing that a blow had been struck on behalf of their comrade, raised a cry, and lifted him from the ground, standing guard round him with threatening looks towards his aggressors. The Chinese mandarin, much incensed by the rescue of his victim, was on the point of ordering his recapture, when he caught sight of the lowering expression of his defenders.

"The man has had enough," he said to his attendants. "He will not easily forget his lesson. The Tibetans are, for the most part, a law-abiding people, and do not often require chastisement. But it is a different matter when one of my own race raises his hand against those in authority over him. Was it not a Chinaman who struck the wielder of the bamboo? If so, let him be arrested."

Philip stood his ground, keeping his eyes on the unfortunate attendants, who did not venture to approach him.

"Your Excellency's attendants seem to be in no hurry to carry out their orders," the young man remarked, when no one stirred. "But I must put Your Excellency right on one point. As you no doubt now perceive, it was not a Chinaman who struck your servant. Although for convenience I wear the national garb, I am an Englishman, and I defy you to arrest me!"

The mandarin flushed beneath his sallow skin, and his dull eye burnt with rage. He would doubtless have persisted in his order had not the Tibetan portion of the crowd gathered round the Englishman, with looks which plainly said he should not be taken without a struggle. The mandarin was once more foiled. In a white heat, and almost inarticulate with rage, he exclaimed—

"The Chinese are always courteous to foreigners, and a mandarin should set an example to others in this respect. In deference to the great nation to which you belong, I will take no notice of your recent conduct, but I warn you that your actions may not always be so readily condoned," and the mandarin, bidding his bearers move on, leant back among the cushions with a look of sullen anger in his eyes.

Philip Harwood, in no way impressed by this speech, was turning once more in the direction of the mission, when the muleteer he had befriended placed himself in front of him and made him a low obeisance.

" The peling " (foreigner) " has saved my life," the man began in grateful accents. " These great mandarins often flog a man to death, and no one is brave enough to interfere. But in my case the peling has taken the risk, and he may yet be made to suffer for it. How can I repay him ? "

" By resuming your journey and getting well as soon as possible," answered Philip. " Your master must make allowances for you, as with those wounds you will not be fit for work for several days."

" I have no master ! " answered the Tibetan. " I was engaged to bring this caravan to Ta-chien-lu, and as soon as I have been paid for it I shall be free. Does the peling want a muleteer ? "

Philip would certainly require muleteers. This fellow was of rough exterior, but he looked an honest man and spoke like one.

" Yes, I shall want some muleteers," said Philip. " Go and settle with your present employer, and if by to-morrow morning you are still of the same way of thinking, come to the English mission at eight o'clock, and I will consider the matter."

A gratified smile illumined the Tibetan's countenance, and, bowing low once more, he answered—

" The peling will find that I do not so readily change my mind, and will see me at the English mission at eight o'clock to-morrow morning."

The midday meal was already prepared when Philip returned, and he sat down to his host's table with an excellent appetite after his morning walk. Mr. Ransome told him that, so far, he had been unable to procure a suitable servant for him, but that he did not despair of doing so in the course of a day or two.

"That reminds me," he continued. "At the last house I visited with regard to the matter before returning home I heard that there was another European in the town."

"Another European!" repeated Philip, unpleasantly surprised. "I hope he has not come on the same quest as myself."

"I do not know his business. My informant, who came into the house as I was about to leave it, said he had just witnessed a most extraordinary scene, in which this European played a principal part."

Philip now understood who this other European must be, but before enlightening his host, he wished to hear how the affair was regarded by an inhabitant of the town. Accordingly he said—

"What was the scene to which the man referred?"

"It appears that the Governor of the neighbouring province of Yunnan, who is on a visit to the Governor of this province, was passing through the town this morning, when a restive mule nearly upset his palanquin. The unfortunate man in charge of the mule was seized at once, and the Governor of Yunnan, Tuen Fang by name, a very cruel mandarin, ordered him to be flogged with a split bamboo. After he had received a couple of strokes the European interfered, knocking down the man with the bamboo. Of course, Tuen Fang was in a great rage, and would have arrested him if he had dared."

"And there the matter ended?" queried Philip.

"For the time being, at any rate; but if this European proves to be an intending explorer of Tibet, you need not fear him as a rival. He has spoilt his chances at the very start."

Philip leant back in his chair with a smile.

"Let me know the worst, Mr. Ransome," he said, "for I was the offending foreigner."

"You!" exclaimed the missionary, dropping his knife and fork and staring at Philip in amazement. "With your knowledge of Chinese ways and habits, I could not have believed that you would have been so foolish. Of course I admire your courage in interfering in such a case, but it does more credit to your heart than to your head!"

"Why, what harm can come of it?"

"Every kind of harm. It is lucky for you that Tuen Fang is not the Chinese Amban (Ambassador) at Lhasa. If he were, and he discovered you travelling in Tibet, there would be little chance of your getting out of the country alive."

"Still, I do not regret having acted as I did, and, after all, Tuen Fang is not the Chinese Amban at Lhasa. Do you know anything of his history?"

"Only that he is reported to have wrung more money from the people in the form of bribes, or by sheer extortion, than any other mandarin in China. His avarice is only equalled by his cruelty."

"Then, as you say, it is a good thing for me that he is Governor of Yunnan instead of Chinese Amban at Lhasa. Let us drink to his confusion!"

It was impossible to quarrel with the young man's irresponsible light-heartedness, and Mr. Ransome humoured the toast which his guest proposed. Philip's spirits were evidently proof against the apprehensions which the missionary entertained on his behalf. After all, there was not much cause for alarm. They agreed that it would be best for Philip not to ask for a passport into Tibet from the

Chinese authorities, as it would almost certainly be refused, and in any case would not be granted for places west of Batang. Philip would have to travel as an Eastern Mongol, this portion of the Mongolian race bearing the most resemblance to Europeans. If arrested, it was very improbable that news of it would reach the Governor of Yunnan, or that, if it did, he would identify the suspect with the man who had flouted his authority in Ta-chien-lu.

The following morning, as Philip and Mr. Ransome were preparing to go out together and make purchases for the approaching expedition, the mission servant announced that there was some one at the door asking for the "peling."

"Perhaps it is a message from my friend the Governor of Ynnnan," said Philip, with a laugh. "Are we to admit the enemy, Mr. Ransome?"

The missionary looked grave, but told his servant to bring the man in. Instead, however, of an emissary from the autocratic Tuen Fang, there appeared, cap in hand, a poorly dressed Tibetan, whom Philip recognized at once as his friend the muleteer.

"This is the man," he explained to Mr. Ransome, "who was unfortunate enough to incur the mandarin's anger yesterday. He asked me if I wanted a muleteer, and I told him that he might call here to see me about it this morning. The matter had escaped my memory. Well, my man," he continued, addressing the Tibetan, "you are still, then, of the same mind as yesterday?"

"I am, Kushok!" replied the man, with a profound obeisance. "What I say one day I do not unsay the next. If the Kushok is in need of a muleteer, I pray that he will let me work for him."

"You have evidently made an impression on him," said Mr. Ransome to Philip. "He has already conferred on you a patent of nobility by addressing you as 'Kushok.' Though rough-looking, I think that he would serve you faithfully. I should engage him."

"What is your name?" asked Philip.

"Mantso," replied the Tibetan.

"Well, Mantso, I require muleteers for the caravan which I am taking into Tibet."

A pleased smile appeared on Mantso's good-natured countenance.

"Then the Kushok will engage me, for no one knows my native country better than I do. Where does the Kushok wish to go?"

"To Lhasa!"

The Tibetan's jolly face assumed as grave a look as it was capable of.

"It will be a difficult matter," he said.

"I shall travel as an Eastern Mongol, but of course I may be stopped and denounced as a peling, while you would be punished for bringing me into the country. Are you prepared to undergo the risk?"

"I will do anything to serve the Kushok."

Mantso was evidently sincere, and Philip no longer hesitated about engaging him. The terms, so much per day, were settled at once, and he was told to bring his personal property round to the mission, where he would stay till the caravan started.

"That man will make a good servant, I think," said Mr. Ransome when Mantso had withdrawn. "He may not be able to cook European dishes, but he is accustomed to caravan work and inured to the rigours of the climate. That is the kind of servant a traveller in Tibet requires."

CHAPTER III

NOW that a satisfactory servant had been obtained, preparations for the journey went on apace. Philip Harwood calculated that a dozen mules would carry all his baggage, including tent furniture and ammunition for three rifles. But in a country where travelling is beset with so many difficulties as in Tibet, it is necessary to have a much larger supply of animals than is actually required for the loads, and Philip decided to take twenty-five. These he purchased by twos and threes, so as not to raise the price by trying to get all of them at once. The first three he bought the day after engaging Mantso, and when they arrived at the mission yard he found the muleteer critically examining the eyes, teeth, and legs of the animals.

"What do you think of them, Mantso?" asked Philip, rather proud of his purchases.

Mantso ran his eye over them once more.

"That one yonder, Kushok," he said, pointing to the furthest one, "must be eighteen years old. It is six years since I drove him last, and he did but little work then."

"Of course, I could see he was an old mule," rejoined Philip, disillusioned by this candid criticism; "but a willing old mule is often better than a stubborn young one. The other two are all right, at any rate."

"I know them both, Kushok. The mare in the middle is so obstinate that if you give her only half the usual load she will not stir. As for the third, he is young indeed, but broken-winded, and we shall never get him up a mountain pass. But they are all three worth keeping, for the Kushok, of course, received them as presents."

Philip burst out laughing at Mantso's naïve deduction.

" On the contrary, Mantso, I bought them. How much do you think I paid for them ? "

Mantso scratched his head as he made a mental calculation.

" Perhaps the Kushok gave fifty rupees each for them ? "

" Can you buy them at that price ? "

" Not so cheap as that, Kushok ; but a good animal may be got for eighty or a hundred rupees."

" You can purchase three for me at that price then, Mantso."

The Tibetan muleteer was delighted with this commission, and set off at once to the market-place. His object in going there was not to buy mules, for he was acquainted with cheaper and better depots for this purpose, but he wished to discover the man who had taken advantage of his master. On arriving at the quarter where the mules were for sale, he made a short inspection and then approached a Chinese dealer who had the largest selection, and was on that account most likely to have obtained his master's custom.

" You have some beautiful animals here," began Mantso, noting at the same time that, though showy and well groomed, they were of little value for hard work.

The Chinaman, who was seated on the ground smoking a pipe, glanced up curiously, and seeing only a poor Tibetan before him, who could not mean business, disdained to make reply.

" I suppose they cost much money," continued Mantso, no whit repulsed by the Chinaman's silence.

" Much more than a half-starved, tsamba-eating Tibetan could afford to pay ! " replied the dealer.

"Ah, we poor Tibetans have no money, it is true, and we are as stupid as oxen. It is you clever Chinese who know how to get rich."

The Chinaman smiled graciously at this flattery, and took a contented pull at his pipe, as if it was no fault of his that he had been born so clever.

"Now, how much would that animal cost?" asked Mantso, pointing to the best mule of the lot. "Of course, I cannot afford to buy it, but a Tibetan muleteer knows a good animal when he sees it, and I am curious to hear the price."

"That mule is worth two hundred rupees," replied the Chinaman, taking his pipe out of his mouth for the first time since Mantso had accosted him.

"Only two hundred rupees!" exclaimed Mantso in well-feigned astonishment. "I should have thought it would have cost two hundred and fifty at least."

The dealer took a pull at his pipe.

"It is cheap, of course," he condescendingly admitted. "But I am not the man to haggle over the trifling sum of fifty rupees. There was a peling here this morning to whom I sold three mules almost as good as that one, and how much do you think he paid for them?"

This was the precise piece of information which Mantso desired to obtain, but no one would guess the fact from the self-possessed way in which he answered—

"Well, they would be worth, of course, nearly two hundred and fifty rupees apiece, but as you did not haggle over the bargain he bought them perhaps for only two hundred."

"I charged him no more than one hundred and fifty rupees," replied the Chinaman, with a touch of regret in his tone.

"That was little enough indeed. But what did the

peling look like? Was he tall, with brown eyes that shone like burnished steel?"

"He was tall, and his eyes, now that I come to think of it, resembled your description of them."

"Then it is my master. He wants three more mules, and he has sent me to select the best I can find. I shall recommend this one we were talking about, but I want two others."

The dealer laid down his pipe and jumped to his feet in order to obtain Mantso's approval for the other two mules. Although the roughly clad Tibetan had no money of his own, it seemed that he could influence those who were possessed of wealth, and he at once became a person of importance in the Chinaman's eyes.

"Here are two mules which I can safely recommend you," he said. "I bought them just after your master was here this morning. This one is strong and can carry a very heavy load. The other is of lighter build, and would make a good saddle animal."

"They are both valuable beasts, I can see at a glance. How much will you want for the three?"

"I could not sell them for less than two hundred rupees each."

"Is that the least you will take for them, and shall I be unable to get them cheaper anywhere else?"

The dealer for the first time had a suspicion that the Tibetan knew more about mules than he seemed to, but Mantso returned his critical glance with a look of such abounding innocence that the man replied—

"Nowhere in Ta-chien-lu will you get mules like these at so small a price."

"I am very grateful for all the information you have given me," said Mantso, "and I shall let you know what my master says. Farewell!"

The muleteer turned back in the direction he had come, but as soon as he was out of sight of the Chinese mule dealer he made his way toward one of the largest caravansaries in the town. As it was at Ta-chien-lu that the goods from Tibet were transferred from the back of Tibetan animals to the shoulders of Chinese coolies, the numbers of mules available for the return journey was usually considerable.

The caravansary which Mantso first visited was one where the richer class of travellers stayed. The mules here had evidently been well fed and had carried light loads. This was not a true test of an animal's capabilities, and the muleteer went on to a caravansary used by those who travelled not for pleasure, but for business. Here he met a small Tibetan trader, for whom he had acted on previous occasions as muleteer, and who had only reached Ta-chien-lu the previous day. With the primitive socialism of pastoral Tibet, where the poorest of a clan associates on equal terms with its chief, the trader welcomed him as a brother, and they sat down to tea together.

Like most Asiatics when intent on business, both Mantso and his host began by studiously avoiding it and exchanged gossip about their mutual friends and acquaintances. At length, after swallowing the sixth cup of tea, the muleteer said he must be going. The moment had come for the discussion of business, and the trader concluded that his guest had come to ask for employment. If so, he would be glad to have him, though it would not do to let the muleteer think so.

" You are, then, remaining at Ta-chien-lu for the present ? " the trader said.

"I don't yet know when we are to commence our journey."

The trader's countenance fell. It seemed that Mantso was already engaged.

"Is it a Lhasa merchant this time?" he asked.

"No; he is an Eastern Mongol."

"The Mongols are mean fellows. I hope you will make sure of your pay."

"I have no fears on that score. Indeed, my master is so free with his money that he charged me to buy three mules for him."

The trader had some mules for sale, as the goods with which he was returning would not require as many animals as the goods he brought from Tibet.

"Your master can take his choice of mine," he said, pointing to his baggage mules.

Mantso cast a careless glance in their direction.

"They look worn out and good for nothing but the crows."

"You know most of them, and have seen the loads they can take."

"Yes, but you have overworked them this last journey. My master will have nothing to do with broken-down animals."

The trader knew that Mantso wished to buy, or he would not take the trouble to decry them.

"He will find them reliable beasts," he answered.

"How much do you want for them?" asked Mantso.

"One hundred and twenty rupees apiece."

"Not one of them is worth as much as sixty."

Each of them having stated his price, they commenced the inevitable haggle for a mean, Mantso the while examining each animal in turn with the greatest minuteness. By the time that he had mentally selected the three animals which he thought to be the best, the price had reached ninety-five rupees on the trader's part. A further reduction of five rupees was necessary before the exact mean between the two outside prices had been reached. But the seller would not give way, and Mantso, gravely bidding him farewell, walked off towards the caravansary gates. He had barely reached them before the trader came running after him.

" It is well, Mantso. The mules shall be your master's for ninety rupees each. To no other person would I have sold them so cheap. But we are old friends, you and I, and shall doubtless work together again at no distant time. It is for this reason and no other I have consented to reduce the price so much."

Mantso hesitated. His pride as a bargainer urged him to wait till next day to see if the trader would still further abate the price. On the other hand, he longed to take back to his master three mules which cost sixty rupees apiece less than those he had bought himself. Accordingly he said—

" As a proof of the esteem in which I hold you, I will agree to the price you mention. Those are the three animals which I have chosen," he continued, pointing each one out in turn. " Send a boy with me, and I will get you the money before the sun goes down."

So much time had been spent in this transaction that it was four o'clock before Mantso set out from the caravansary with the three mules and the trader's boy. He went a little out of his way so as to pass the Chinese mule dealer in the market. As the muleteer walked some distance ahead of his purchases, the Chinaman did not think they belonged to him, and said—

" Well, has your master sent you for my mules ? "

" It is only a question of price," replied Mantso. " Is two hundred rupees the lowest figure you can take ? "

" I could not sell them any cheaper," said the man.

" Then I bid you good day," answered Mantso. " I have just bought three for ninety rupees each," and calling to the Tibetan boy to follow with the mules he marched off, much pleased with his revenge on the Chinaman who had taken advantage of his master.

On reaching the courtyard of the mission he brought Philip out to inspect his purchases. The young man was not favourably impressed by the animals, with their drooping heads and ill-kept coats.

"I do not think much of your selection, Mantso," he said.

"But they are excellent animals, Kushok," the muleteer protested. "I know each of them and the work he can do."

"They may have done good work in their time, but I don't think they will do any more. How much are they?"

"Ninety rupees apiece," replied Mantso, very proud of his bargain.

Philip looked at them again, and then said—

"They are cheap enough, at any rate. I will take them on your recommendation, and if they turn out badly it will be your fault."

Philip Harwood's stay in Ta-chien-lu was now drawing to a close. He had bought all his camp furniture and laid in his provisions. In excess of what would be required for consumption, he took a large quantity of brick tea, as throughout Tibet there is a steady demand for it, and in some parts it forms the only currency. For purposes of exchange he also provided himself with a number of Tibetan boots with cloth legs and raw-hide soles. Finally, he took four or five dozen "khatas," or ceremonial scarves, which are presented at every interview and sent with every letter in Tibet. To omit them in these cases is to commit a breach of good manners hardly excusable in the most ignorant nomad of the Chang.

As for the baggage animals, the three mules which Mantso bought picked up so rapidly, and gave promise of such good work, that Philip commissioned him to buy the remaining eighteen, a task which he performed to his master's complete satisfaction. Owing to the number of baggage animals being so much in excess of those required for the baggage, the loads had to be made small, so as to give each of them a share of work. In some instances, of course, the articles could not be thus broken up, but on the whole the loads were evenly distributed. Finally, it only remained to engage the other muleteers.

"How many will you require, Mantso?" Philip asked.

"Three men will suffice, Kushok."

"Do you think that you could get them?"

Mantso's eyes glistened with pleasure at this further proof of his master's confidence in his judgment.

"Assuredly, Kushok," he answered. "When will you want them?"

"I start in two days. Let them come before sunset to-morrow."

Mantso bowed with his accustomed profundity, and hastened away at once upon his errand. But he did not make his selection in haste, and returned that evening with no report to make to his master. The following day, however, at sunset, the muleteer marched into the mission yard with three men at his heels. Philip, who happened to be there, regarded them with some astonishment, for they looked almost as ill-kept as Mantso's mules. The muleteer, unabashed by their appearance, drew them up in a line and bade them make obeisance, which they did in the usual Tibetan fashion, with bowed backs, extended tongues, and their long hair hanging down on either side of their faces. When Mantso considered that this attitude of humility had been sufficiently prolonged, he ordered them to resume a vertical position and exclaimed—

"Come forward, Phendi!"

The right-hand man advanced a step or two, and Mantso,

eyeing him from head to foot, as if he were running over the good points of a mule, began—

" Phendi is a native of the central kingdom, and comes from the same village as myself. He is strong of limb and endures fatigue well. You will find him a good muleteer."

Phendi was a tall man of melancholy appearance, with a long, thin face, the cheeks of which were furrowed with deep lines from constant exposure to the dry, cold winds of his native country. He attempted to accompany Mantso's introduction of him with a smile, but beyond a slight gleam in his hollow eyes and a deepening of the wrinkles round his mouth no evidence of his sentiments became apparent.

" Your countryman does not look very happy at the prospect before him," said Philip. " I presume, however, that he knows his own mind. Who is the next man ? "

Phendi had already retired, and a fat man with quick, jerky action stepped forward in his place.

" This man's name is Esa," said Mantso. " He belongs to the Drupa tribes who live in tents. A sojourn in Ta-chien-lu has made him fat, but he will be thin enough after he has been on march for two or three weeks."

Esa bowed and grinned with much animation, and Philip thought that even if his fat remained he would, at any rate, perform his work with cheerfulness.

The last to be introduced was in general appearance the most presentable of the three, his features being more regular and his dress less slovenly than either of the other two. But he had a pair of shifty, restless eyes which Philip did not like at all. Mantso seemed to divine his master's thoughts, for he began in apologetic tones—

" This man, by name Jasi, is a half-caste Tibetan from

Ladak. I have never travelled with him, but am told that with a little supervision he makes a good muleteer."

Though far from liking the man's appearance, Philip had seen enough of life to know the futility of relying on first impressions, and he engaged all three men. They were shown the mules and the baggage, and told to have the animals loaded by daylight the next morning.

CHAPTER IV

WHEN Philip rose at dawn the following day he found the work of loading the animals all but completed. Five mules had been reserved for himself and his four men, while Mr. Ransome's mule had also been saddled, as he intended to ride a part of the way with his guest.

Having fortified himself against the fatigues of travel by making a good breakfast, Philip gave the order for the caravan to start. It was an interesting and at times diverting spectacle to watch. Phendi led the way on a mule of such small proportions that its rider's legs almost reached the ground. He held the reins in his left hand, while in the right he carried a prayer wheel, which he rotated unceasingly. With his long, unkempt hair, a far-away look in his eyes, and his Tibetan sword hanging transversely across the front of his body, he had the appearance of an Eastern Knight of La Mancha setting out on his famous travels.

Half a dozen pack mules followed him, and then came Esa, his ample proportions bulging out on either side far beyond the slender frame of the animal he rode. Esa was unable to twirl a prayer wheel, for under his right arm he carried a pole some twelve feet long. Philip could not understand what purpose this pole served, but learnt, on asking Mantso, that it was a lance for self-protection if attacked by robbers. Jasi carried no ostensible weapon, but the handle of an ugly knife peeped out beneath the folds of his garment.

As for Mantso, who brought up the rear, his desire to

maintain the gravity which became a chief muleteer contended with the gaiety of spirits natural to a Tibetan, so that only the thought of his responsible position prevented him from bursting into song and laughter. Philip Harwood and Mr. Ransome rode side by side not far behind him. It was a lovely morning. The sun, rising in the east over the flowery land of China on which they had turned their backs, shone upon the snow-capped mountains of Tibet in front, making them sparkle in its glorious light. Some twenty years previously Mr. Ransome had set out on such a morning from Ta-chien-lu, with the object of reaching Lhasa, and in spite of the ill-success which attended this effort the missionary felt his blood stirred once more within him by Philip's venture.

"If there was only some one who could take my place in Ta-chien-lu," he exclaimed, "I should like to have made in your company another attempt to gain the forbidden city."

"It is not too late," said Philip. "You could send for a substitute from one of your other stations."

Mr. Ransome shook his head.

"It would take six weeks or a couple of months to get any one even from the nearest station, and I could not leave the mission here unattended for that period."

If Mr. Ransome had not been working alone in Ta-chien-lu, Philip felt that he might perhaps have been able to persuade him to make the journey. Although no longer young, as testified by his iron-grey hair, the missionary had led so wholesome a life that he would probably have borne the fatigues of travel quite as well as his young friend. But it was useless to speculate about what might have been, and Philip made no further reference to the subject.

At length Mr. Ransome reined in his mule at a small stream which ran across the road.

"This little stream forms the boundary between China and Tibet," he said. "I have passed it once each way, but I will not cross again, unless I am called to take up my residence in the country."

"If I ever get to Lhasa," replied Philip jestingly, "I will see if I cannot persuade the authorities to give you an invitation."

"I will take the will for the deed," replied the missionary. "And now I must say good-bye. I can do no more than wish you success, and pray God to watch over you in your dangerous journey."

Philip bade adieu to his kind-hearted host with a feeling of genuine regret, and watched his retreating figure, a trifle less erect than usual, till he disappeared round a bend in the road. Then, resolutely facing the task before him, he plunged into the stream. A moment later he had crossed the Rubicon and entered the confines of the forbidden land.

After some two hours' march the caravan began to ascend a mountain pass. Under their light loads the animals made good progress, and clambered up the steep path at almost the same rate as along the level ground. Indeed, the saddle mules had more to carry than the pack mules, and for this reason, as well as to give the men some exercise, Philip ordered them to dismount, setting them the example by doing so himself.

In accordance with this order, Phendi stepped off his animal and strode up the hill without any change in his abstracted expression. Jasi, too, seemed in no way inconvenienced by the change in his method of progression; but Esa, who had armed himself against the cold of his native country with several layers of clothes, besides carrying a large assortment of household goods in the central fold of his outer garment, soon began to puff and blow with the exertion. The sojourn in Ta-chien-lu had made him fat and short of wind. In addition, his twelve-foot lance proved a great embarrassment to him. He was constantly running the point of it into the ground in front of him, or hitting with the other end the head of the mule which followed him. This mule would sometimes stop and back in order to avoid the blow, thus communicating the disturbance to the rest of the caravan, till poor Esa earned the abuse of each of his fellow-muleteers in turn.

At length they reached the top of the pass, where stood an "obo," or loose stone monument raised by grateful travellers to the presiding deity of the mountain. Each of the muleteers added a stone to the structure, and tied "lung-ta," or "wind horses," to the poles erected round it. These "lung-ta" were pieces of cotton or linen with the Buddhist sacred formula, "Om Mani padme hum," inscribed upon them. Kept in perpetual movement by the wind, they performed the same functions as prayer wheels turned by water, and were believed to accumulate merit for the donor. Phendi, who found himself unprovided with a legitimate "lung-ta," improvised a substitute by tearing a strip of cloth off the edge of his garment. This he attached to a pole with an air of quiet satisfaction, knowing that although it lacked the mystic formula, the wind horses of his companions, on which the words appeared, would in a few weeks be no more legible than his own.

Half-way down the descent, on the further side of the pass, Philip halted the caravan in a grassy nook, with a clear stream running by the side of it. The mules, with their loads still on them, were allowed to graze or rest according to their fancy, while the men prepared their midday meal. Jasi collected "argol," or animal droppings, rendered fit for fuel by the dry Tibetan air. Lighting the fire with a tinder-box and slow match, he suspended the kettle from a tripod he had already erected. Meanwhile Esa pounded up with a stone on the top of a boulder a piece of brick tea, the fragments of which he threw into the kettle as soon as the water boiled. After letting it stand for a few minutes, he poured the tea into a churn, added butter, and set the churn in motion.

When the mixture in the churn began to thicken it was considered ready for consumption, and the men sat down, each of them producing a wooden cup from the folds of his garment. The cup was filled from the churn and a bag of "tsamba" handed round. "Tsamba" is the staple article of diet in Tibet, being barley parched over a fire and then ground. Each man took a handful of the meal and added it to the churned tea, stirring the mixture with his fingers till it became thick enough to roll into a ball. The ball was then eaten, being washed down with fresh tea, on the surface of which floated a piece of butter, together with the broken twigs of which brick tea is chiefly composed. This meal, as may be imagined, did not prove very attractive to Philip, who was fortunately provided with food for several days from Mr. Ransome's stores.

After two hours' rest the march was resumed. The lower they descended the more beautiful the country became. Crops of barley, with a few patches of wheat, had ripened in the valley below. Thickets of wild gooseberry lined the path, which soon grew into a wide track enclosed by hedges, like an English country lane. The fields were divided by similar hedges, or by wattle fences, or by post and rails. Nothing he had seen in his journey through China reminded Philip so much of home as his first introduction to Eastern Tibet. Intoxicated with the keen mountain air and with the delight experienced by all travellers at being once more on the move after a few days' sojourn in one place, the young man became full of enthusiasm for his venture. The brook by the side of which he now rode gurgled musically as it fell over the boulders in its bed, while the jingling mule bells—every mule carries a bell in Tibet—maintained a pleasant accompaniment to it. Nowhere in the world could there be a more smiling, fertile country than that which lay before him. Surely, thought Philip, the dangers and discomforts of travelling in Tibet had been exaggerated by his predecessors.

That evening at sunset they arrived at a small village, where Philip intended to put up for the night. As he entered it the place looked very deserted, though from a distance he had seen a good many people moving about in the main street. The young man knocked at three doors in turn without receiving an answer, and then turned to Mantso for an explanation.

"They are afraid of having to provide mules for your caravan, Kushok," he said. "The Chinese always make them furnish transport, and pay them nothing for it."

"But I, of course, am willing to pay," replied Philip. "See if you can persuade any one to give us shelter for the night."

Mantso jumped off his mule and knocked persistently at the door of the nearest house, till a woman's voice responded—

"Cease knocking, or we will not unbolt. What is it you want?"

"Open, friend," said Mantso. "My master desires a night's lodging."

"Let him go to some one who is rich enough to supply his wants."

"My master is not a Chinaman, but an Eastern Mongol, who will pay for all he has."

Philip could hear a whispered consultation, after which

the bolts were withdrawn and a good-looking woman made her appearance.

"Is this the Kushok?" she asked Mantso, indicating Philip with a motion of her head.

"Yes, sister," answered the muleteer. "We have travelled far to-day, and shall be glad of food and rest. The Kushok will repay you well."

The woman looked at Philip critically. Though not resembling the ordinary type of Eastern Mongol, she saw, at any rate, that he was not a Chinaman, and accordingly replied—

"You are welcome, Kushok, to such poor food and shelter as I can supply. Come in."

She led the way through the open door into a courtyard, on one side of which stood the house. The ground-floor consisted of stables, which together with the yard could accommodate all Philip's animals. The staircase to a balcony on a level with the first floor consisted of a stout beam with holes in which to put the feet. The woman ascended this beam with practised ease, and Philip followed her. Crossing the balcony, they entered a fairly large room, the ceiling of which was supported by beams. A stove was burning at the further end of the room, but there was no chimney, and the smoke escaped by an oblong hole in the ceiling. A section of a tree did duty for a table, and a few cushions served as chairs. Philip, being invited to take one of the cushions, sat down and looked around him. The occupants of the room consisted of a man lying on the floor and smoking a pipe in front of the fire, an old woman seated near him weaving cloth, a girl of twelve, and two small boys with bright eyes and merry countenances.

"Is that your mother?" inquired Philip of the woman who had brought him in.

"Yes, she is my mother," the woman answered.

"And that, no doubt, is your husband," continued Philip, indicating the man with the pipe.

"He is one of them, Kushok."

Philip knew, of course, that polygamy existed in Tibet, and was interested by this first introduction to it.

"How many others are there then?"

But this was a matter which concerned the man. Evidently flattered by the curiosity which the visitor evinced in his family affairs, the man took his pipe out of his mouth and answered—

"Two more, Kushok. My two brothers!"

"Where are they now?" asked Philip.

"They are both away from home. One is doing some work at Batang; the other is on the road to Lhasa as muleteer to a caravan."

"We Mongols, as you know," continued Philip, "have a wife apiece, and could not be reconciled to the idea of sharing her affection with others. Tell me, are not your brothers jealous of you, when they are away from home?"

Both wife and husband laughed at this suggestion, and even the old grandmother was observed to smile.

"They are no more jealous of me when I am at home," answered the man, "than I am of them when they are at home."

"And are you all three content to have no wife to yourselves alone?"

The man evidently thought that Philip had strange ways of putting things.

"We each of us have a wife," he replied, "only she is the same woman for the three. She works well for each of us and is always cheerful. This would not be the case if there were two other wives in the house for her to quarrel with."

"Your brothers might have houses of their own if they had wives."

The man shook his head, as if he found it very hard to make the Kushok understand.

"The piece of land we inherited from our father is not large enough to be divided into three and keep three families. Even now we have to go out and seek work elsewhere. But when we are away we need have no anxiety about the house, for one of us is always taking care of it."

From a practical point of view there seemed to be something in the man's argument. But how the woman regarded the matter was another question, and turning to her Philip said—

"Are you quite content to have three masters instead of one?"

Again laughter convulsed the Tibetan household.

"There are no masters in this house, Kushok," the woman answered. "I am mistress of the household, and everything is entrusted to my sole charge. My husbands do not hire themselves for any work, nor make any bargain without first consulting me. Tibetan women work hard, but they are better off than Chinese women. When a Chinaman goes on a journey he leaves his house defenceless, and if he dies his wife becomes a widow. I am never left unprotected by a husband, and with three of them I should indeed be unlucky if I ever became a widow."

Thus it seemed that matters were arranged to the satisfaction of all parties, and Philip had nothing more to say on the subject. In fact, his attention was now drawn to a matter which concerned him more immediately, namely, the cooking of his dinner. The appetizing effects of Tibetan air have been experienced by every traveller in that country, and Philip proved no exception to the rule. To judge by the clumsy utensils used, the prospect of an inviting dinner seemed somewhat remote, but nevertheless savoury odours began to mingle with the pungent smell of the burning fuel.

Meanwhile the grandmother plied her distaff industriously, and kept a keen look out upon the movements of her grandchildren. She was evidently the disciplinarian of the household, and having had, no doubt, to manage three or four husbands in her time, found the task of keeping children in order a comparatively light one. The young girl was made to wind yarn, and received a sharp rebuke if her eyes wandered to the stranger and her work for one instant ceased. The two young boys were being schooled by the old lady, and had to repeat sentences from the sacred book of Buddhism. As long as their grandmother's eye was upon them they remained as demure as possible, but if anything else attracted her attention they began playing furtively with each other, or pulled the tail of her favourite cat.

At length the dinner was cooked, and a boiled leg of mutton brought to Philip on a wooden platter. With his own knife and fork—for none were provided—he cut himself two large slices, and much surprised his hostess by refusing to take any more. The grandmother next cut off, with a knife which hung from her waist, a large piece for herself and three smaller pieces for the children. When the wife had taken her share the husband claimed the rest of the joint himself, picking the bones with such completeness that not a particle of flesh was left upon them. There is a proverb in Tibet that you can tell a man of affairs by the thorough way in which he picks a bone. Judged by this standard, the husband would have qualified for a very high place in the administration of his native country.

At the conclusion of the meal Philip lit his pipe, and as a cold wind blew in upon him from the open doorway he moved to the unoccupied side of the fire. But he had no sooner thrown himself upon the floor, with his feet resting on a log which did duty for a fender, than the women folk raised a loud scream, and the man jumped up and dragged him away to the middle of the room.

"What is the matter?" asked Philip, much surprised by this treatment.

"You had taken the corner reserved for the household god," replied the man. "I am afraid you have offended him greatly."

Philip realized at once the mistake he had made.

"I owe your household god a thousand apologies," he said. "I might have guessed that the place reserved for him had it not been the custom in Mongolia to put the opposite side of the fire at his disposal. Where is he to be found in the daytime?"

"He sits in the doorway as long as the sun is there; that is from eleven to four o'clock."

"You give him, of course, the choice of the best position in the house. But how do you get in and out of the room when he is there?"

"We use that window."

The window indicated was merely an opening in the wall on the same side as the door, though a good deal smaller.

"The smallness of the window must make it inconvenient for you."

"It was worse before we made the window. Last year my eldest daughter was married, and after the wedding feast we found that, although the winter had not passed, the deity had without any warning transferred his seat to the open doorway. Of course, you know that a bride may not pass when he is there."

"So you had to make the window before the bride could get out?"

"No, that would have taken too much time, so we moulded the image of a horse in dough, and after placing tea and beer beside it, entreated the deity to go for a ride. He granted our prayer, and my daughter passed safely out of the house. After that I began to make the window."

Philip produced some money from his pocket.

"In order to appease your household god," he said, "I will give six rupees for a lama to come and pray to him to-morrow. As for to-night, I will make him an offering in wine."

The family received this announcement with much satisfaction, hoping to help the deity consume his wine. Philip had brought a dozen bottles from Mr. Ransome's cellar, and sent Mantso for a couple of them. When they arrived a small vessel of the liquid was placed on the side of the fire which the household god occupied, and then the wooden cups of the three adult Tibetans—the children had been sent to bed—were filled. The wine had an exhilarating effect. The wife began to sing Tibetan airs, and proved that she had a very pretty voice. The proceedings terminated by Philip singing the English National Anthem, which he had learnt, he said, from the "pelings." The Tibetans regarded his performance with a puzzled expression, and were only restrained from giving vent to their habitual merriment by a feeling of respect for a man who was so lavish with his money and who carried about with him such excellent wines.

CHAPTER V

IN spite of the smoky atmosphere of his apartment—for the family had retired to an adjoining chamber, leaving him in possession of the living-room—Philip Harwood slept soundly till roused by the housewife, who, according to the national habit, was astir at four o'clock. The young man, however, was not sorry to be up at that hour. In Eastern Tibet it is advisable to commence the day's march early in the morning, for at noon the rays of the sun in the clear, dry atmosphere are very powerful. Breakfast accordingly was served to the light of pine splinters and butter lamps, the latter being practically candles, for the low temperature made the butter as hard as wax. The smell of burnt grease which these lamps gave forth, mingled with the smoke from the fire and the pungent fumes of the pine splinters, might have affected a more squeamish appetite, but Philip made a capital breakfast. By daylight the meal was concluded, and the animals loaded ready to start.

The entire household, with the exception of the man, who they said was indisposed, descended into the yard to see the caravan depart. The housewife's face beamed with a happy smile, induced by the liberal pay she had received for Philip's lodging; nor had the grandmother and children been forgotten by him. Philip was just at the point of starting when the husband appeared on the balcony and began to descend the tree-trunk ladder. On reaching the ground, he approached Philip and asked him if he could give him any medicine for a headache.

The young Englishman, before leaving Shanghai, had realized how useful a little medical knowledge is to a traveller, both to maintain his own health and to prescribe for those in need of medical advice. With this object in view, he had studied with an English doctor and attended the Shanghai hospital. He thus acquired a fair knowledge of the use of ordinary drugs, and had brought a box of them with him. The present case was an easy one to diagnose, and after feeling the patient's pulse and looking at his tongue Philip came to the conclusion that the debauch of the previous evening was the cause of the mischief. Mantso was told to bring the medicine chest, from which his master drew forth a bottle of magnesia. The blue colour of this bottle elicited a murmur of admiration from the family group, as well as from the muleteers, who gathered round to watch the proceeding.

" Fill your tsamba bowl half full with cold water," said Philip. The man drew a long face, for Tibetans believe that cold water is injurious to the health.

" Will not hot water do ? " he asked.

" No ; the water must be cold."

The wife put an end to the discussion by taking her husband's tsamba cup and filling it half full with cold water as desired.

" Now, you must drink the medicine directly I hand it to you. Are you ready ? "

The man nodded, and Philip emptied a small quantity of the magnesia into the cup, stirring it round with the handle of his riding whip. When ready, he gave it to the patient, who, though evidently alarmed by the effervescence, resolutely swallowed it. The onlookers gave a shout of laughter at the man's expression when he took the cup from his lips.

" What was it like ? " demanded his wife.

" I could not tell you," he replied, wiping away the water it had brought to his eyes. " I only know that the Kushok bewitched the cold water with the handle of his whip, so that as it went down my throat it boiled."

Another burst of merriment greeted these words, the children clapping their hands in keen enjoyment of their father's perplexity. Philip hastily packed the bottle of magnesia and gave the order to start before the spectators should begin to clamour for a taste of the magic water.

Travelling along the Lhasa road in Eastern Tibet consists in climbing over a series of mountain ridges lying parallel to each other, like the furrows in a ploughed field. As the villages are situated, for the most part, in the valleys, an ascent has usually to be made on leaving them. The scenery during the next few days resembled alternately Switzerland and England. The pine woods, the ravines, and foaming torrents of the former were to be found on the flanks of the mountains; whilst in the valleys could be seen the green grass, the corn, and the hedges which form the familiar features of an English landscape. The grass, however, was of that rich variety that only grows in countries where the soil is covered for four or five months in the year with snow. Amongst the trees there were numerous holly oaks, often mistaken for the giant holly, and Philip passed large plantations of apricot trees. The fruit was just ripe, and men were busy gathering it.

" What do you do with all this fruit ? " the young Englishman asked one of the workers.

" It is dried in the sun and stored for winter."

" But I notice that you pick the rotten fruit as well as the fresh, though you will not be able to preserve it."

" No ; but from the stones we crush oil for cooking and for lamps."

A Wife from the Forbidden Land

It was clear that Tibetans wasted nothing of the scanty products of their land.

In one of the villages through which Philip passed the wheat harvest was in full operation. The mode of reaping followed was the primitive one of pulling up the wheat by the roots and tying it in bundles. This method naturally involved much labour, and the lamas had turned out in large numbers to assist the laymen. But the help they rendered was more spiritual than material, and consisted in sitting comfortably round the edge of the field twirling their prayer wheels and exhorting their brethren to persevere in their labours.

Baggage animals carried the bundles of corn into the village, where it was trodden out in the various courtyards by eight or ten oxen walking round in a circle. The mixture of grain and chaff which resulted from this process was carried up to the house-tops. Here women threw it up by handfuls into the air, the strong wind carrying off the chaff, while the grain collected on the roof. In the glorious rays of the setting sun it seemed as if a golden rain were falling on the village street.

As the caravan ascended towards the lofty tableland of Central Tibet the land became more barren, and the spaces available for cultivation smaller. So as not to encroach upon these spaces with buildings of any kind, the houses of a village were raised one above the other on the face of a cliff, with the result that many of them could only be reached by a ladder from the roof of the house beneath. The labour of climbing up to these eagle nests when carrying a sack of tsamba or a pail of water was very considerable. Yet Tibetan women performed the ascent thus laden a dozen times a day, and not only suffered no ill effects, but always seemed to be merry and cheerful. The fact that such heavy work could be borne by them without any injury was a proof of the invigorating influence of the climate of Tibet.

For eight or ten days Philip Harwood made regular and fairly long marches without losing a single baggage animal. It was instructive to observe how the best mules, like the best men, when no artificial restrictions are put upon their labour, worked their way to the head of the caravan. The leading mule occupies an arduous and dangerous post. A great deal depends on his sagacity. He not only makes the pace, but he has to find for himself the best path over an awkward place. As a reward for his toil and his intelligence he is given the heaviest load of the whole caravan, so as to test the weight-carrying capacity of the rotten wooden bridges which abound in this part of Tibet.

In some of the ravines the path consisted of nothing more than a few planks supported by horizontal beams driven into the face of the cliff. On reaching these narrow passages the muleteers kept up a continuous shouting, to warn travellers approaching from the opposite direction to halt, as one mule could not pass another in them.

Philip was one day traversing a defile of this character, and had just left behind him a length of wooden scaffolding, when a large stone came thundering down over the head of the mule immediately in front of the one he rode. The first mule stopped suddenly, and in spite of repeated blows from Philip's riding-whip, began to back against his own mule. The latter could not back in turn, as the succeeding animals had closed up to him. The frightened mule hugged the face of the cliff, and pushed Philip's mule towards the brink of the precipice. The animal was powerless against the leverage thus obtained, and Philip, feeling that the beast could no longer keep his footing, jumped off just in time to save himself. There was a hurried scuffling of feet, a crash of hillside shrubs, and the rumble of the falling mule. Then all was still.

Philip, who had in the meantime seized the bridle of the animal which had done the mischief, looked down the abyss, and thought he could distinguish the form of his mule on the bank of the foaming stream beneath. The animal, he concluded, must have been killed, but the saddle was a greater loss than the mule, as it could not be replaced. For this reason Philip decided to try and recover it, and, in spite of the protests of Mantso, who warned him he was risking his life, began to descend the cliff.

By means of the bushes and projecting rocks, the young man succeeded, notwithstanding the difficulties of the descent, in reaching the bottom in safety. To his surprise, he found the mule alive, quietly grazing the scanty grass at the edge of the stream. It was plain that the animal could not return the way he came, even if Philip himself succeeded in doing so. Yet the young man was loath to abandon a serviceable beast, and determined to make it swim down stream till a point was reached from which the path could be regained. Accordingly he remounted the animal, turned his head towards the torrent, and clapped the spurs into his side. The mule reared up, and, after a momentary hesitation, plunged headlong into the stream.

The shock of the ice-cold water coming from the snow-clad heights was very severe, and Philip became too numbed to steer a course. He had no recollection afterwards of the way in which he made the passage. It seemed a phantasmagoria of whirling waters, and giant boulders springing up suddenly in the centre of the torrent and hurling themselves headlong at him. The distance down stream to the more level ground was covered in an extraordinarily short space of time, and then Philip found himself on firm land again, with a shivering mule beneath him, and surrounded by his four astonished muleteers. Neither rider nor animal appeared, on examination, to have sustained any more injury than a few cuts, and the journey was resumed in a pleasant valley, where a powerful sun soon dried Philip's clothes upon his back.

The fifteenth day out from Ta-chien-lu arrived, and Philip hoped to reach Batang that evening. The march would be a long one, and the caravan started early, so as to gain their destination in the daylight. They halted for their midday meal on the further side of the final pass, and on resuming the march came to a point where the road forked in two different directions. Mantso, after a moment's hesitation, selected the road to the right, but Philip thought it looked less worn than the other, and called the muleteer's attention to the fact.

"But see, Kushok," the man replied, "here are recent droppings from pack animals, so it is plainly the main road."

Philip acquiesced in the decision of his guide, and they entered the road, which became more rough and narrow the further they went. At length a sudden turn displayed to their view at the distance of some two hundred yards another caravan, which had apparently just come to a halt. No sooner, however, did the men of this caravan perceive the new-comers, than they hastily threw their loose baggage on their yaks and drove them up a narrow ravine.

"They take us for chukpas!" said Mantso with a grin.

Philip had been warned to be on his guard against brigands, or "chukpas," as they are called, but he had hardly expected to be mistaken for a chukpa himself.

"Get out a couple of rifles, Mantso," he said. "We must be prepared in case they attack us."

Although Philip had brought three rifles with him, he had instructed Mantso alone in the use of them, so that the third one could not be used on the present occasion. The mule which carried the rifles and the ammunition always marched near to the leader of the caravan, and the weapons were quickly procured. Philip told Mantso to bring up the rear of the caravan, while he himself would remain at the head. The other three men, disposed at equal distances along the line, were ordered to dismount and lead their mules. Phendi drew his Tibetan sword with no change of expression in his melancholy countenance at the prospect of a fight. Esa was visibly alarmed, and handled his lance nervously, while his eye sought the ravine down which the strangers had disappeared. As for Jasi, it was impossible to tell, from his shifty, uncertain look, in what light he regarded the situation. He obeyed, indeed, the instructions to dismount, but he kept his only weapon, the murderous knife, in its sheath.

Philip, who had dismounted like the rest, was now approaching the mouth of the ravine, where, at a distance of barely eighty yards, three men became visible, the muzzles of their matchlocks resting on the forked antelope horns used for that purpose. Higher up the ravine stood the baggage animals and their drivers. As Philip drew near he saw the three men ignite the slow matches which were to discharge their weapons. No time should be lost if a needless conflict was to be avoided. Walking straight towards them with his rifle on his shoulder, he raised his hand and cried—

"We are travellers and not chukpas. Put out your slow matches, if you do not wish us to return your fire."

Whether his action in walking so fearlessly towards them convinced them of his sincerity, or whether they recognized the European repeating-rifle which he carried, and knew that their weapons were useless against it, Philip could not say. The result, at any rate, was that they removed their slow matches and awaited his approach.

"Whither are you bound, brother?" asked the centre one of the three men—a short, pleasant-featured Tibetan.

"I am bound for Batang," answered Philip, careful not to mention any destination beyond it.

"Batang?" repeated the man in evident surprise, and with a sidelong glance at his companions, "but this is not the way to Batang."

"Then my guide, as I thought, must have made a mistake. We ought, I suppose, to have taken the road to the left, but he saw traces of a caravan having just passed to the right, and that decided his choice. It must have been your caravan that led us to take the wrong turning."

The stranger smiled.

"That is the last thing which we wished to do," he replied. "When we caught sight of you in the distance we took you for chukpas, and, although we were bound for Batang, we turned down this road, in the hopes you would pass on without discovering us. But now that you have overtaken us and are going to the same place as ourselves, let us travel in each other's company. Two caravans are safer than one."

There was no reason why the man's proposal should not be accepted, especially as he would be able to prevent Mantso from making any further mistakes about the road. Matters were soon arranged, and Philip and his new acquaintance rode off at the head of the combined caravans.

"I wish my journey ended, like yours, at Batang," said Philip's companion.

"Have you much further to go?" asked Philip.

"A long way, for I am going to Lhasa."

The mention of the goal which he himself had in view made Philip thoughtful. Could this man, he wondered, help him to achieve his object?

"I am an Eastern Mongol," he said at length, "and am

travelling with the view of acquiring business clients in Tibet. Batang was the original limit of my journey, but if I saw any prospect of opening up a trade with Lhasa, I should like to go there."

"There is plenty of trade to be done with Lhasa. I am a Lhasa merchant myself. You ought certainly to go there. We will travel together. I see you have one of those strange guns which ignite without a slow match, and can fire six or seven shots without reloading."

The Tibetan merchant made no attempt to conceal the reason he had for desiring Philip's company. The young man determined to make the most of his opportunity.

"Yes, it is a wonderful gun," he said, "and will kill a man three li" (i.e. a mile) "away."

"Three li distant? It seems impossible. With that weapon to defend you, a chukpa could never come near enough to do any harm. I should much like to travel to Lhasa in your company."

The man's candour was amusing, but Philip hoped to make use of his dread of the chukpas, and replied—

"I have no passport from Batang to the sacred city, but if we joined caravans, as you suggest, there would be no need for me to have one."

"That is true," replied the Tibetan, delighted to find that the young stranger had a selfish reason for being willing to accompany him. "As a Tibetan, I can travel wherever I like in my own country, and no questions are asked with regard to those who compose my caravan. I could call you master of it, if inquiries were made. My name is Purdung."

"And mine is Khangsar," replied Philip, on the spur of the moment.

The compact was made forthwith, and the young Englishman became more hopeful of accomplishing his object than he had ever been before. The only risk now was that Purdung might discover his nationality, and refuse to travel with him in view of the penalty he would incur for bringing a "peling" into Lhasa. There were, however, several points in Philip's favour. European types were comparatively common in Central Asia, especially amongst the Eastern Mongols. Philip had dark eyes, and exposure to all weathers had tanned his skin as brown as that of a native of the soil. Moreover, he spoke Tibetan so well that no one would suspect him from his accent of being a European.

Purdung proved a very pleasant companion. He possessed the Tibetan cheerfulness of disposition, and Philip had reason to congratulate himself on the chance encounter of the afternoon. As part of Purdung's caravan, he would not be exposed to the inquisition of the Chinese officials at Batang, who would otherwise have wanted to see his passport, and to be informed of his next destination. The lamas, too, having no reason to suspect his nationality when in the caravan of one of their countrymen, would not prevent him from penetrating any further into Tibet. Everything seemed to be going well with him, and it was with high hopes that he entered Batang and put up with Purdung at the principal inn in the town.

CHAPTER VI

ALTHOUGH Purdung proved an admirable companion in many ways, there was one respect in which Philip Harwood found it hard to bear with him, namely, his Asiatic disregard for the value of time. On the day following their entry into Batang the Lhasa merchant announced his intention of remaining there five days. The journey before him would prove long and tedious. He had comfortable quarters now, and he meant to make the most of them. What difference could five days make in a journey of two or three months ?

In spite, however, of his chafing against the enforced delay, Philip found much to interest him in Batang. This town marked the point where the temporal rule of the Dalai Lama began, and the Tibetans showed themselves already more independent in their attitude towards the Chinese officials put in authority over them. Although the Chinese governor had a garrison at his command, the inhabitants paid but little attention to him. It is true that very few of the soldiers were armed, and that one could only tell a warrior from a civilian by the fact that he was the more timid and helpless of the two. Moreover, as the governor received no salary, he recouped himself by reducing the garrison by one-half of its nominal size. Of course, in case of trouble, he could always obtain the requisite troops from China, though the knowledge of this fact was not sufficient to obtain for him the respect of those over whom he was supposed to rule.

A Wife from the Forbidden Land

For other reasons than his desire to be moving, Philip Harwood was glad when his sojourn at Batang came to an end. A muleteer on the journey does not require much supervision, but it is a different matter when he is cooped up in town with nothing to do. Mantso, of course, was fairly well occupied in waiting on his master, and attending to the mules. Phendi, too, found occupation with the animals, and beyond looking a trifle more melancholy, seemed to smoke his pipe in silent submission to the fate which kept him idle in the yard of an inn. But Esa was of a less phlegmatic disposition. He liked good cheer, and would sit surrounded with kindred spirits drinking chang and singing songs far into the night. He also began to put on flesh again, thus losing the training he had acquired on the journey from Ta-chien-lu.

As for Jasi, though there was little in his conduct to which exception could be taken, Philip never felt perfect confidence in him. The ladaki did not drink, nor behave himself riotously, but there was always something mysterious about his movements. He would be absent from the inn for hours together, and if, on returning, he happened to meet his master, he would slip past him furtively, as if he half expected a rebuke. The young man would almost rather have seen him drunk than moving about in this covert manner.

But the day of departure arrived at length, and troubles of this kind were done with for the time. The difficulties, however, of travelling in Tibet began to appear in unmistakable form. Though the harvest had only just been gathered in, the first snowfall of the winter season occurred. The powerful rays of the sun, it is true, made all traces of it disappear by midday, but the country was evidently becoming more barren and inhospitable. Towards sunset, after a tedious march, Philip and Purdung came to a halt near a nomad encampment, for they would pass no village, nor even a solitary house where they could shelter, for the next six days.

The black tents of the nomads squatted like huge spiders on the plain, their watch-dogs baying loudly as the strange caravan approached, and straining at the leashes which bound them to the tent pegs. Philip was surprised at the speed with which Purdung had his tent erected, and a stove burning brightly in the centre of it. As in Tibetan houses, there was no chimney to carry off the smoke, but a rectangular opening in the centre of the flat roof prevented the fumes from becoming unbearable.

Purdung invited Philip into his tent, and while he was there, the chief of the nomad camp came to pay a formal visit. He was accompanied by six of the leading men, all of whom followed him into the tent. They formed a curious assembly, with their long sheepskin garments hitched up by a girdle at the waist and hanging in a large fold all round below it; their top-boots, with woollen uppers and raw-hide soles, and their tangled, greasy locks. Not being able to afford shades for his eyes against the glare of the sun and snow, the nomadic Tibetan lets his hair grow long and pulls it over his eyes when travelling. Not one of the seven men retained a full set of teeth, and several of them, though barely middle-aged, had only two or three teeth left. The Tibetans say that the piercing winds of their country are the cause of this deficiency, but a wind that will blow the teeth out of your mouth is a little too strong for general credence, and the real explanation is the constant use of soft food which requires no mastication, so that the teeth, having no hard work, get loose and fall out.

At the tent door stood a group of the humbler members of the tribe, and with the fitful light of the pine splinters playing on their dishevelled locks and weather-worn faces, they formed a picture which Philip could not easily forget. Tea, of course, was provided for all, even those at the door pulling their wooden cups out of the folds of their garments for a share in the national beverage. Tsamba and butter were also handed round, each man helping himself to the latter with his fingers, and applying any remnant that adhered to them either to his hair or to his boots, according to which end of him stood most in need of it. Nothing, however, could exceed the good-nature of these simple nomads, and they laughed and joked with as light hearts as if their existence were the most enjoyable that could possibly fall to the lot of man.

The chief explained that they had just taken up their winter quarters on the present spot, having come from the higher country which had to be traversed on the way to Lhasa. He warned Purdung that the road was very heavy, snow having fallen during the last three days of his march. Travelling in Tibet at any season of the year has its own disadvantages. If in summer, the rivers are swollen with melted snow, and all but impossible. In winter fallen snow impedes progress, and biting winds cause the most intense discomfort.

The following morning Philip rose at dawn and found the nomads already at work, collecting argol or grinding tsamba, some of the latter, in spite of the low temperature, having their right arm and shoulder bare. For convenience of travelling, the nomad's day clothes must also serve the purpose of bed-clothes, and what is not warm enough at night with 20° of frost, is much too hot at noon with the thermometer 60° or 70° in the shade. Consequently, when working in the daytime the nomads slip their right arms out of their sheepskin coats, or even bare themselves to the waist. At night they loosen the girdle and let the garment fall to its full length to cover their feet, or else they strip altogether, and, lying on felt, put their clothes on the top of them.

When the caravan started, two or three of the nomads' dogs, which had managed to get loose, came yelping at the heels of the animals. To any one unacquainted with his character, the Tibetan mastiff, which sometimes attains the size of a small donkey, is a terrifying object, with his loud bark and shaggy muzzle. But his bite is not as bad as his bark, and the skilful use of a thick stick soon sends him howling back to his master.

Philip had now to experience his first formidable mountain pass. The ascent commenced from the camp itself. Over the snow which covered the ground Philip's mules did not make such good progress as the yaks which composed the majority of Purdung's baggage animals. A biting wind blew in the teeth of the travellers, cutting the face like the lash of a whip. The dazzling rays of the sun reflected from the snow inflamed and almost blinded the eyes. Purdung had hoped to get over the pass that day, but it soon became evident that they could not do it. The mules staggered beneath their loads, and had to halt every now and again to get their breath in the rarefied atmosphere. It seemed to Philip, who had dismounted, as if leaden weights were attached to his legs. The *mal de montagne* gave him much the same sensations as *mal de mer*. He felt sick and giddy, with such a helpless lack of energy, that he could not walk without holding on to his animal's tail.

" It is the poisonous fumes arising from the ground that make you ill, Kushok," said Mantso, in accordance with the Tibetan superstition. " Eating onions is the best remedy."

Mantso had been chewing onions from the time the ascent commenced, and if one could judge by his appearance, for he looked as cheerful as ever, they had the desired effect. Philip tried the remedy, but derived no benefit from it. Matters grew worse as the day declined. The pack mules blundered hopelessly upwards, falling frequently with their loads. The muleteers found great difficulty in getting them on their legs again. One of them could not be made to stir, in spite of the blows that were rained upon him, and lay panting on the ground till Mantso drew his knife, and before Philip understood what he intended doing, had slit both the animal's nostrils. Strange to say, this drastic remedy seemed to have the desired effect. The mule, breathing more easily, struggled to its feet, and performed the rest of the journey with less signs of distress.

Towards sunset it became evident that the top of the pass could not be reached that day. Six hundred feet still remained to be climbed, and the animals were worn out with fatigue. Even the hardy muleteers had become exhausted, and after struggling to assist a fallen mule on to its legs again, would throw themselves flat upon the ground, in which position they found it easier to recover their breath. When the sun went down all intention of continuing the march was finally abandoned, and the caravan was compelled to encamp on a spot exposed to the full force of the wind. Worse still, argols could not be found in sufficient quantities to make a good fire. The wretched men burrowed beneath the snow in the fading light, and only managed to collect a scanty store. With this they attempted to make tea, but at that altitude the water boiled at so low a temperature that no essence could be extracted from the leaves, while the tepid mixture froze as soon as it was transferred to a bowl. Owing to the hardness of the ground and the strength of the wind, it was found impossible to pitch a tent. With the thermometer standing at 20° below freezing point, Philip threw himself down supperless behind the shelter of a boulder, and tried to compose himself to sleep beneath the angry sky.

It may be imagined that the members of the caravan obtained little rest that night, and that, as soon as dawn broke, they were all anxious to leave such a miserable camping ground. Philip had always insisted, contrary to the Tibetan custom, on unloading the pack animals every night. On this occasion, however, he had allowed them to remain loaded, and it was fortunate that he did so, for the men with their numbed hands and stiffened limbs would have spent two or three hours replacing the packs. As matters stood, they resumed their march at six o'clock, and reached the top of the pass at nine. For the first time Philip understood the sentiment which prompted the Tibetans to record their gratitude to the deity of the pass, when the summit had been gained.

But their troubles were not over yet. On the further side lay a plateau which was but little lower than the top of the pass. The scene was one of typical Tibetan desolation. Not a single tree nor blade of grass was visible, huge blocks of granite alone breaking the dull uniformity of the barren waste. The only sign of life was a young eagle, which came flying towards the caravan from the further and comparatively sheltered side of the pass. Philip watched its flight with curiosity, as it attempted to breast the icy wind which caught it at the summit of the mountain. The struggle was a brief one. The wind seemed to wither the young bird like the blast of a fiery furnace, its wings lost the power of sustaining it, and it fell lifeless at Philip's feet.

The storm-clouds, which from the valleys looked so high in the heavens, swept over the face of the plateau as if it were in reality the roof of the world. In the rarefied atmosphere of the great altitude which they had reached sound travelled with great difficulty. The ticking of a watch could not be heard unless pressed against the ear. If a mule stumbled over a stone no sound came from the scuffling feet. Mantso's usually penetrating voice was inaudible at a few yards' distance, and though his lips moved, no words proceeded from them. The place possessed all the haunting unreality of an oppressive dream.

The toll in baggage animals which this plateau had taken from caravans which had passed that way was very great. In one part the skeletons lay in such quantities as to resemble a cemetery in which the bodies were exhumed. Purdung's yaks, inured to the freezing temperature of their present elevation, stood the test well, but Philip's mules fared badly. He had been unable to bring away any provender from Batang for them, and they could not eat the scanty grass, which grew here and there beneath the protection of a granite boulder. This grass becomes so stiff in the dry wind of Tibet that it has been known to pierce a camel's foot. It is not surprising that Philip's mules refused to touch it, and that two of them died on this plateau from sheer exhaustion.

Happily, towards four o'clock, the descent to a less inhospitable region began, and at sunset they reached a sheltered camping ground, with a stream of fresh water and a good supply of argols. The tents were soon erected, good fires lighted, and hot tea infused life into the exhausted members of the caravan. Philip made a hearty meal from Tibetan fare, and then smoked his pipe in front of the camp fire. Before he withdrew to his tent, Mantso approached him and said—

"We must tether the mules close to the tent to-night, Kushok. This is the district where the wild men are found, who kill the baggage animals and sometimes the members of a caravan."

Philip had heard tales of these wild men, but was inclined to be incredulous with regard to their existence.

" Have you ever seen one, Mantso ? " he asked.

" Only once, Kushok, though I have known many animals to be killed by them."

" What was he like ? "

" He was some distance from me, but I noticed that he wore no clothes, and had long hair, and a clumsy walk."

Philip could make nothing out of this vague description, and merely telling Mantso to call him if a wild man attacked the animals, turned into his tent.

Mantso soon had an opportunity of obeying this order, and roused his master at dawn the following morning with the news that a wild man had killed one of the mules, and, being disturbed, had only just made off. Philip jumped up and accompanied Mantso to the slaughtered animal. It had evidently broken its tether, for it lay some little distance from the camp with a large gash in its throat.

" Which way did the wild man go ? " asked Philip.

Mantso pointed to the road by which they had reached their present camp, and on it could be seen an upright figure moving clumsily along at a distance of three hundred yards. For a moment the young man was in doubt, and then the figure turned its head, and displayed to view the pointed muzzle of a bear.

" That is only a bear, Mantso," he said.

" I don't know what is the proper name, Kushok," replied Mantso, " nor have I ever seen them close, for it is wiser to run away. But that figure yonder walks upright like a man, and our name of ' wild man ' is the best that we could give it."

Philip's first impulse was to get his rifle and go in pursuit of the beast, but realizing that it might be a long business, and interfere with the day's march, he thought it better to give up the project.

Just as they were starting Purdung came up to Philip and informed him that the district on which they were now entering was infested with robbers, and that he had heard they were already hovering round the caravan. He advised Philip to be fully prepared, and to carry his rifle ready loaded for immediate use. Accordingly, the young man, though somewhat sceptical about the presence of robbers, slung the weapon over his shoulder.

However, whilst crossing an open plain about an hour after starting, half a dozen horsemen appeared on the right of their path, and rode along parallel to it at a distance of some four hundred yards, evidently watching the caravan. Purdung declared that they were chukpas, and recommended returning to the camp they had just left, where they would be able to fortify themselves. But Philip refused to be intimidated by six horsemen, who might be just as much afraid of Purdung's caravan as Purdung was of them. Accordingly the march was continued, and at noon they halted for their midday meal. The six horsemen, seeing them stop, drew nearer, but when Philip and Mantso rode out to meet them they turned and trotted off.

"I do not think those fellows will trouble us much," said Philip, as he sat down to his meal in Purdung's tent. "If two of us can frighten them away, they are not likely to attack the whole caravan."

Purdung shook his head lugubriously.

"They have only gone away to get reinforcements," he answered. "I know them too well. We have not seen the last of them yet."

The march was resumed at two o'clock, and until five no other human beings came into sight. At that hour, however, the six horsemen whom they had seen in the morning reappeared, followed at a short interval by a dozen more.

"What did I tell you?" said Purdung to Philip in doleful tones.

"They have done as you said," replied Philip, "but even with their increased numbers I shall be surprised if they have the courage to attack us."

At this moment one of Purdung's men came up and pointed to another body of perhaps twenty horsemen on the side of the road opposite to that on which the eighteen had just appeared. There seemed to be little doubt now that the two parties were acting in concert with the object of robbing the caravan. Purdung was much alarmed.

"Why did we venture through this district with so small a caravan?" he said. "I have never travelled here before with a party of less than one hundred men. We are now at the mercy of these chukpas, and even your wonderful gun will not serve you against such numbers. What is to be done?"

The situation certainly looked more serious. At the distance of a couple of miles the road entered a deep defile. The chukpas would probably attack them while passing through it. Philip made up his mind at once.

"We must pitch our tents where we are," he said.

"But there is no shelter here," protested Purdung. "It would be better to enter the defile while we yet have time, and find a nook where we can protect our baggage animals."

"I can protect them better in the open plain," replied Philip, "for my gun carries further than the weapons of the chukpas. In a narrow defile, where they could shelter behind rocks, I should be at a disadvantage."

Purdung reluctantly agreed to Philip's proposal, and a halt was called. The two parties of the chukpas also halted and seemed to discuss among themselves the new situation.

Apparently they decided not to attack, and as the sun declined they rode off in opposite directions and disappeared.

This action put neither Philip nor Purdung off their guard, and they arranged a strict watch for the night. Purdung, who had half a dozen Tibetan mastiffs, tethered them in a circle round the camp. Philip's four muleteers mounted guard two by two in turn. The young man himself kept on the alert, visiting the pickets now and then to make sure they were awake. But when midnight came, and no alarm had been raised, he concluded that the chukpas did not intend to return, and prepared to turn in.

As, however, he proceeded to his tent, a peculiar sound, like the cry of some wild animal, caught his ear. One of the watch-dogs at once gave tongue, and the others took up the cry. Philip, whilst passing Purdung's tent, at the entrance to which its owner stood, asked what animal it was which had set the dogs barking.

"It was no animal, but the cry of the chukpas," Purdung answered. "They make that cry to see if our mastiffs are on the alert. Now that the dogs have replied, they will not dare to make an attack. I shall take some rest, and I advise you to do the same."

As Purdung felt no uneasiness, Philip had no occasion to do so, and, following the Tibetan trader's example, he retired to his tent to get some sleep.

CHAPTER VII

WHEN morning broke the chukpas were nowhere to be seen, but on going beyond the area guarded by the dogs Philip found tracks such as would be left by a man crawling on his hands and knees. These must have been made by the chukpas, though they had not ventured within fifty yards of the dogs. Purdung, who accompanied Philip, seemed relieved by the latter fact, and began to hope they would give no further trouble.

Half an hour after starting, the caravan reached the entrance to the defile. The path was steep and the banks on either side were strewn with boulders, which would afford excellent cover to a determined enemy. Though Philip did not credit the chukpas with courage to attack the caravan, he took the precaution of marching at the head of it himself. More than half of it had been traversed, when the young man fancied he saw a figure move behind one of the boulders, at the same time a musk deer made its appearance on a projecting rock some three hundred yards ahead. If the chukpas were in hiding, it would be well to let them see the range of his gun. Accordingly Philip took a steady aim at the deer, and the report of his rifle was followed by the animal falling headlong over the rocks on to the path below. Almost immediately a number of men emerged from behind the boulders on either side, and, scrambling up the banks, disappeared at the top. A man who could shoot a deer at that distance was not the kind of antagonist the chukpas wished to meet.

Purdung was delighted at the ease with which the

robbers had been put to flight, and his former high spirits returned. With the aid of this Eastern Mongol and his wonderful gun, he now had no doubt that he would reach Lhasa in safety. The chukpas, in truth, did not make their reappearance, but other troubles, inseparable from travel in Tibet, attacked the caravan. In the first place, the keen winds cut Philip's skin till it was raw, and the glare of the sun set up inflammation in his eyes. Purdung recommended butter, the Tibetan panacea for every ill, but Philip had recourse, with good effect, to the vaseline he carried in his medicine chest. As for his eyes, a horse-hair shade in the form of a fringe protected them sufficiently to prevent any further suffering on that score. Another source of trouble arose from the presence of wolves in the district through which they passed. In spite of tethering the baggage animals close to the tents at night-time, the wolves managed to pass through the cordon of watch-dogs, and killed three of Philip's mules. The muleteers on guard—Esa and Jasi—relying on the mastiffs, had evidently fallen asleep. Philip rated them soundly, and bade them be more careful in future. Esa received the rebuke with penitence, but a lowering look could be seen in Jasi's eyes, in spite of his air of submission.

Three days later they reached a village called Namcho, where the shelter of an inn was very welcome after the severe weather experienced in their recent marches. Both men and animals sorely wanted a rest. Half of Philip's baggage mules had been lost in accidents, had succumbed to hard work, or fallen a prey to wild beasts. As Philip heard that the Lhasa road after leaving Namcho became more suitable, on account of its roughness, to yaks than to mules, he took the opportunity of exchanging his baggage animals for the favourite beast of burden in Tibet.

On the strength of Purdung's report that the lamas of

Namcho were apt to deal very harshly with strangers, Philip kept to the inn during the two days they were to stay in the village. On the morning of the third day, however, the Tibetan trader announced that he could not start till the morrow, and the young Englishman, tiring of his enforced seclusion, went out into the village. A little further down in the main street he found a crowd collected round the door of a house. Glad to find something that would divert attention from himself, he approached the crowd to see what was going on. The house round which they were gathered appeared to be an inn, and through the open doorway he caught sight of a group of gesticulating lamas. On making inquiry from a bystander, he heard that a Chinese mandarin of high position who had taken lodgings in the inn was discussing with the lamas the amount of "ula," or free transport, which should be furnished by the village to take him and his baggage to the next stopping place on the road to Lhasa. Having been unable to come to an agreement, they had referred the matter to the "Deba," or Tibetan chief of the district, who lived some little distance from Namcho, and whose arrival they now awaited.

At this moment the sound of an approaching cavalcade could be heard, and there swept into the narrow street of the village a brilliant troop of horsemen. The leader, who rode a fine white animal, wore a dark brown satin garment lined with Siberian fox-skin, and a yellow satin cap faced with sable. The clothes of his retinue displayed an equal profusion of colour, though the material was not so rich. Having never seen a Tibetan of the upper classes, Philip was much struck by this man's appearance. His fellow-countrymen were considered to be the poorest and most barbarous of any of the old-world nations. Yet this man, with his sumptuous dress and his long hair falling in curls upon his shoulders, carried himself with the well-bred air of a cavalier of King Charles the First's Court. It was not however the Deba's general appearance, but the expression of his countenance, which made the greatest impression upon Philip. There was a look of capacity and determination in his face which would have made him remarkable even amongst the governing classes of the leading European nations. Where could he find a field for the exercise of his talents in a country which was subject to the yoke of the decrepit Chinese Empire ?

But the lamas now came pouring out of the inn to welcome the ruler of the district, who received their homage with easy dignity as nothing but his due, and still remained on horseback. His object was clear. He did not wish to show deference to the Chinese representative by hastening to dismount and pay his respects to him, preferring that the mandarin should come to the door himself to greet him. The struggle for a victory on this point of etiquette was soon decided. The Chinese mandarin realized that he must give way, and rising with an ill grace went to the door to welcome the Deba.

Philip recognized him as soon as he made his appearance. It was Tuen Fang, the mandarin whom he had defied in the streets of Ta-chien-lu. The young man concealed himself from view, and asked his previous informant if Tuen Fang was merely going on a visit to Lhasa. The man looked at him in some surprise.

"Have you not heard ?" he answered. "This mandarin has been appointed the Senior Amban at Lhasa !"

It was an unwelcome piece of news for Philip. As Senior Amban, or Chinese Ambassador at Lhasa, Tuen Fang would hold a powerful position in the city. If the young man succeeded in getting there, and happened to be recognized by the amban, his situation would be a perilous one. Mr. Ransome's warning might be justified after all.

But Philip's thoughts were soon diverted to what was going on before him. As soon as the Deba saw Tuen Fang at the door he leapt lightly off his horse, and taking a "khata," or "scarf of greeting," which one of his retainers held ready for him, he presented it to the amban. The latter made an effort to accept it with good grace, and said—

"Welcome, Deba! Enter, and let us discuss this matter quietly within."

"Nay," replied the Deba in clear, decisive tones. "We will settle it here in the presence of the lamas and inhabitants of this village, so that they may learn the demands which the Chinese Amban makes upon them. What 'ula' do you ask?"

Tuen Fang's complexion turned to a deep shade of yellow and his dull eyes burnt angrily. If he only had two or three score Pekin soldiers armed with European rifles, he would soon teach these insolent Eastern Tibetans better manners. As, however, the small Chinese garrison in Namcho did not possess a single firearm he was entirely at their mercy.

"Chinese mandarins are not in the habit of discussing their affairs in the presence of an ignorant public," he answered. "But as you Tibetan noblemen hold other views, I am willing to act in accordance with them. It is only a trifling matter after all. I shall want sixty baggage animals."

"That is somewhat in excess of the number usually required by a mandarin when entering our country. We have a saying that he comes into Tibet with one suit of clothes and leaves it with a caravan of a thousand yaks."

A tinge of warm colour appeared in the mandarin's yellow face.

"The fact remains that I am entitled to sixty baggage animals or their equivalent in money. With which do you intend to furnish me?"

"You certainly will not get the money, and as for the animals there are not as many as sixty in the village. The heavy exactions of you Chinese mandarins as you pass to and fro is depopulating the country. Look at the empty houses in this street. The 'ula' has ruined the occupants and they have been obliged to go elsewhere. At this rate you will soon empty all the villages on the high road to Lhasa. But you will not get anything from my district for which you do not pay, even if you bring your fine soldiers from Pekin to collect it. We are a free people here, and it is better to be killed outright than to die of slow starvation."

The conclusion of this speech was greeted with loud applause by the Tibetan crowd. Tuen Fang was visibly alarmed, and his Chinese retinue shrank back as though in expectation of an attack. The mandarin saw that it would be best to change his tone at once.

"The Chinese Government has no wish to be oppressive in its dealings with Tibet. If the 'ula' is depopulating the country to such an extent, some change must be made in the law respecting it. Meanwhile, as you assure me that this village in particular is suffering from the custom, I will waive my right to claim three score baggage animals. I will ask for no more than just sufficient to carry my baggage, and I will pay for them at the current rate."

The Deba refrained from smiling at this sudden volte-face. "I am glad to hear you say so, mandarin," he answered. "Let me know the number you require, and you shall have them to-morrow morning. I have the honour to bid you good day."

In accordance with Tibetan custom, Tuen Fang presented the Deba with a khata in return for the one he had received, and then the latter mounted his horse and, accompanied by his retinue, rode off amidst the cheers of the crowd.

Philip saw that it was time for him to go if he was

anxious not to attract attention, and passing down the street he entered the open country beyond. A short distance from the village stood a large lamasery built of stone on the face of a cliff. Slipping by it as quickly as he could, he came to a fertile and well-tilled valley. The autumn still lingered here, though on the high tableland, which he had lately traversed, winter had already appeared.

Tempted by the pleasant country to go further than he meant, it was some two hours later when he once more approached the village. A mule stood at the monastery gates, and as Philip drew near to them a man came out, mounted the animal, and rode briskly off towards the village. The mule bore a strong resemblance to Mantso's saddle-mule, though the rider, from the distant view which Philip had of him, reminded him more of Jasi than of Mantso. Yet it could not, of course, be Jasi, for what would he want at the monastery, and how did he come by Mantso's mule?

On reaching the inn Philip went to the part of the yard where his saddle-mules were stationed. There stood Mantso's animal quietly munching hay. His breathing seemed regular, and his back showed no recent traces of a saddle. Yet the animal at the lamasery gates was very like this one. Philip decided to question Mantso about the matter. In answer to his master's summons Mantso issued from the inn.

"Where are the men?" asked Philip.

"They were all here a little while ago, Kushok, except Esa," Mantso replied. "Esa has relations in the village and has gone to see them. But the other two are here," and he called Phendi by name. No one answered, and Mantso continued—

"Then Phendi must have gone out too, but one of them of course remained to look after the mules. Jasi! Jasi!"

A sleepy voice replied to the second call, and a bundle of clothes, rising up from a distant corner of the yard, approached them.

"How long have you been here?" asked Philip.

"How long?" repeated Jasi, as if endeavouring to collect his thoughts. "Why, I have been here ever since the Kushok went out."

If the man was acting, he acted very well.

"Have any of my mules been taken out of the yard to-day?"

"No, for we have kept a watch upon them."

"Even when you were asleep?"

"I thought Phendi was on watch as well, or I should not have gone to sleep. But the Kushok will not punish me for that?"

There was nothing further to be said. As none of the men seemed to have been in the yard with Jasi, it was impossible to prove if he were telling the truth or not. After all, even supposing he had taken the mule, no very serious offence had been committed. He might have had a friend or relation at the monastery, and selected the best animal in the caravan to take him there.

The following morning at daybreak Philip was in the yard superintending the preparations for departure, when six lamas made their appearance and asked for Purdung. On hearing that he was within, they entered the house in search of him. The young man thought no more about the matter, and was busy with the loading of the animals when Purdung and the lamas issued from the inn. The Tibetan trader showed some embarrassment, and warned Philip with a look to be on his guard.

"This is the man Khangsar," he began aloud, indicating Philip. "He is an Eastern Mongol, and manages the caravan."

The lamas looked at Philip closely. Exposure had tanned his skin; his clothes were such as Mongols wore, and even his features were of a mould not unknown in Mongolia. Still they were not satisfied, and their leader, a man of capable and determined physiognomy, said—

"Where is his passport?"

This was the question which Philip had feared. He did not attempt to answer it himself, but Purdung, forcing a laugh, replied—

"As a member of my caravan he needs no passport. When did you begin requiring a passport for every muleteer?"

"But this man had a caravan of his own when he entered the country."

Purdung was struck dumb. The lamas knew everything, and it would be useless to try and brazen the matter out. Feeling that nothing he could say would remove their suspicions, he left Philip the task of exonerating himself.

"I have told you all I know," he answered. "If you want any further information, you had better ask Khangsar himself."

The lama turned to Philip and demanded his passport.

"I have no passport, and this is the first time I have been asked for it."

"That is because you pretended to belong to this merchant's caravan."

Philip wondered how they found out that he did not belong to it. Speculation on the point, however, was idle, and he continued—

"If a passport is necessary I could no doubt obtain one from the Deba of the district."

But the suspicions of the lamas were fully aroused, and their spokesman replied—

"The Deba has no power to grant you a passport. You must return the way you came."

This was a pretty ending to Philip's plans, which, since he had joined Purdung's caravan, seemed in a fair way towards accomplishment. The thought stung him so acutely that he felt an impulse towards defiance. With his three repeating rifles all the matchlocks in the district could not stop him. But the young man realized at once that such action would only render failure more certain in the end. Swallowing his disappointment as best he could, he answered—

"As I cannot get a passport, I suppose I must return. But when I get to my own district, where I have some little influence, I shall know what account to give of Tibet to those of my countrymen who might think of visiting it."

The lamas smiled at this threat, which Philip had uttered more because he thought it in keeping with the part he played than from any expectation of its efficacy. Eastern Tibetans have a contempt for Mongols, and do not care in what light the latter may regard their country. Having accomplished their object, the lamas prepared to depart, their leader saying as he went, "In three days' time, at the latest, you must set out on your return."

"I shall leave before then," replied Philip.

As soon as the lamas had gone, however, Purdung broke out into loud lamentations. How with his small caravan could he ever hope to reach Lhasa in safety, now that his good friend Khangsar of the quick-firing gun was not allowed to accompany him? The lamas were worthless busybodies who were always interfering in matters with which they had nothing to do. How did it concern them whether an Eastern Mongol had a passport or not? If the officious Chinese authorities had raised an objection there would have been less occasion for surprise. But it was too bad of the lamas to break up the caravan of one of their own countrymen merely because a member of it did not possess a passport. Why should they not insist on travelling together, and see if the lamas dared to separate them by force?

To Philip, in his present angry mood, the suggestion was a tempting one, but he soon saw that it would only be putting off the evil day. With their rapid means of intercommunication the lamas would doubtless warn the villages through which the caravan would have to pass, and the opposition to them would increase till it became too formidable to be brushed aside. For a moment the young man entertained the idea of accompanying Purdung's caravan disguised as a muleteer, sending back his own caravan in charge of one of his men, who would have to personate his master. But none of his four untutored muleteers could be expected to play the part without detection, and Philip abandoned the idea.

A third plan occurred to the young man's mind. Should he consult Purdung as to its feasibility? Philip had already begun to suspect that there was some informant in the camp. Purdung might thoughtlessly divulge the plan to one of his attendants, and the lamas might in this way get to know of it. Philip decided to keep his own counsel, and in reply to Purdung's suggestion that they should travel together in defiance of the lamas' orders said that, much as he would like to accompany him, he felt certain that the attempt would end in failure. Accordingly, with much bewailing from Purdung and genuine regret on Philip's part—for the Tibetan merchant was a pleasant and light-hearted companion—Purdung's caravan started from the inn, leaving Philip in the middle of the street gazing wistfully after it.

CHAPTER VIII

AS soon as Purdung's caravan disappeared from view Philip Harwood returned to the yard of the inn with his mind made up. The pack animals were already loaded, and nothing could be gained by unloading them and remaining at the inn. As the lamas were not likely to alter their decision the sooner he started on the road to Ta-chien-lu the better. Philip found his four muleteers waiting to learn what he intended to do. They had, of course, overheard his conversation with the lamas, and wondered what would be the outcome of it. Mantso was visibly crestfallen at the check his master had sustained. The muleteer had now identified himself with Philip's object, and felt his reputation at stake in the endeavour to reach Lhasa. Phendi had his usual abstracted air, as if it were the same thing to him whether he journeyed from Ta-chien-lu to Lhasa or from Lhasa to Ta-chien-lu. Esa evidently viewed the situation with disfavour. To retrace his steps seemed more toilsome than to keep marching forwards. As for Jasi, he gazed at Philip with a curious expectancy, as if much interested to learn his choice.

The young Englishman did not leave them long in doubt. Briefly announcing that he meant to return to Ta-chien-lu, he gave the order for the march to be commenced. The members of the caravan wore a dejected air as they rode slowly eastward out of the village that morning. Travelling back over ground already trodden, when you are particularly anxious to go forward, is a disagreeable occupation. Each stage reminded Philip of his buoyant hopes on the outward journey, and made his retreat the more distasteful. The gloom pervading the caravan was intensified by the slowness with which the yaks travelled, their movement being almost a crawl in comparison with the walk of the mules.

This tedious day's march came to an end when barely ten miles had been covered. As soon as Philip's tent was pitched Mantso served his master's supper in silence. The usually merry muleteer had been very taciturn all day, hardly saying a word to Philip or to his fellows. When the meal was cleared away the young Englishman lit his pipe and considered the situation. The result of his reflections was that he summoned Mantso to his tent.

"Mantso," he said, "to-day's march has been all in the wrong direction!"

Mantso's face lightened immediately. It seemed that his master was not going to submit to fate without a protest, after all.

"Yes, Kushok," he answered; "we ought to have been going towards Lhasa instead of away from it."

"Do you know this part of the country well?" continued Philip.

"I have been travelling in it for twenty years, Kushok," he answered simply.

"Then you could take us by a roundabout route to the south and afterwards to the west, so that we should avoid Namcho and join the Lhasa road again some distance beyond it."

"No one could do it better, Kushok."

"Well, then, we will strike camp at three o'clock tomorrow morning and get away while it is still dark, so that no one will see us leaving the main road."

Mantso's good-natured face was wreathed in smiles as he replied that he would go and tell the men to be ready at that time.

The order was duly carried out. Mantso roused Philip at half-past two, and served his breakfast to the flickering light of a butter lamp. On leaving his tent at the conclusion of his meal the young Englishman found all the yaks loaded but one. This animal proved refractory, and would not let the men put his pack upon him. Mantso at once applied the usual remedy. Seizing one of the animal's horns in his two hands and telling Phendi to take the other, they jerked the horns outward with all their might, till it seemed as if they must snap or burst the skull asunder. After this operation had been repeated two or three times the animal became quite dazed, and submitted without a murmur to the fixing of the load. Everything was ready by half-past three, and the march began.

For the first two miles Mantso led them by the side of a stream, the faint shimmer of which only intensified the darkness of the muddy banks on either side. Philip's mule floundered helplessly along, hardly able to drag its legs out of the boggy soil. As for the yaks, their great weight—a wild yak bull has been known to scale over 1500 lbs.—caused them to be still worse bogged, and on two occasions the packs had to be removed before the animals could extricate themselves. These two miles took a couple of hours to cover, and then the path lay up a mountain pass, which, in spite of the steep ascent, seemed a pleasant relief after the clinging mud-banks of the stream.

But it was not long before this path became as difficult to follow as the one just traversed in the valley. Being little more than a track made by herds of antelope and wild yak, it was quite unsuitable for tame animals with loads upon their backs. Half-way up the pass a succession of huge boulders had to be crossed. They rose up one above the other like the steps of a giant staircase, with the difference that gaps of two or three feet were often to be found between one step and another. On reaching the spot Philip declared that the yaks could never mount them with their heavy loads.

"They will ascend better than the mules, Kushok," said Mantso. "Let the yaks go first. You will soon see whether I am right."

They drew to one side of the path and allowed the leading yak to reach the lowest boulder. After inspecting the height of it, the animal, urged on by Phendi, leapt up on to the top of the boulder as lightly as a cat. Then it went on from step to step, sometimes, as it paused to select the best spot towards which to make the following jump, balancing itself on a piece of rock only just large enough to hold its four feet bunched close together. In fact, the yaks seemed positively to enjoy poising themselves in hazardous positions, and grunted with satisfaction at the task to which they had been set.

The mules, however, as Mantso said, proved much less agile and surefooted. Although relieved of their riders' weight, they found difficulty in jumping the necessary height. Nor could they judge their distances well, either going beyond or falling short of the required spot. Their feet did not give so good a hold upon the rocks as the cloven hoofs of the yaks, and they frequently fell between the boulders. Philip's chief surprise was that they should all have escaped without a broken leg.

The day's march proved to be a tedious one. They were obliged to halt for the midday meal on almost the top of the pass, where argols could not be found in sufficient quantities to boil the tea. Then, as they began to descend the other side, a dense mist rolled up the mountain and made the journey slow and dangerous. Even Mantso, who knew the country so well, became confused and lost his way. In addition to the difficulty of finding the right path, there was the difficulty of making the whole caravan keep to it. The muleteers could only see the animal in front of them, and if they strayed from the path the sense of hearing was the only means by which they could regain it. The direction of sound is very deceptive, and matters were made worse by the rarefied state of the air at that elevation and the resulting difficulty in hearing. Philip was half inclined to call a halt and pitch camp till the fog disappeared; but the severe cold, in conjunction with the impossibility of procuring fuel, made the project impracticable.

Accordingly they groped their way down the mountain pass in the dense white mist as best they could. All the men went on foot, leading their mules and driving the yaks in front of them. Mantso, of course, headed the caravan, and Philip followed him. The chief muleteer led them on two occasions down a gully from which there was no exit except by retracing their steps. Once Philip found himself standing on the edge of a precipice, his position being revealed to him by a puff of wind which momentarily cleared the view in front of him. Three times his mule fell down, either knocking or dragging his master to the ground with its fall. The nervous strain of such a journey made itself felt on all the members of the caravan.

At length, towards five o'clock, Mantso confessed himself lost, and asked Philip what was to be done. They had evidently descended some distance, for the atmosphere became much milder. Both men and beasts were quite worn out. The fear of a fall at every step makes a journey more fatiguing than three times the distance in clear weather. All the men, including Philip, were bruised by falls, and many of the animals were badly cut. Under these circumstances the young man decided to pitch camp, and began to search for a suitable spot for the purpose.

Whilst thus engaged Philip found to his surprise a well-worn track. The fog at the same time began to disappear, rolling up the mountain like the drop scene of a theatre and displaying in its place a magnificent view. The newly found track ran at right angles to the direction in which the caravan had been travelling. Towards the north the trend of the path was hidden by a projecting rock, some twenty paces from where the young man stood. As he glanced in that direction a man and a boy, the one on a horse and the other on a mule, rode into view from behind the rock. By the side of the mule a Tibetan mastiff ran. This dog, engaged in barking playfully at the boy, did not notice Philip till he was close upon him, when the unexpected apparition sent him with a yelp into the middle of the road. As he went he tripped up the mule, and in a moment the mule, its rider, and the dog were rolling on the ground together.

Philip rushed forward, and dragging the boy clear of the kicking mule knelt down to see if he was injured. The man too jumped off his horse, and came running up to where the boy lay.

"He has a cut over his forehead which has stunned him," said Philip, "but I cannot find that any of his bones are broken."

At this moment the boy, a bright Tibetan lad of about ten years of age, opened his eyes and smiled.

"How did it happen, father?" he said.

"He has regained consciousness," said the man to Philip, "but his wound bleeds badly. What can be done?"

The members of Philip's caravan had now come up, and Philip told Mantso to get the small case in which he carried a few medical appliances for use in accidents. As soon as the case was brought the young man bound up the wound and stopped the flow of blood.

"This bandage will serve for the time being," said Philip to the father. "How far away from here do you live?"

He looked at the man for the first time, and though his face seemed familiar he could not recall where he had seen him.

"We live about two miles further along this road—that is, about eight miles from Namcho."

Philip at once recognized the man's face. It was the Deba who had treated Tuen Fang so cavalierly at Namcho. He did not, of course, know Philip, and the latter continued—

"The boy had better be taken home at once. As he cannot ride in his present state, I will have a rough stretcher made, and two of my men shall carry it."

The Deba gratefully accepted this offer, and a suitable litter was made out of a couple of tent poles and a stout rug. Meanwhile the Deba insisted that the whole caravan should accompany him, and he would give accommodation to both man and beast for the night, a proposal with which Philip was very willing to fall in. Accordingly they set out together, though the stretcher, accompanied by Philip and the Deba, soon outpaced the slow-moving yaks. The boy, although his head throbbed painfully and the fall had covered his body with bruises, bore the journey well. Fortunately for him, it did not take much more than half an hour.

From the gorgeous retinue with which the Deba had been attended at his interview with Tuen Fang, Philip had been prepared to find him the owner of a well-built house, but he had hardly expected to see so fine a castle as that to which he was now conducted. It was built of solid stone three stories high, and surrounded by a moat. A garden lay on one side of the castle within the moat, the banks of which were planted with trees. As they approached, a drawbridge, as in European castles of the Middle Ages, was lowered for them, and crossing it they passed under an archway into a large courtyard. Here the Deba, giving the animals in charge of attendants who came to meet him, led the way to the main entrance into the castle.

The chatelaine, who had, it seemed, just heard of the accident, now came running out in great alarm.

" Calm yourself, Phagmo," said the Deba. " Maru has had a fall from his mule and cut his forehead. This good friend," indicating Philip, " bound up the wound and made a hammock, in which two of his men carried the boy. Let him be taken up to his room at once."

" Praise be to Buddha that he is alive, Phala," answered Phagmo, looking into the hammock and seeing her son's eyes wide open. " Bring him this way."

Entering the castle, she took them through a lofty chamber resembling the banqueting hall of an old English castle, and up a flight of stone steps to a room on the first floor. Here the boy was laid upon his bed, which consisted of a mattress and bed-clothes stretched upon the floor. Philip knelt down at his side, undid the bandages, and bathed the wound. Then, taking a needle and thread from the medicine case which Mantso had brought him, he sewed the gash up neatly, for he had had some practice at this kind of work in the hospital at Shanghai.

" It is a clean cut," he said, " and should heal well. Give me a little water in a cup, and I will mix him a sleeping-draught."

Phagmo gave the order to get the cup to some one who left the room with a light, quick step and soon returned. Philip, who had meanwhile procured the ingredients for the draught from his case, turned to find the cup held out to him by a young girl of seventeen years of age. She bore a strong family likeness to the boy, and the young man saw at once that she must be his sister. What struck him more than anything else about her was her beautifully fresh complexion. All the Tibetan women whom he had hitherto seen had smeared their faces with black paste, and even the chatelaine had slightly discoloured her skin. But her daughter's complexion was as rosy as an English country girl's. She was dressed in a garment of yellow silk tied up at the waist by a girdle, after the national custom, and hanging down to just above her ankles. On her feet she wore the usual high boots, the upper parts of which were made of wool and the soles of untanned leather. There was little in the costume to distinguish it from that worn by men, and she might have been mistaken for a lad but for the thick tresses of rich black hair which hung down her back some distance below her waist, and were adorned with coral and turquoise.

As she handed the cup to Philip her dark eyes gazed in wonder at the drugs he had prepared.

"This medicine," he said as he mixed the draught, "will make your brother sleep as soundly as—as I can see you always do."

"He will sleep well indeed then," she answered with a smile, displaying two rows of exquisitely white teeth.

The boy took the draught without a murmur, and in a few minutes fell into a peaceful slumber. Much relieved by this result, the Deba conducted Philip to the room prepared for him and told him supper would be served below as soon as he was ready.

When the young man descended from his room the sun had set and the hall was illumined with rows of butter lamps. The lofty pillars and brightly coloured banners covering the walls made the resemblance to a medieval castle more marked than ever. Down the centre a long low table was laid for the retainers, who stood in a group conversing with the Deba. A smaller table ran at right angles to the top of the hall, with cushions arranged for only two persons. When Philip entered the Deba conducted him to one of the seats and took the other himself, while the retainers placed themselves at the table in the centre. Attendants at once brought in the viands, and the chatelaine and her daughter helped to wait on the Deba and Philip. The fare consisted of roast and boiled joints of mutton, followed by scones, cakes, and fresh and dried fruit. As may be well imagined, Philip, who had eaten scarcely anything since four o'clock that morning, did ample justice to the meal.

At its conclusion the retainers withdrew to their quarters and the tables were cleared, the women taking their dinner in another apartment. When Phala and Philip had lit their pipes and drawn their cushions near to the fire, which was burning brightly at the top of the hall, the former thought that he might at last try to satisfy his curiosity about the stranger.

" In what direction were you travelling when I met you this afternoon ? " he asked.

Philip hesitated for a moment as to whether he should mention his real destination, and decided to do so.

" Lhasa," he answered briefly.

" Lhasa ? " repeated the Deba in surprise. " But you were not on the Lhasa road."

Philip came to the conclusion that it would be best to be quite frank.

" I got as far as Namcho on the Lhasa main road, but the lamas made me turn back, so I am following a circuitous route in order to avoid the village."

Phala smiled. The stranger evidently did not know that he was Deba of the district and in sympathy with the lamas.

" What reason did they give for sending you back ? " he asked.

" Because I did not have a passport."

The Deba was silent for a while. Then he resumed—

" The Tibetans, as perhaps you know, are very jealous with regard to foreigners entering their country. What is your object in going to Lhasa ? "

" I want to trade with Lhasa merchants.'

" To what country do you belong ? "

" Eastern Mongolia. My name is Khangsar."

Phala looked at his guest, and then, after a pause, he said—

" If it were not for your dark skin, and your knowledge of our language, I should have said you were a peling (foreigner). But I know that many of your countrymen resemble, like you, the pelings in feature. Perhaps the lamas suspected you of being one, for they would have no reason to prevent an Eastern Mongol from journeying to Lhasa."

" And if I had been a peling," answered Philip boldly, " why should they object to my going to Lhasa for purposes of trade ? The more merchants you have there, the cheaper will all commodities become, and the whole country would benefit by it."

Phala shook his head.

" Trade is not the first necessity of a nation. It is no gain to get your merchandise cheaply if you lose thereby your independence."

" How could one peling affect the independence of your country ? " Philip asked.

" By himself, perhaps, he could do no harm, but others would join him, till a large number of them dwelt in our sacred capital. Then they would combine, and if they did not get their own way, they would pick a quarrel with those in authority and appeal to their fellow-countrymen for help."

"You give the pelings a very bad character."

"We judge by what has happened in neighbouring states. There is a saying in Tibet that wherever a peling gets a foothold, there he remains, till the whole country becomes subject to him."

"He has had a foothold in Kashmir, Sikkim, and Nepaul for many years, yet he has not interfered with the independence of these states."

"In Kashmir, so my father told me, they used to say—'The world is Allah's, the land is the pasha's, but it is the company that rules.'"

Philip had heard the saying himself, and saw the appropriateness of the quotation. But there was one more point he wished to raise.

"If the Tibetans are so opposed to foreigners, why did they admit the Chinese, who have done just what you are afraid the pelings will do, and have practically seized the government of your country?"

It was a home thrust and hit the Deba hard, for he frowned and answered—

"According to the teaching of the great Buddha, whom we worship, men should live in peace together and not shed each other's blood. We Tibetans attempted to follow this precept, and the Chinese took advantage of us and invaded our country. But they do not rule it so easily as you think. In Eastern Tibet they exist on sufferance, and even at Lhasa they are not all-powerful. Perhaps some day we shall drive them out of the country altogether."

Philip realized that Phala was a patriot, and that his treatment of Tuen Fang was part of a deliberate policy. Perhaps, after all, there were greater blessings that a nation might enjoy than mere cheapness of commodities.

CHAPTER IX

WHEN Philip Harwood went to pay a professional visit to his patient at dawn the following morning, he was surprised to find his room untenanted. Thinking that the boy had been moved to other quarters, he descended to make inquiries about him. There was no one in the hall, but, on going to the entrance, he caught sight of Maru's sister feeding pigeons in the courtyard. Although the temperature was still below freezing point and the ground hard with frost, she had no covering on her head nor any kind of outdoor clothing, and seemed quite indifferent to the cold. As she stood with the pigeons circling round her, her dark hair and rosy cheeks lending a little colour to the grey monotony of the castle walls, the young girl made a pretty picture.

"You are early," said Philip as he approached her.

"Do you call this early?" she answered on seeing who it was. "I have been up an hour at least."

"Then you rose when it was dark. But let me know your name."

"Lotzung," * replied the girl, smiling.

"It falls to you to feed your namesakes, then."

"Yes, and I am glad my parents gave me the name. In my next life I should like to be a dove. It must be pleasant to fly through the air as they do!"

"You must take care to be a dove in Tibet only then," rejoined Philip. "In any other country you might be killed and eaten."

* *Lotzung*, a dove.

" Is that really so ? " asked Lotzung, raising her dark eyes to his with a look of surprise. " We do not even kill the crows which destroy our crops. How can men shed the blood of animals in which there may reside the souls of their dead relations ? "

" Yes, it does seem a sacrilege," replied Philip gravely. " For this reason you spare the lives of the rats and mice which swarm in your temples, in case former lamas should be doing penance in these shapes. But we will not talk about our future incarnations. The present interests me more. Where is your brother Maru ? "

" I saw him pass through the courtyard into the orchard," answered Lotzung.

" What ! " exclaimed Philip in surprise. " Did he escape from those who were set to nurse him ? "

The young girl gave a merry laugh.

" No one was set to nurse him. When I went to his room this morning I found him ready dressed. He said he felt quite well and was going to practise with his bow and arrow."

" I must see him at once. Where is the orchard ? "

" I will show you," she replied, and taking his hand with the frank action of a child, she led him through a long, narrow archway on one side of the courtyard into the garden which he had noticed on approaching the castle the previous evening. Here, amongst some apricot trees by the side of the moat, they found Maru shooting at a target which he had fixed to a tree trunk. On catching sight of Philip and Lotzung he called to the former—

" Come and see if you can hit yonder target with an arrow ! "

Philip took the bow which the boy held out to him. Then, looking at him reprovingly, he said—

" You ought not to be out here with that cut on your

forehead; the cold may get into the wound and prevent it healing properly."

"My wound!" repeated the boy in accents of surprise. "That happened yesterday, and to-day I am quite well. It hurts no longer."

The wound certainly had the appearance of healing satisfactorily, and the boy looked as well as if no accident had happened to him. Still caution was necessary, and Philip said—

"If you are not careful you will burst the stitches, and then the wound will take some time to heal. Here comes your father—now you will be scolded!"

But the boy ran up to his father laughing, and said—

"The Kushok says that you will scold me for practising with my bow and arrow. Is it not the duty of every Tibetan to learn the use of arms?"

The Deba looked down smilingly upon his son. Tibetans are often so fond of their children that they even shrink from correcting them for their faults. This is especially the case with sons, of whom they think a good deal more than of their daughters. Maru was evidently the favourite child, and as his father took his hand and walked towards Philip he said to the boy—

"The Kushok means that it is not wise to practise shooting before the cut has healed. But it seems to be doing well," he added, stooping down and examining the wound.

"Then let us go and hunt the musk deer as you settled yesterday," rejoined the boy, seeing his parent inclined to yield. "We can take the Kushok with us. It is only a short ride to the hills."

"The Kushok will not encourage you to ride," answered Philip, "by being one of the party. Besides, I must resume my journey to-day."

"You cannot start to-day, my friend," rejoined the Deba. "I still have much to say to you. As for the musk deer hunting, since you do not happen to approve of it for the lad, we will not go. But let us return to the castle; it is time for breakfast."

The party began to retrace their steps, and on nearing the entrance Maru said coaxingly to his father—

"Give me permission to sit at table with the Kushok and yourself. I am old enough to be with men, instead of still consorting with the women-folk."

The Deba hesitated, and might perhaps have given way had not the chatelaine appeared in time to hear the request and to give it the proper answer.

"Come with me, Maru," she said, taking the boy's hand. "It will be time for you to sit with your father when you are strong enough to draw his bow and ride his steed."

Thus it happened that Philip and the Deba breakfasted, as they had dined, alone with the retainers, waited on by Phagmo and Lotzung.

During the meal Philip again said that he must resume his journey that day, but Phala would not hear of it.

"After breakfast I will show you my armoury, and then we will practise shooting, I with my bow and arrows and my matchlock, and you with the new-fashioned gun I saw at your saddle-bow yesterday. You are my prisoner for to-day," he added, smiling. "I am the Deba of this district, and no one may travel through it unless I give him leave."

Philip did not reply that he knew him to be the Deba, and allowed the statement to pass without comment. He was not at all sorry to enjoy a day's rest in such comfortable quarters, and made no further protest. At the conclusion of the meal Phala took him to the armoury, a small room full of the old-fashioned armour of the Deba's ancestors. The protective armour consisted of copper armlets, greaves, and coats of mail. Amongst the weapons Philip noticed some curious arrows, lances, and three-headed spears. The protective armour had not been worn since fire-arms were introduced in Tibet, but bows and arrows were still used for warlike purposes. As most of the Chinese troops in Tibet had no other weapons, the issue of a battle might depend upon them. In the armoury there were also a dozen matchlocks, which the Deba kept in excellent order, and of which he was very proud.

"Let us arrange a shooting match," the Deba said. "You bring your new gun and I will take my bow and arrows and my matchlock. I will give orders for the tent to be put up."

Shooting at a mark was evidently a pastime with the Deba. The range lay about a couple of miles from the castle, and a tent was necessary, he explained, so that they might have their midday meal in comfort, protected from the bright rays of the sun. It was evident that the Deba intended to have a field-day at the butts.

The horses were soon announced, for a Tibetan nobleman never walks to any place, however near, if it is possible to ride there. In the courtyard they found two horses and two mules, while half a dozen mounted retainers were waiting to accompany their chief.

"Who is to be the fourth of the party ?" Philip inquired of Lotzung.

"Are there not four of us ?" she answered, for Maru had persuaded his father to let him go.

"Are you coming with us then, to practise shooting ?"

"No, I only help to bring back the arrows."

"And which is your animal ?" he asked.

"This one," she answered, taking the reins of one of the

mules, which, as Philip noticed, had an ordinary man's saddle.

"Do you ride astride like the men?" he asked.

The young girl looked upon him with wondering eyes. "Of course," she answered, "how else could I ride?" She had tied up her long garment at the waist, so that it only reached to the knee, displaying to view trousers and boots similar to those her father and brother wore. Then, as Philip offered to help her mount, she waved him aside and swung lightly into the saddle.

"I see that you are accustomed to riding," the young man said.

"Yes, I often help my father's men lassoo the yaks, and love riding full gallop after them."

The start was now made, but on account of Maru they did not go above a walk. In spite of this, they reached the ground in little over half an hour. The range had been marked out in a field with a hill on the further side proving an excellent background for the target. The field was cut off from the road by a loose stone wall about four feet high. The Deba's servants had removed the pole which usually lay across a gap in the wall. Through this gap the Deba and his son passed. Philip reined his horse in, so as to allow Lotzung to go next, but the young girl, who had dropped a short distance behind, told him not to wait, and turned her mule's head towards the wall. The animal did not look like a jumper, and the slow trot at which he approached the obstacle made Philip think that he would not even try to jump it. But the young man was mistaken, and the mule, pricking up its ears, rose slowly up on his hind legs, poised himself for a moment on them, and then dropped clumsily but safely over the wall.

"You did not think my mule would jump the wall, did you?" asked Lotzung with a smile, as she trotted up to

Philip. "He is very slow, but he jumps better than any of the others."

The party dismounted at the tent, and the Deba led the way on foot to a position some hundred yards from the target. Two attendants followed with his bow and arrows and matchlock. Fitting an arrow to the string of the bow, the Deba took a steady aim and released the missile. It flew so swiftly that Philip could not follow its course, but he saw an arrow quivering in the centre of the target.

"Now you shoot an arrow," the Deba said to his guest. Philip had not shot with a bow and arrow since his early childhood, but he accepted the Deba's challenge. Putting an arrow in its place, he tried to draw the bow but it refused to bend. Phala smiled and the children clapped their hands with delight. Thus spurred to make a second effort, Philip drew the string perhaps a couple of inches, whereupon the arrow escaped his grasp and struck the ground at a distance of some twenty yards. It evidently required knack as well as strength to draw a Tibetan bow.

Phala handed Philip another bow, which bent more readily, and at a shorter range the young man began a match with Maru. The boy, of course, beat him easily. In fact, the strength and skill he displayed was marvellous at his age. Lotzung, as she walked to and fro, bringing back the arrows from the target, laughed heartily at Philip's efforts.

"Perhaps you think you could beat me yourself, Lotzung," said Philip, after one of her outbursts of merriment. "Come and try."

"Lotzung cannot draw a bow!" said Maru, with the conscious superiority of his sex. "Women only attend to household matters. It is the men who fight."

Phala smiled at these sentiments and patted the boy's head, while Lotzung, evidently accustomed to such speeches, only laughed. Practice with the bow and arrows lasted till the midday meal, after which Phala called for one of his matchlocks. Resting the muzzle on the pair of antelope horns attached to it, he knelt down on one knee, lit the slow match, and waited. The match missed fire, an apparently common experience, for Phala, in no way disconcerted, lit another and resumed his watch. This time the match ignited the powder, the explosion was followed almost simultaneously by the sharp pinge of the bullet against the target, and Lotzung, who ran to find the effect of the shot, pointed to the centre.

"It is your turn now," said Phala to Philip, with the composed air of a man who has only done what he anticipated. "But if the distance is too great for your gun, go a little nearer."

Phala had fired from about one hundred and fifty yards, and Philip, feeling that he could double the distance, answered, "I will not fire at your target, for my bullets are small, and it might be difficult to find the hole they make. But if one of your men will stand this log of wood on yonder ledge of rock I will see if I can hit it."

Phala smiled incredulously, for the ledge was twice the distance of the target. But he sent the man with the log, and when it had been put up, Philip took a steady aim and the log fell over. Phala gazed at the spot in amazement.

"The wind must have blown the log over!" he said. On examination, however, they found a small hole in the centre of the log and the bullet flattened on the ground beneath the rock.

"It is a marvellous gun," confessed Phala. "If we Tibetans had such a weapon, we would soon drive the Chinese out of the country."

Philip's performance put the Deba out of conceit with his old matchlocks, and he spent the rest of the afternoon examining his guest's rifle and trying to understand its mechanism. The evening was devoted to music. Phagmo, who had complained of a headache in the morning, had been given a cooling draught by Philip and felt much better. Phala had also been successfully treated for a troublesome cough, so that the whole family, with the exception of Lotzung, had availed themselves of his medical skill. The musical entertainment consisted of songs by Phagmo and Lötzung, both of whom had very sweet voices, while the Deba accompanied them on a stringed instrument.

Before retiring for the night Philip announced his intention of departing in the morning, and presented Phala with one of his three rifles. The Deba was greatly pleased with the gift, and insisted on Philip staying another day to instruct him thoroughly in its use. Though the young man was anxious to get away at once, he saw that it would be well to fall in with the wishes of a powerful nobleman like Phala. He therefore consented to remain on the understanding that no attempt should be made to detain him more than one day longer.

Philip's reputation as a physician had one result which he had not anticipated. When he descended to the courtyard the following morning, Lotzung, whom he found at her daily task of feeding the pigeons, ran to him and said—

"I want you to give me some medicine!"

"Medicine!" exclaimed Philip in surprise, as he saw her rosy cheeks and bright dark eyes. "What do you want medicine for? Are you feeling unwell?"

"No, I am not feeling unwell, but I should like some medicine!"

"Put out your tongue," said Philip gravely.

Lotzung displayed a tongue of a healthy red colour.

"Let me feel your pulse."

It beat as strong and rhythmically as that of a well-trained athlete.

"I think you said that you sleep well?"

"I suppose I do. I remember nothing from the time I lie down to the time I wake, and it usually seems like a few minutes instead of hours."

"I need not ask if you have a good appetite," continued the young man, for Lotzung had eaten with them in the tent on the previous day, and he had noticed that she did full justice to the fare. "Have you any aches or pain?"

"None at all," said Lotzung.

"Well, I can find nothing the matter with you, absolutely nothing, unless perhaps it is exuberance of health."

Lotzung looked extremely disappointed.

"You have given medicine to all of them—father, mother, and Maru," she protested, with all but tears in her eyes. "Even the servants have not been forgotten. Surely you can spare a little for Lotzung."

Philip was quite taken aback by the earnestness of her appeal.

"I can certainly spare you some medicine, Lotzung," he said with becoming gravity. "I assure you that it was no intentional slight that I have not prescribed for you already. I will send Mantso for my medicine case at once."

Mantso, who generally managed to be within call when Philip wanted him, answered his master's summons, and was dispatched to get the case. The sight of the precious box in Mantso's hands induced most of the household to follow him into the yard in order to see who would be the lucky recipient of a portion of its much prized contents. Philip, with great deliberation, measured out and mixed half a cupful of sherbet and gave it to Lotzung to drink. The effervescing liquid made as great impression upon the spectators as the magnesia which he had administered to his host at the first stage of his journey. Lotzung was highly gratified at being the object of so interesting a demonstration, while Maru muttered beneath his breath that it was a shame to waste such good medicine on a woman.

During the day Philip instructed Phala in the use of his newly acquired rifle, and presented him with a hundred rounds of ammunition. In return the Deba, as they sat together that evening, went into the question as to how he could best assist his guest in his enterprise.

" You tell me that your object is to open up a trade with Lhasa ? "

Philip assented.

" I will do all I can to help you get there. As far as my own district is concerned, I will give you safe conduct, but I cannot answer for other districts. No passport given by me would ensure a safe passage to Lhasa. Only one signed by the Emperor of China or the Dalai Lama himself could do that. Therefore I warn you to be careful. I do not ask for any credentials from you, nor for any account of yourself. In fact, I would rather not have it. But you have told me that the lamas of Namcho have sent you back. They may have found out something against you. Be careful, therefore, next time you are stopped by lamas that no particulars of an unfavourable character should reach their ears."

" I shall be content if you give me a safe passage through your district. For the remainder of the journey I understand that I shall have to depend on my own resources."

"Even supposing you get to Lhasa," continued Phala, " your troubles are not over. A stranger is always liable to have false accusations made against him. When I lived in Lhasa I could have been of service to you, but I have little influence there now."

" How did you come to leave it ? " asked Philip.

The words were no sooner out of his mouth than he repented them, for a cloud passed over his host's face.

" I left Lhasa because my enemies succeeded in having me banished the city. The power is all in the hands of the regent, a man who is not worthy of such a position."

Philip remained silent, wishing to avoid any further indiscretions ; but Phala continued.

" Of course you know whom I mean. The present regent has acted for three Dalai Lamas in succession. His position is almost unassailable, for he is supported by the wealthy lamasery of Sera. Then he takes care to win over the Chinese amban for the time being, or, if the amban is not to be bought, he intrigues at Pekin for his recall. The late amban was proof against bribes, and he is replaced with another mandarin, who is more likely to fall in with the regent's plans."

Philip saw that the Deba referred to Tuen Fang, but he made no comment, and Phala went on—

" If we had an honest regent, the Chinese would have no more authority in Lhasa than you have here. I opposed this man and he proved too strong for me, banishing me from Lhasa. However, though I have no influence amongst his partisans, I will give you a letter to a friend of mine in the sacred city who may be able to assist you."

CHAPTER X

BY dawn the following morning all the pack animals were loaded and the caravan was ready to start. Half an hour earlier Phagmo had prepared a substantial Tibetan breakfast, to which Philip sat down in company with his host. At the conclusion of the meal Phala said that he could ride part of the first day's journey with him. This offer was very welcome, for should the lamas of Namcho have heard where Philip was, they were hardly likely to interfere with him if accompanied by the Deba of the district.

Mantso brought his master's mule to the principal entrance and Philip took leave of his hostess with many expressions of gratitude for the hospitality which she had shown him. As Maru had persuaded his father to let him accompany the caravan as far as he himself was going, there only remained Lotzung of whom to take farewell. Strange to say she was nowhere to be seen, and Philip now remembered that he had not noticed her feeding the pigeons as usual that morning.

"I should like to wish Lotzung good-bye," he said to Phala. "Where can she be found?"

Phala did not know, and repeated Philip's question to Phagmo. The latter expressed herself equally ignorant.

"Perhaps she is still in bed," said Philip.

Phagmo smiled at such a suggestion.

"A Tibetan girl soon learns to perform the various duties which women have to do. Lotzung gets up at four o'clock to churn the butter, and I saw her at that hour myself this morning."

"She must be riding somewhere," said Maru. "When I went to get my mule, I noticed that her mule was not in the stable."

"Then she has gone to help the men with the cattle," Phagmo observed. "I will tell her that Khangsar sent her a farewell message."

As Philip mounted his mule he could not help feeling somewhat piqued at Lotzung thus absenting herself. After having coaxed out of him a special dose of medicine she might at any rate have deferred her ride till his caravan had started. But it was absurd to expect gratitude in a girl so young and irresponsible as Lotzung.

Their journey lay along a fertile valley, where the glorious tints of autumn still lingered in the land. As the road was good Phala proposed riding ahead of the slow-travelling yaks to await the caravan at the house of a friend some ten miles distant. Philip soon recovered his spirits in the pleasant company of Phala and his son, attended by six gaily-dressed retainers. If he had been successful in gaining the confidence of the Deba of one district, why should he not be equally fortunate with the Deba of the next district? The Tibetan gentry, if one could judge by Phala, seemed remarkably intelligent and broad-minded, and as long as he kept out of the way of the lamas, he might yet accomplish his design of reaching Lhasa.

Thus Philip trotted gaily along with Phala and Maru either side of him, and the attendants close behind, the tinkling bells which the animals carried making a pleasant accompaniment to the rhythmic clatter of their feet. Occasionally, on coming to an open stretch of springy turf, they would break into a canter, when the bells would clash together as the animals came into step, ringing out irregularly again, like a peal of church bells, as soon as the uniformity of the movement ceased.

At ten o'clock they reached the farm where Phala wished to halt. The owner came to the door to welcome the Deba and his company, and they were soon sitting down to a well-served meal. At noon the caravan arrived, and Philip ordered a halt to rest the animals. Shortly afterwards Phala took the young man aside and drew a letter from the folds of his garment.

" Here is a letter to my friend Rashwa, of whom I spoke to you," he said. " Do not lose it, for should you succeed in reaching Lhasa it will be of service to you. Above all, be careful not to arouse the suspicions of the lamas. They are patriots, but over-zealous in their efforts to exclude foreigners from Tibet. Two of my attendants will accompany you to the boundary of my district, which you should reach by sunset to-morrow. I have told them to keep away from the main road to Lhasa, and, on leaving my district, I should advise you to do the same. The track is bad, but you will run less risk of interference."

Philip thanked the Deba for his kindness and promised to be guided by what he said. He then accompanied him to the door, where they found Maru already mounted.

" Tell your sister," he said jestingly to Maru, " that if I ever come this way again I shall reserve that beautiful medicine I gave her for some one who will appreciate it more."

" I thought at the time that you were only wasting it," replied Maru regretfully. " When you come again, you will give some to me, will you not ? "

Philip laughingly promised to do so, and then the Deba and his son rode off, accompanied by their four attendants.

After the pack animals had rested for a couple of hours Philip gave the order to resume the march. The country still remained very beautiful, and the two retainers were full of interesting information with regard to it. As a rule Philip brought up the rear of his caravan, to help any animals which got into difficulties, and to see no straggling occurred. On this occasion he anticipated no such difficulties and rode at the head in the company of his guides.

Diverted by their conversation Philip failed to remember that the saddle-mules would travel much faster than the yaks, and rode a considerable distance in front of his caravan. When he discovered the fact it was already four o'clock, and the village where the guides proposed he should spend the night had come into view. Accordingly he told the two men to ride on and arrange about accommodation while he waited for the caravan to overtake him.

When the men had gone Philip found himself in a pretty grove, with a bank of rich turf on the further side of a sparkling brook. He crossed the stream by a rough log bridge, and, dismounting, lay down full length on the grass. The sun was still sufficiently powerful to maintain a pleasant temperature, the birds twittered in the trees, and the water gurgled musically as it fell over the moss-grown boulders in mid-stream. The scene once more reminded him of England, and, shutting his eyes, he fancied himself again in the woods adjoining his distant home. If the rest of his journey were as pleasant as this stage of it he would be fortunate indeed, and, with that agreeable sense of drowsiness which follows a long ride in the exhilarating Tibetan air, he allowed himself to fall asleep.

A pleasant dream accompanied the sleep. He saw himself overcoming one by one all the dangers of the journey, and escaping the vigilance or disarming the suspicions of the lamas he encountered on the way. He experienced the thrill of his first view of the sacred city of Buddhism, and of his successful entry into it; his reception by Rashwa, and the first evening spent under his host's roof, with a group of young Tibetan girls,—amongst whom, by that disregard of the unities of time and place displayed in dreams, stood Lotzung,—celebrating his arrival with songs of welcome.

When he awoke these songs still seemed to linger in his ears. Yes, there was no doubt about it, the sound of girls' voices came from the direction in which the village lay. Philip jumped to his feet, and in the distance, through the trees, he saw a group of young girls coming along the path towards the stream. They were dressed in holiday attire, and decked with garlands of wild flowers from the woods. As they went they sang a pretty air, with the sweetness of voice for which Tibetans, both men and women, are justly celebrated.

Philip made up his mind at once. This was evidently some quaint Tibetan custom connected perhaps with the betrothal or marriage of one of the girls composing the party, and would be interesting to observe from a place of concealment. Accordingly he walked in the direction of the rough wooden bridge, by which they would have to cross the stream, and took up his position behind a tree, from which he could watch them pass without attracting notice himself. As the girls came nearer he saw that one of them carried a wooden platter filled with fruit. This must be intended as a present for the couple in whose honour the fête had been arranged.

The girls, who numbered about a dozen, were now nearing the bridge, and Philip noticed that as they went they peered through the trees as if in search of something. He wondered what they could be looking for, and in order to discover it he incautiously bent forward too far from the protection of the tree. In a moment the leader of the band, a pretty girl of seventeen or eighteen years of age, had caught sight of him, and calling to the others ran up to him and took his hands.

"We have found you at last then!" she cried. "I was afraid that we had passed you. Come and sit down and partake of the fruit which we have brought you." And, still holding his hands, she led the bewildered young man to the trunk of a fallen tree, and made him sit upon it. Then, before he could ask for any explanation, she presented him with a khata of welcome, and threw a garland of flowers round his neck. This ceremony finished, she took the platter of fruit and held it out to him.

"Eat," she said. "Fruit is welcome at the end of a toilsome journey."

Philip selected a magnificent pear, but before commencing to eat it he took the opportunity of a momentary lull in the laughing voices round him to say—

"It is extremely kind of you to deck me with these flowers and to offer me some of your beautiful fruit, but before swallowing this pear I think I ought to tell you that I am not the man you are looking for. Having made this explanation I feel at liberty to eat the fruit you have already given me," and Philip took a hearty bite at the pear.

A peal of merry laughter followed this speech with its accompanying action, and the leader said—

"Whom do you think, then, we are looking for?"

"I cannot tell," replied Philip, "but it is doubtless some happy youth of your acquaintance whom for some reason you wish to honour."

"Then you are wrong," the girl answered with a smile. "The youth we are looking for is not known to any of us, but he is a friend of the Deba of our district, and that is why we wish to know him. His name is Khangsar. Are you not he?"

The young girl evidently knew all about him, and it would be useless to disown the name he had chosen to assume.

"Yes, I am Khangsar," he said, "and count myself a very lucky person to be the object of such a pleasant demonstration. That last pear was a very good one. As you say they are for me I will take another one."

Again the girls laughed heartily, and, seating themselves on the grass in a semicircle round him, began to weave fresh garlands, singing tunefully as they did so. Philip munched his pear and surveyed them at his leisure. They were certainly a very presentable lot, those who were not good-looking making up by pleasantness of expression what they lacked in regularity of feature.

"So you heard all about me from the two guides who went on ahead," he said. "I don't know how you found the time to arrange such a pleasant reception for me."

They all laughed at this observation, and the leader said—

"We like to do honour to our Deba's friends." Then turning to her companions she continued: "Let us dance before him now."

They sprang to their feet with a chorus of consent, and commenced a quaint but by no means ungraceful dance on the grass plot in front of him, singing the while, and keeping measure to their song. It was a pretty sight, these Tibetan girls executing the national dance in their native groves, and Philip watched the performance with interest. First came a general movement in which all took part, but presently one of the girls advanced in front of the others and performed alone, whilst her comrades stood round and sang to her. This *pas seul* showed more animation than the general ballet, and the performer after a time turned towards Philip and seemed to dance to him alone.

After a particularly energetic finale, she threw herself at his feet and held out a flower for acceptance. Philip took it, but the girl still remained on her knees, looking up at him with a smile upon her lips. The situation threatened to become embarrassing, and, as something further was evidently expected of him, he bent forward and said—

"Thank you very much; I consider your performance excellent."

Peals of merry laughter greeted this remark, and the young girl, rising hastily, rejoined the rest, when another *pas seul* was commenced.

In this way each member of the band performed before Philip, and ended by prostrating herself at his feet, his compliment on her dancing being received with the same merriment, while its recipient retired with haste and confusion to her place. There followed a short pause, and Philip was coming to the conclusion that the performance had ended, when a girl emerged from the shelter of the surrounding trees and joined the group. She wore a mask of black silk, which, with the exception of two holes for the eyes, left only the lower part of the face, including a very pretty little mouth, exposed to view. The girl began to dance at once, and from the first moment it was plain that she far excelled the others in the grace and lightness of her movements. A bewitching smile played round her mouth, and as she joined now and then in the singing of the chorus the sweetest notes issued from her lips. Little wonder that when she at length prostrated herself at Philip's feet her companions greeted her performance with rapturous applause. The young man, gazing down through the eyelets at the sparkling eyes, and attracted by the pretty smiling mouth, to which the black mask acted as a foil, felt a very natural desire to see her face, and said—

"You have danced very beautifully, and I am sure your features are as pretty as your voice is sweet. Take off your mask and let me see if I am right."

But the young girl only shook her head, though she still remained kneeling before him, looking up at him with smiling lips. Her non-compliance only confirmed Philip in his desire, and seizing her outstretched hands, he placed her on the tree trunk on which he sat, with the intention of removing the mask himself. No sooner, however, was the girl seated at his side than a wild burst of applause rose from her companions, and their leader ran up to the couple and joined their hands.

"Om mani padme hum!" she exclaimed, repeating the familiar Buddhist formula in solemn tones.

"Om mani padme hum!" cried all the others.

"What is the meaning of this?" asked Philip, much perplexed at the turn which the proceedings had taken.

"You an Eastern Mongol, Khangsar, and yet ignorant of our customs?" answered the leader. "Surely you know that when a man at these dances selects a girl to sit beside him he takes her for his wife."

Philip nearly jumped out of his seat at her words, and in spite of the declining temperature, great beads of perspiration broke out on his forehead. Fancy being saddled with a wife just when the real difficulties of his journey were about to commence, and when he would have trouble enough to look after himself without being hampered by a woman. Besides, his father-in-law would probably want him to settle down in the neighbourhood of the village, instead of taking his daughter on the perilous journey to Lhasa.

"I must confess to ignorance of this custom," he replied, "and on that account must claim release from the contract it entails."

But this plea only raised a storm of protests, and cries of "Hail to the bride and bridegroom!" rose on all sides. To make matters worse Philip discovered that his caravan had now arrived, and that his four muleteers, reinforced by the two guides, who had returned from the village, were pressing forward with beaming countenances to offer their congratulations. The number of witnesses was overwhelming, and the young man realized that he was in an awkward fix. What was he to do? The thought struck him that he might persuade his newly-wedded wife, who during all the hubbub had remained silent at his side, to repudiate the bargain. But on turning to her, he found the mask had been removed, and recognized, to his amazement, the Deba's daughter, Lotzung.

"You, Lotzung?" he exclaimed.

"Yes, it is Lotzung!" the girl answered, smiling. "I am glad you did not take any of the others, Khangsar!" she added with a little laugh.

"Well—but—I say, Lotzung, this is of course only a pretty little open-air play. We had better return to the realities of life again. It is getting late, and I must push on with my caravan to the village. When do you go back to your father?"

"Go back to my father?" repeated Lotzung, with her eyebrows arched in pretty surprise. "A daughter when she is married leaves her father and mother and accompanies her husband wherever he goes!"

"Yes, of course, but then you are not my wife!"

"But the wedding has this moment taken place. Were we not properly married?" she continued, appealing to the band of girls.

"It is a lawful marriage!" they all responded, much amused at the perplexed expression of the bridegroom's face. The six men also added with a laugh—

" Yes, Kushok, she is your wife ! "

Against such a unanimous verdict it was useless to protest, and Philip ordered his muleteers to resume the march. The two guides led the way, the baggage animals came next, while Philip and Lotzung, escorted by the band of girls, brought up the rear. The latter were once more singing merrily, and gave Philip the opportunity for reflection which he desired. How did it all happen ? Was it a plot of Lotzung's, who, for some reason best known to herself, wished to appear for a day at any rate as his wife ? If so, she had laid her plans with much skill and forethought. She must have learnt on the previous evening the direction which his caravan would take. In the early morning, after her mother had seen her at her usual work, she must have slipped away to the stable, taken out her mule, and ridden hard for the village they were now approaching, in order to collect a band of girls in time for his arrival. What could have been her object ? It was certainly not a case of love, for nothing of the kind had passed between them. Was she merely a tool employed by the lamas to get him into trouble ? If so, they had not taken her into their confidence, for no one could look at her smiling, open face and believe that she was knowingly betraying her companion. Perhaps, after all, it was only a childish freak, the origin of which was capable of some simple explanation.

But what gave Philip much more concern than the young girl's view of the matter was the light with which the Deba would regard it. No doubt he would consider that his guest had made a very ill return for the hospitality extended to him. Philip saw that he must be informed at once, and he decided to send Mantso back to the Deba's castle that very night, to explain exactly how matters stood. Meanwhile he would take care that no misconstruction could afterwards be put upon his present relations with the Deba's daughter.

On approaching the village Philip realized that every one had been informed of the recent ceremony, for the inhabitants came out to welcome him. He was escorted to the house of the chief, who had prepared a dinner in honour of the wedding. To this repast they sat down at sunset with as many guests as the room would hold. Of course there was no opportunity for private conversation with Lotzung, who took the honours paid to them with smiling complacency, as nothing but her due. Philip, who caught the happy gladness of her dark eyes, and the music of her laughter, found it impossible to regard her as anything but an irresponsible child of nature, without any of the feelings or sentiments looked for on such an occasion from her European sisters.

The merry-making was carried on after the meal had been cleared away, but before the guests began to depart, Philip called for silence, and said—

"I must thank you all, and especially the chief of this village, whose hospitality we are enjoying, for the kind reception you have given me. I attribute it to the high regard in which you hold the Deba of this district, who is my friend. You have, of course, all heard of the ceremony which took place this afternoon. In my country it is the custom for a newly-married couple to sleep in different houses for the first three nights after the wedding. I therefore wish to bid you all good night before I withdraw to another building."

This announcement was received at first in astonished silence, and then with a ripple of incredulous laughter. Lotzung, the person most concerned, smiled pleasantly, as if Philip's proposition was the most natural one in the world for a bridegroom to make. The chief's wife, who had gone to much trouble in preparing the bridal chamber, was the most disappointed, but her expostulations had no effect on Philip. Wishing them all good night he left the house for the shelter of the village inn. On his way thither he gave Mantso a letter which he had found time to scribble to the Deba, with instructions to ride off with it at once. He then entered the inn, feeling that he had done all that was possible to put matters straight.

CHAPTER XI

As Philip Harwood got up the following morning he debated what his best course of action would be. With regard to the Deba, whether he came himself or sent a message by Mantso, no news of him could reach Philip at the earliest till the afternoon. Meanwhile it would look strange if he avoided his bride, and the young man saw no reason why he should do so. In fact, by paying her a visit he might arrive at some explanation of her conduct, which so far was quite unintelligible to him.

Accordingly, after an early breakfast, he walked across to the chief's house, and found Lotzung in the yard throwing bread-crumbs to the pigeons.

"You have not forgotten your pets, I see," said Philip.

Lotzung smiled pleasantly up at him, and, continuing her occupation, asked—

"When do we start on our journey?"

"That depends, Lotzung," he replied. "I want information on several points before I answer that question. In the first place, who planned that little surprise in the grove yesterday?"

"I arranged it all," replied the young girl, as if she were rather proud of the achievement. "Nobody at home knew anything about it."

"Did you wish to be my wife then?" inquired Philip.

"Yes, of course," she answered quite naturally, "or why should I have taken the trouble?"

"I might have chosen one of the other girls."

" I wished to give you your choice, but I am glad it did not fall on anybody else."

" But why should I marry at all ? "

This was a question which Lotzung had evidently never anticipated.

" I do not know," she replied, " except that everybody who visits this country has a wife while he is here."

" And leaves her behind when he goes ? "

" She would not, of course, be able to accompany him."

" But even supposing it is the usual custom to contract such marriages when paying a visit to this country, that does not explain why you should wish to marry me. It cannot be because you love me ! "

" Oh no, that is not the reason."

" What is the reason then ? " asked Philip, a little piqued by so ready a confession.

" I will tell you if you promise not to be angry with me ! "

" I promise," answered Philip.

" Well, then, I wanted to go to Lhasa, and that was the only way in which it could be done."

" Why do you want to go to Lhasa ? "

" In order to see my brother who lives there."

" I did not know you had another brother."

" We do not speak of him as a brother."

It seemed to be a delicate subject. Perhaps the young fellow had committed some youthful folly and been disowned by his parents, though it was not unnatural that he should still hold a place in his sister's heart.

" How old is he ? " asked Philip.

" Fourteen," she answered.

Fourteen was very young for a boy to have irretrievably disgraced himself in the eyes of his family. Philip's curiosity prompted him to ask one more question.

" What does he do in Lhasa ? "

"I must not tell you," the young girl replied.

Philip saw that he had gone too far.

"I ought not to have asked you," he said, "and I am glad to see you take his part. But you have not gone the right way to work to get to Lhasa. You should have waited till there was some one going there to whom your parents could entrust you."

Lotzung shook her head.

"My mother would not let me leave the house except to be married. Although my father is rich, I have to work hard, and nearly all my time is occupied in household duties. The only way I could get to Lhasa was as some one's wife. So when I heard that you were going there, I arranged the ceremony by which a girl may choose her husband if he is willing to take her. Do you want to get rid of me already?"

"I am not the only person to be consulted," Philip replied. "Your parents have the first say in the matter. I sent a messenger last night to tell them what has occurred."

"Did you say that you would not take me with you?"

"There was no occasion to do so, because, of course, they will send some one to take you back."

Strangely enough this statement seemed to set Lotzung's mind at ease, and she asked no more questions. The festivities in connection with the marriage were still being kept up by the chief, and the two principals had to grace them with their presence. Lotzung acted her part with a smiling composure, as if she had been wedded to some one she had known from childhood. But Philip could not dissemble his feelings, and, for a bridegroom, wore a look of decided perplexity.

The hours passed by and no news came from Phala. On his good horse he could easily have reached the village early in the afternoon, but the sun set and he did not appear. Philip sat silent and preoccupied amidst the festivities which were going on around him. What was he to do if the parents refused to take their daughter back? But at length he heard that Mantso had returned, and, hurrying out into the yard, he found his servant just dismounting from his mule, whose drooping head and panting nostrils testified to the pace at which he had been ridden.

"Has the Deba arrived, Mantso?" asked Philip.

"The Deba is not coming, Kushok," answered Mantso. "He gave me this letter for you," and the muleteer produced a letter from the folds of his garment.

"How is it you have been so long?"

"I arrived at the Deba's castle at eight this morning. He had left to hunt the musk deer three hours earlier, and they expected him back at noon. As my mule was tired, and I should have gained no time by going in search of him, I waited for him at the castle."

Philip took the letter to the light of the open doorway and read as follows:—

"HONOURED FRIEND,—Your letter informs me that you have been married unwittingly by a band of young girls to my daughter Lotzung, and you ask what I wish you to do in the matter. There is nothing to be done. We received from Lotzung, by a messenger who arrived a short time before your muleteer, a certificate of the marriage, signed by all the girls who witnessed it. Such a certificate in our country makes the marriage legal. We shall miss Lotzung greatly, for she is very useful in the house. But she has been lawfully married, and we no longer have any claim upon her. Since she must leave us, I am glad she goes with you, for are we not friends, and have you not given me a proof of your friendship by presenting me with one of your beautiful guns? You will find Lotzung a hard worker, who will serve you well in every way. Farewell.—PHALA."

Here was a pretty state of affairs! Just when he was

about to enter on the most perilous portion of the journey to Lhasa, Philip found himself tricked into a marriage with a girl whose parents regarded the contract as binding. He had no desire to make a lifelong partner of a Tibetan woman, nor did the idea of a temporary marriage find favour with him. Although he was not in love with Lotzung any more than she was with him, he respected her too much to consent to an alliance of this character. What was he to do? He could not send her back to her father, after the letter he had just received from him. It would be worse still to leave her behind at the very village where her marriage had been celebrated as an event which had called for general rejoicing. He decided to see what Lotzung herself thought of her father's letter.

On re-entering the house Philip found the young girl performing a dance by herself in the centre of the room. As she did not catch sight of him he stood and watched her for a while. Moving on a level floor instead of the grass, she danced even better than the previous evening. Her figure was good, and the silk robe she had donned was very becoming. But her sparkling eyes and joyous expression proved even more attractive than her graceful movements. She was not the kind of bride one would expect to find a newly-wed husband planning to get rid of.

The performance ended amidst great applause, and then Philip led her to a corner of the room.

"I have just heard from your father," he began.

"What does he say?" asked Lotzung, her happy expression undergoing no change.

"What did you expect him to say, after getting the certificate you sent him?"

"I knew they could not order me to go back to them, and as you did not do so they must of course agree to the marriage."

"What is to be done then?"

"It is very simple. Am I not your wife, and does not a wife accompany her husband wherever he goes?"

"Listen to me, Lotzung. Though you may be my wife according to Tibetan law, you are not according to the law of my country."

"But we are in Tibet, and therefore I am your wife."

"Suppose I leave Tibet, you could not then come with me. You ought to marry a Tibetan, so that you would never be separated from him."

"But you do not mean to leave me here?" rejoined Lotzung, with a look for the first time of anxiety in her eyes.

"There is only one thing to be done. Have you any friends in Lhasa?"

"I have an uncle."

"Well, I will take you with me on the understanding that we are husband and wife in name only, and that as soon as I get to Lhasa, if I ever do, I hand you over to your uncle, when our temporary partnership will be dissolved for good."

"That is all I want," replied Lotzung, evidently pleased with the arrangement. "In return I will work for you as faithfully as your wife, though I shall only be your servant."

As soon as the matter was settled Philip went out into the yard and summoned his men.

"We start at dawn to-morrow," he said.

Mantso, Phendi, and Esa were evidently gratified with the news, but Jasi said—

"Which route does the Kushok wish to take?"

"The same as before, running parallel to the main Lhasa road."

"That route is now impossible, for there was a heavy fall of snow last night."

"Is there any other way open?"

"Yes, there is a road to the right shortly after leaving the village."

"But that joins the main road," said Mantso.

"No, you bear to the left again, after passing round to the north of Mount Miri-La."

Mantso said he did not know the road, and both Phendi and Esa agreed with him. Under these circumstances Philip decided to take no notice of Jasi's unfavourable report against continuing on the road they had been following, and merely repeated his order for the caravan to be ready to start in the morning.

After an early breakfast at the inn Philip went over to the chief's house and found Lotzung waiting for him at the entrance to the yard. She was dressed in a simple costume of grey Tibetan cloth, the sober colour of which only served to heighten the effect produced by her rosy cheeks and sparkling eyes. Seeing that Philip was ready to start she mounted her mule, which one of the chief's attendants was holding. As she rode out into the street a fine Tibetan mastiff bounded joyfully in front of her.

"Whose dog is that?" asked Philip, admiring its huge proportions and shaggy coat.

"That is my dog Champa," answered Lotzung. "You will not forbid its coming with us?"

Philip was glad to have a dog to accompany the caravan. Tibetan mastiffs are useful to their owners, though annoying enough to every one else. He had several times thought of procuring one, but was afraid it would be difficult to gain its affection. A dog, however, that was already attached to a member of the caravan would no doubt prove of service to it.

In spite of the late hour at which the festivities had ceased the previous evening, nearly all the merry-makers were up to witness the departure of the caravan. Philip waited till all the pack animals had gone, and then took leave of the chief who had honoured his marriage with such lavish hospitality. As a farewell present the young Englishman gave him a compass, which he carried on him, and which was more ornamental than useful. The chief, however, had admired it and was delighted with the gift.

The ascent of the pass over the Miri-La mountains began about an hour after they left the village. Jasi's report with regard to the snowfall proved to be correct. The higher they went the deeper the snow became and the more slowly the animals progressed. All the men dismounted, and Lotzung insisted on doing the same, though her comparatively light weight could make little difference to her mule. The snow had obliterated all signs of the path, and Mantso himself was frequently at fault. When they halted for the midday meal no argols could be found with which to light a fire. One of the chief disadvantages of following a by-path was the scarcity of argols. The consequent inability to boil water means the loss of a meal to a Tibetan, for besides using the hot tea as a drink he rolls his tsamba balls with it. Even if everything went well the top of the pass could not be reached under four hours. If difficulties were encountered another hour or two would have to be added. What was to be done? Should they go on, or camp where they were for the night?

Philip decided on the bolder course, and after an hour's rest gave the order to resume the march. The effects of the altitude they had reached were now severely felt. The mules, though relieved of their riders, staggered wearily upwards, while even the hardy yaks showed symptoms of exhaustion. As for the men, the familiar signs of *mal de montagne* made themselves visible, the effort of dragging the animals out of snowdrifts proving a great tax upon their strength. Lotzung suffered from dizziness and headache, but, refusing to mount, tramped pluckily along behind her mule, holding on to its tail for assistance. Philip himself had made his way to the head of the caravan, Mantso being the only person in front of him. Oppressed with mountain sickness, his head throbbing violently, and with a sensation of leaden weights on his feet, he struggled resolutely on, determined not to give in till nature refused to go any further.

Thus plodding painfully upward and hardly conscious of his surroundings, he suddenly missed both Mantso and the mule. Had he passed him without noticing it ? He was on the point of turning round when a cry seemed to come out of the bowels of the earth in front of him. Peering forward he caught sight of the top of Mantso's cap in a hole in a snowdrift made by his mule and himself. The caravan was halted, ropes were brought, and Mantso was, after considerable exertion, hauled out of his self-made pit, for the top of his head had been some five feet below the level of the snow. Still greater difficulty was experienced in recovering the mule; but it was at length dragged out on to firm ground again.

The exertion caused by the last effort prostrated all the men, and they threw themselves full length upon the ground to recover their breath and ease their palpitating hearts. Lotzung had sunk upon a rock, and Philip alone remained standing face to face with this fresh obstacle. The cold was intense. His breath, exhaled in short, quick gasps, froze into snowflakes as it left his lips. Still he was resolved not to give in as long as he had the power to move.

" Have you lost the path ? " he asked Mantso, when the muleteer at length rose to his feet.

" No, Kushok, the path here runs in a hollow between two walls of rock. The wind has filled the hollow with snow."

"We had better keep along the top of one of the walls then."

Mantso shook his head.

"They are too rugged and uneven."

"We must press on somehow," said Philip resolutely.

"It can only be done in one way," replied Mantso. "The yaks must be unloaded and made to tread down a track along the course of the path."

Reluctantly the men set about undoing the packs which would cost them so much labour to replace. In their exhausted condition, and with their fingers numbed with cold, it proved a troublesome task, but they accomplished it at last. The leading yak, a powerful animal with shaggy coat reaching to the ground, was then led up to the hole from which Mantso and his mule had recently been dragged. At the edge it halted, looking down into the cavity with startled eyes and blowing intermittent jets of vapour from its distended nostrils. The sagacious animal understood, but did not relish the work which was required of it. A blow from Mantso put an end to its hesitation, and with a series of short expostulatory grunts it felt its way slowly to the bottom of the hole. There it halted, waiting patiently for the next step in the operation.

A second yak had now been brought up, and was being driven down into the hole. It descended on the top of the first one, and then made a fresh hole for itself in front of its predecessor, and in the desired direction. A third yak came and, walking along the backs of the other two, still further extended the passage. When this manœuvre had been performed by each yak in turn, the first animal to descend into the hole was made to jump on the back of the next one and walking along the whole line, make a fresh place for himself at the head. The others followed, and the operation was continued till the end of the drift was reached

Even then the task was not completed. The snow at the bottom of the passage thus made was still very yielding, and the yaks had to be driven backwards and forwards two or three times before it became firm enough to carry them with their loads on their backs. It wanted now only half an hour to sunset. Both men and animals were exhausted with their long day's work and scanty food. Even Mantso's endurance was coming to an end, while Jasi openly murmured against doing anything more that night. It seemed imperative to encamp where they were. The animals could not have their packs replaced upon them before dark, and then they would have in front of them a long and trying passage through the snowdrift. Yet, in spite of these objections, Philip gave the order to reload, and, though the men complied reluctantly, they knew the order was a wise one. For if a snowstorm occurred in the night all the labour of making the passage would have to be performed again on the following day. Accordingly the packs were slowly secured upon the animals' backs, an operation which occupied the men till some time after nightfall. Then followed the tedious march along the prepared track, the snow at portions of it being still soft enough to allow the yaks to sink to their girths in it. It was nearly ten o'clock before they all arrived at the other end, and then animals and men alike were so exhausted that they sank upon the snow-covered ground to rest. Philip found a sheltered spot beneath a boulder for Lotzung, and she lay down in it, protecting herself from the wind by Champa's shaggy coat, Then, clearing a space for himself in the snow, the owner of the caravan stretched himself upon the hard ground and fell into a well-earned sleep.

CHAPTER XII

AS soon as the first faint streaks of dawn appeared in the eastern sky Philip awoke. He had slept soundly, the surrounding snow keeping him as warm as in a comfortably heated chamber. His first visit was to the boulder where Lotzung lay. He found the young girl sleeping peacefully, with a sheepskin garment rolled up for a pillow, and one hand buried in Champa's woolly coat. As she lay there with her long black eyelashes showing in relief against her waxen skin, the cheeks just tinged with the rosy hues of the rising sun, and a happy smile upon her lips, Lotzung made a very pretty picture, and Philip marvelled at a constitution which seemed so little affected by the rigours of the altitude which they had attained.

The young man then turned his attention to the muleteers. Jasi alone had taken the trouble to make a bed for himself in the snow, the others lay on the top of it, just as they had thrown themselves down the previous night. Esa, indeed, who had become hot when driving the yaks through the narrow passage, and had, in Tibetan fashion, slipped his right arm and shoulder out of his sheepskin coat, had not even re-covered them, but lay with his bare skin upon the snow. As for the animals, Philip found the mules huddled together in a dejected group, having evidently despaired of extracting any sustenance from the rocky soil beneath the snow. The yaks, however, seemed to relish the withered tufts of grass which they found here and there beneath the shelter of a boulder, and which the dry air of the country had rendered hard enough to pierce the sole of a raw-hide Tibetan boot.

By this time Mantso had risen and come to Philip for orders. It was useless to attempt to boil water at that altitude, even if any argols could be found for the purpose. The boiling point was so low that on removal from the fire the tea would have frozen in the bowl. The only thing to be done was to resume the march at once. Fortunately the yaks were ready laden, as the men had been too exhausted on the previous evening to relieve them of their packs. The fodder they had managed to find had somewhat renewed their strength, and they commenced the march with a fair reserve of energy.

Even supposing they did not encounter another snowdrift, a couple of hours' journey still remained before they could reach the summit of the pass. If hindered by a snowdrift their position would become really serious, for the exertion entailed by it, and the further postponement of their much-needed meal, might incapacitate the men from further effort. Philip trudged resolutely on behind Mantso and his mule, fearing every minute to see them disappear in a drift as on the previous day.

In this way three-quarters of the ascent was safely accomplished when a faint cry caught Philip's ear. Turning round he saw that Lotzung's mule was no longer followed by its mistress, who had sunk upon the ground, while Champa stood over her and licked her hands. Philip caught the mule's bridle and led the animal back to where the young girl sat. The colour had gone from her cheek, but she summoned a brave smile to her lips as she said: "I am taking a little rest. It is want of food, I think, which makes me feel so weak."

In spite of her youth and vigorous constitution Lotzung was, after all, only a woman, and could not endure the hardships of such a journey like a man. It would be useless to put her on her mule, for the animal was too weak to carry her. Accordingly Philip said—

"We are quite near the top now, Lotzung. Make one more effort and we shall be there. I will help you." He assisted her to her feet, and, holding the mule's tail in one hand and supporting Lotzung with the other, resumed the march. Champa, conscious that something had gone wrong, followed with lowered head and tail between his legs. Philip found this last portion of the ascent a very great strain, weakened as he was by want of food, and by the effects of the altitude. Towards the end Lotzung became so faint that he could only support her by putting his arm round her waist. Half lifting, half dragging her, he toiled slowly upwards till the summit was gained. Mantso had already reached it and tied a lung-ta to one of the poles belonging to the cairn of stones. He was now prostrate before it, returning thanks to the deity of the pass. Lotzung, revived by the fact of having reached the summit, produced a khata and said to Philip—

"Let us also attach a lung-ta to the pole."

Philip humoured her wish, and the khata, fastened to the pole, was soon flapping gaily in the wind.

"Now let us offer our prayers to the god of the mountain," she continued when he returned to her. "We have much reason to be grateful to him."

She took Philip's hand and drew him towards the cairn. Then, falling on her knees, she looked up to him and said—

"Will you not pray at my side? Otherwise our journey is sure to be unlucky. Husband and wife should offer up their thanks together."

She looked up to him so imploringly that he yielded to her entreaties and knelt down at her side. But while the young girl was repeating the meaningless formula of the

Lamaist Church Philip returned thanks to the God of his childhood for having brought him thus far safe upon his journey.

The descent on the further side of the mountain now began, and in two hours' time Philip halted on the site of a former camp. Sufficient argols were found to cook the breakfast, and kettles were soon singing on the camp fires. The spot was too high and exposed to form a camping place for the night, so, after an hour's rest, the downward march was resumed. By five o'clock they had reached a suitable spot for the purpose. The animals were unloaded, the two tents (Philip had brought a separate one for Lotzung) erected, and the evening meal prepared, after which the members of the caravan retired to a well-earned rest.

The marches of the next few days proved very trying. A series of mountainous ridges ran at right angles to the course, and the whole time was occupied in alternately ascending and descending them. On the main road they could have counted on sufficient argols for the camp fires, and on falling in with a house or a village every two or three days. But on the bypath they were following both argols and habitations were very scarce. Only the danger of interference from the lamas prevented Philip on more than one occasion from striking out for the main route.

On the fourth day an accident occurred which still further augmented the young man's troubles. Mantso, as usual, led the caravan and Philip brought up the rear. While thus engaged Lotzung came riding back with a very white face.

"Mantso's mule has slipped," she said, "and they both rolled down the mountain-side together."

Philip hurried forward to the front as quickly as possible. They were ascending a path cut in the rock on the side of a ravine. There was just room enough for him to pass the pack animals, and at length he reached the head of the column. Phendi and Esa were gazing in horror down the cliff over which Mantso had disappeared, while Jasi sat down upon the path, unconcernedly preventing the animals advancing any further.

"Why do you all stay here doing nothing?" exclaimed Philip angrily. "Mantso must be rescued. Get me some rope."

"No one can descend a cliff like that," said Jasi, not offering to move.

"The ropes at once, blockhead!" cried Philip, with a look which made the man rise without further delay and go in search of the yak which carried them. As soon as he returned with a long coil of rope, Philip made one end fast to the tree and began the descent. It was much more steep than the place where his own mule had fallen, and he had little hope of finding either the animal or its rider alive. They had been invisible from the path, but after he had descended some thirty feet he caught sight of them lying on a ledge of rock, the mule's further descent being stopped by the trunk of a tree. Both were motionless, and from the helpless manner in which the mule's head, with protruding tongue, hung over the precipice, it was plain that he was already dead. Was Mantso also beyond recovery?

Philip descended to the ledge on which the muleteer lay and knelt down at his side. He had evidently received a violent blow on the forehead which had closed up both his eyes. But to Philip's intense relief Mantso, though stunned, was still breathing. There was no time to be lost. The young man called for another rope to be lowered, and, having taken the saddle off the dead mule, tied it round Mantso's body with the end of the second rope. He then gave the order to his men to heave up the injured man, and, climbing up the first rope himself, he assisted the muleteer's helpless body over the obstacles on the side of the cliff, which from time to time obstructed his passage.

In this way Mantso was at length brought safely back to the path again. Restoratives were applied and, as soon as he regained consciousness, his wound was bathed and dressed. As it was impossible for him to travel in his present condition the camp was pitched in an open space some hundred paces further on. The wounded man was taken into Philip's tent and soon fell into a healthy slumber.

Such was the muleteer's vitality that on the following morning he seemed none the worse for his terrible fall, except that the swelling over his eyes still prevented his seeing out of them. He insisted, however, that he was well enough to travel, and in proof of his assertion he scrambled to his feet and groped his way to the tent door.

" But who is to be the guide, now that you cannot see ? " asked Philip.

" The other three muleteers know the road well enough," Mantso answered, " to take you the route you wish to go."

Philip summoned the three men to his tent, and said to Phendi : " As Mantso is unable to see, can you take his place as guide ? " Phendi shook his head regretfully.

" I have never been this road before, Kushok," he answered.

" And you, Esa ? " continued Philip.

" I have only travelled once this way, and do not know it well enough to act as guide."

This was unfortunate, for Philip had more confidence in these two men than in Jasi. Still, there was no help for it.

" Do you, Jasi, know the route ? " he asked.

" I have followed it many times, Kushok," he replied.

" Well then, you shall act as guide, remembering that in no case are you to lead me to the main road to Lhasa. Do you understand ? "

Jasi cowered before the penetrating glance which accompanied these words, but recovering quickly, answered that he understood quite well and would take care to do the Kushok's bidding. Whereupon Philip dismissed the men, telling them to load the animals and resume the march.

As Mantso had lost his mule Philip selected a quiet yak to carry him, and the march began. The young man kept a sharp look out on Jasi, checking by his compass the direction in which he led them, especially when the path forked in two directions. For three days matters went on satisfactorily. The road, it is true, became rougher, thereby increasing the labour of the pack animals, and resulting in the loss of three of them. But the general direction of the march seemed to be as Philip wished, and to judge from the wildness of the country and the absence of habitations they could be nowhere near the high road to Lhasa.

"Jasi seems to make a good guide," said Philip to Lotzung, as they rode side by side the third morning after Mantso's accident.

"It appears so, Khangsar, but I do not like him," responded Lotzung.

"Why?" asked Philip.

"I don't know why; I only know I cannot trust him. Besides, he is a Ladaki."

Philip laughed. He knew the prejudice which the native of Tibet proper entertains for those of Little Tibet, who have become dependent on English rule.

"There may be honest men in Ladak," he rejoined.

"Jasi may be honest, but I do not like his eyes," she answered.

There was nothing further to be said. Women are always led by instinct, and no amount of reason will make them change opinions formed by intuition only.

That night they encamped in a sheltered spot, near which

they were able to collect a plentiful supply of argols. The camp fires burnt brightly, and the muleteers indulged to the full their love of boiling tea. Lotzung, delighted with their comfortable quarters, served Philip's meal in more tempting fashion than she had yet been able to do. Everything seemed to be going smoothly, and Philip's hopes once more rose high.

But misfortune generally comes when least expected. The following morning Phendi and Esa appeared at the door of their master's tent with most lugubrious countenances, and Philip saw at once that something serious had occurred.

"Well, what is it, Phendi?" he asked.

Phendi, never very eloquent, could on this occasion find no words to express himself, and nudged Esa to reply for him. Esa, usually so talkative, was also dumb.

"I suppose you have broken something or lost something between you, and are afraid to confess it. I had better call Jasi to hear what he can say."

"It was of Jasi that we wished to speak to you, Kushok," said Esa at last. "We cannot find him anywhere!"

"What!" exclaimed Philip, a presentiment of the truth taking possession of him.

"We knew nothing of it, Kushok," protested Esa, alarmed by Philip's look. "He took the early morning watch, and when we got up we found that he had gone."

"And with him has gone his mule and three of the best yaks, together with their loads," said Phendi, finding his tongue at last.

"Which way did he go?"

"We tracked him down to the road into which this path runs a little further on, and found that he turned to the left."

"Then saddle my mule; I will soon bring him back."

Again the men hesitated. They had not yet come to the end of their bad news.

"That road, Kushok," said Esa at length, "is the main road to Lhasa."

So Jasi had played him false after all, and crowned his treachery by carrying off three of the best yaks with their valuable loads. Philip had never liked the look of the man from the day that Mantso presented him in the courtyard of the mission house. He now felt convinced that it was Jasi he had seen paying a visit to the monastery outside Namcho, and that in consequence of the information then given the lamas had ordered him to return the way he came. The young man remembered that Jasi wanted him to travel in the direction of the main road on leaving the village where the marriage festivities had taken place, and that Mantso's accident had given him the opportunity he sought. To gain his purpose he might, indeed, have caused the accident. On considering the matter, it really looked as if Jasi had been the agent of the lamas from the first. Philip recollected that in every town where they had halted he used to absent himself from the inn, and seemed out of countenance when he was discovered doing so. No doubt at each place he had communicated to the lamas all he had been able to learn about his master. If Philip had only acted on his first instinctive dislike of the man, and had refused to engage him, none of these misfortunes would have befallen him.

However, it was the time for action, not for vain regrets.

"Are you both sure that the road into which this path runs is the main road to Lhasa?" he asked.

"Quite sure, Kushok."

"How far is the nearest village?"

Phendi scratched his head and looked at Esa.

"About six miles," replied Esa, unhampered by any scruples in the matter of accurate calculation.

"Then we shall have time to retrace our steps before the lamas can reach this spot."

"There is a large monastery on the road about one mile from here," said Phendi.

Jasi had certainly arranged the betrayal of his master very cleverly, pitching the camp within a mile of a large monastery, and getting away in the early hours of the morning to give information before the caravan could start. Some decision must be arrived at without delay, for the lamas might already be marching on the camp. Philip made up his mind at once, and went in search of Lotzung, whom he met coming out of her tent. Her smile of greeting was arrested by his serious look.

"You have bad news, Khangsar," she said. "Tell me what it is."

"Jasi has deserted with his mule and three yaks and their loads."

"Then Lotzung was right after all," she answered. "But is that the only thing that makes Khangsar look so grave? The loss of the animals and their loads is not a very great matter, and we are the better off for being rid of Jasi."

"That is not all. A large monastery lies within a mile of this spot, and he has doubtless laid information there against me." Lotzung saw that the matter was more serious than she had anticipated.

"What are you going to do?" she asked.

"It is too late to try and run away. I shall divide the caravan into three portions. With the smallest portion, consisting of two or three yaks at the most, I shall attempt to pass the monastery. Jasi knows that I must have discovered his desertion by this time, and will conclude that

I shall decide to retrace my steps. He would not suspect me of marching along the main road in full view of a large monastery."

There was a short pause.

"And what will you do with me, Khangsar ?" the young girl asked in a low voice.

"If you came with me, and the lamas discovered that I was the same person who had been ordered back from Namcho, they might treat you roughly for being found with me. You must therefore accompany one of the other caravans under Phendi or Esa, whom I shall instruct to make a detour on either side of the main road, and meet me again twelve miles on the Lhasa side of the monastery."

"The lamas will not hurt me. I would rather go with you," she answered.

"You will have to put up with many hardships then. We must wear the rough costume of the nomads, take only three yaks for our baggage, and travel on foot ourselves. But here comes Mantso."

The swelling on Mantso's forehead had now gone down sufficiently for him to use his eyes. He had just heard from the other two men of Jasi's desertion, and came to beg Philip not to be angry with him for having recommended him as a muleteer. He said that he had travelled with him once before, and that he had worked well for his master then. Philip assured Mantso that he did not blame him in any way for the occurrence, and proceeded to explain his plans for dividing up the caravan.

"You will come with Lotzung and myself," he said. "So load three yaks with only sufficient food and baggage for six days' journey. We will start as soon as we have changed our clothes for coarser garments. Phendi and Esa can pack up the tents and set out on their march when we have gone."

CHAPTER XIII

THREE-QUARTERS of an hour after the discovery of Jasi's desertion Philip left the camp accompanied by Lotzung, Mantso, three yaks, and Champa. Lotzung had begged that the latter might be allowed to go with them. Philip had at first intended to leave the dog behind, lest it might assist Jasi in recognizing the party. But at a distance one Tibetan mastiff is very much like another, and it was not probable that Jasi would in person assist the lamas to intercept the caravan. The Ladaki, having seen the range and efficiency of Philip's rifle, would have no desire to act as a target for it. He would probably content himself with pointing out at a distance what he took to be Philip's caravan, leaving the monks to make sure of the fact by themselves.

On reaching the point at which the path ran into the main road Mantso recognized the spot, and said that the monastery lay to the left about half a mile distant on the way to Lhasa. To the right a caravan of twenty yaks could be seen approaching. As this was about the same size as Philip's before the division took place, it might serve to mislead Jasi and give the small party in advance a better chance of avoiding the lamas' scrutiny.

Accordingly Philip set out at once along the road in the direction of the monastery. The trio might easily be mistaken for the members of a poor Tibetan family. Lotzung had smeared her face with black ointment and had put on the shapeless sheepskin garment which Tibetan women of the poorer classes wear. The two men would be taken for brothers, married, in accordance with the custom of polyandry prevalent in Tibet, to one and the same woman. The appearance of poverty would be emphasized by the fact that they were all on foot, for nearly every Tibetan rides an animal of some kind, and only the very poorest walk.

After travelling about a quarter of a mile the lamasery came in view. It was a fine building, capable of holding some five hundred monks. A large party of mounted lamas were collecting at the gates, while others on foot were hurrying towards the road, separated from the building by a space of perhaps a hundred yards in width. The mounted lamas were probably preparing to ride to the place where Jasi had told them Philip was encamped, while those on foot were sent to see that he did not pass along the Lhasa road.

All the three members of the small party wore horsehair fringes over their eyes, so as to render recognition as difficult as possible. They peered through these fringes as they approached the group of lamas to see if Jasi was amongst them, but there were no signs of the muleteer. It seemed at first as if they would be allowed to pass unchallenged, but one of the lamas put up his hand and bade them halt.

"Whence do you come?" he asked.

Mantso, whom Philip had instructed to answer all questions, put out his tongue in the submissive manner of the poorer classes of Tibet, and bowing low replied—

"From the village of Riuchi, Kushok."

"And whither are you going?"

"To Garthok, if Buddha permits," he answered.

"Have you seen a caravan of some twenty yaks about a mile from here?"

"A caravan of twenty yaks is now approaching."

A murmur ran through the group of lamas. That must be the caravan for which they watched. The lama who had just spoken, a man evidently of some authority, was about to dismiss the small party when a sharp-featured monk at his side, who had been scanning them narrowly, said—

"Let us not be in too great a haste to send these good folk away; they might be able to give us some more information. The caravan we are looking for belongs to a foreigner, who calls himself an Eastern Mongol." Here the keen eyes of the hollow-cheeked lama seemed to be piercing through their scanty disguise. Mantso made no remark, and the lama continued—

"With the Eastern Mongol is his wife, the daughter of the Deba of a province several stages distant from here. He has also three muleteers. Is that the caravan which you say is now approaching?"

Philip waited in anxious suspense to hear what Mantso would reply. If his courage failed him they were lost. But the muleteer retained his self-possession and rejoined—

"I know nothing of the members of the caravan, Kushok. We saw them coming down a bypath into the main road about half a mile from here, but they were not near enough for us to tell what they were like."

"How are we to know that you are not a part of the caravan we want? That fellow yonder"—pointing to Philip—"may be the Eastern Mongol himself, and this girl his wife, the Deba's daughter."

"I am the wife of these two brothers," interposed Lotzung, speaking in the dialect of the nomads and with their usual bluff directness, "but no one can say I married Eastern Mongols. I am a Tibetan by birth, and would not associate with such poor-spirited folk. Perhaps this lama is a Mongol himself."

This speech was greeted with laughter by the monks, though Philip failed to understand what Lotzung had said. It was evident, however, that she had disarmed their suspicions, for the small party were allowed to go on.

A Wife from the Forbidden Land

Philip breathed more freely as they set the yaks once more in motion. They had a respite, though it might only prove a short one. The party of mounted lamas who had assembled at the monastery gates were already moving off. Philip had instructed Phendi and Esa to travel slowly along the main road in an easterly direction away from Lhasa. They were to try and sell the five mules or exchange them for yaks. When they were overtaken by the lamas, as he felt sure they would be, they were to confess that they belonged to the Eastern Mongol's caravan; that their master, hearing that the lamas had been informed of his presence in the neighbourhood, had resolved to abandon his attempt to reach Lhasa, and that he had gone on ahead of his caravan with his wife and chief muleteer, all mounted on mules. On hearing this, it was improbable that the lamas would go any further, for the fugitives would be travelling in the right direction for leaving the country. As soon as the lamas were gone Phendi and Esa were to set out from the main road on their respective detours.

If everything happened in accordance with this forecast Philip and his two companions would get a good start, as several days would elapse before the lamas could verify the story of his retreat to the eastward. On the other hand, if anything should reawaken the lamas' suspicions with regard to the small party they had allowed to pass, the pursuit would begin at once.

Accordingly Philip urged his patient yaks along at the utmost limit of their speed. Fortunately the road was good, and by ten o'clock six miles had been covered. At this point they halted, for they had touched no food that morning as yet, and Lotzung was feeling faint for want of it; while Mantso had not quite recovered his normal strength. After a couple of hours' rest the journey was resumed, and by four o'clock they came in sight of the village, outside which they were to wait for Phendi and Esa. As it would not do to remain in the road, Philip turned up a stony ravine, where even the sure-footed yaks found it hard to pick their way, and where the lamas would be very unlikely to try and ride their ponies. At about one mile from the road a good camping-ground was found, and in the absence of the tents they set to work to make themselves as comfortable as possible for the night.

In spite of the few utensils and scanty supply of food at her disposal, Lotzung contrived to cook a very palatable meal. As the trio sat round the camp fire after its conclusion Philip thought of Lotzung's speech which had amused everybody so much, and which he had not been able to understand.

" What did you say to the lamas this morning, Lotzung, which they found so laughable ? " Philip asked.

Lotzung had washed the black varnish from her face at a brook which gushed down the centre of the ravine, and in the bright light of the camp fire her rosy complexion seemed to take a deeper hue.

" It was nothing," she answered. " I spoke in the Drupa tongue, and that made them laugh."

" But what did you say ? " persisted Philip.

" I said we were Tibetan nomads, not Eastern Mongols."

Here Mantso burst into a laugh, which he endeavoured to smother on a meaning glance from Lotzung. Philip saw that the guileless muleteer had betrayed the situation, and continued—

" You, Mantso, seem to have heard something more than what Lotzung has told me. What was it ? "

Mantso managed to restrain his merriment, and, in spite of Lotzung's frowns, replied—

" She said she was a Tibetan by birth, and would have nothing to do with poor-spirited Mongols." Philip laughed

A Wife from the Forbidden Land

"So you look down on Eastern Mongols, Lotzung?"

"I thought it best to say so, Khangsar," the young girl answered, smiling through her evident embarrassment. "I knew you would not understand me, and you would have heard nothing of it but for this foolish Mantso here."

"I like to know what people say of me," rejoined Philip. "So you have been taught to despise Mongols, and yet you married me?"

"You are not like other Mongols I have seen," she replied.

"Well, you got us out of a difficulty by what you said, and I don't mind how much you talk against us Mongols as long as you persuade the lamas to leave us alone."

In spite of sleeping in the open, Philip passed a very good night and awoke refreshed at dawn the following morning. Although he did not expect either Phendi or Esa to arrive till the evening at the earliest, he took it in turn with Mantso to watch the main road from the shelter of a projecting rock. Darkness fell without any signs of the two muleteers, and another night was spent in the ravine. On the third day neither of them had appeared by noon, and towards four o'clock Philip was getting anxious when he saw a tall, thin figure stalking along behind half a dozen yaks, and recognized Phendi. The yaks were soon driven up to the camp, and when he had been supplied with tea and tsamba by Lotzung the muleteer allowed his story to be gradually extracted from him.

It appeared that with the eighteen yaks which remained in the camp Phendi and Esa started off shortly after Philip's small party had left. According to instructions, they travelled slowly along the main road in the opposite direction to Lhasa, and came upon a small caravan consisting of two men, a woman, and a couple of yaks resting by the roadside. The yaks carried the goods of the family, and though their packs were small the animals, on account of their poor condition, were exhausted. The trio bewailed their misfortune, as they were anxious to get to Litang as quickly as possible.

Phendi and Esa saw they were just the people to take their five mules, and offered them in exchange for the two yaks, explaining that they were going to cross some very rough country, where mules would be almost useless. The poor family accepted the offer with delight, and having shifted their packs on to two of the mules rode off in the highest spirits.

About half an hour later a party of mounted lamas overtook the two men, and Esa repeated the prearranged story that the caravan belonged to an Eastern Mongol, who had gone on ahead with his wife and chief muleteer in order to reach the next village by sunset. The lamas appeared satisfied with the story, and rode back in the direction of the monastery. When they were out of sight Phendi and Esa separated, the former starting on a detour to the right of the Lhasa road, and the other to the left of it.

Phendi found the country very rough, and being totally unacquainted with it gave his animals and himself much unnecessary labour through taking routes which proved to be impracticable and having to retrace his steps. In his three days' journey he lost three yaks from exhaustion and two from falls down cliffs. One of the latter carried Philip's tent, which could not be recovered. The loss was an unfortunate one, but Philip did not rebuke poor Phendi, for he had evidently had a trying journey and had done his best. Lotzung's tent, at any rate, he hoped Esa would bring safely in.

But on this point Philip was also destined to disappointment. Esa arrived at sunset in a worse plight than Phendi, and with only four remaining out of his ten yaks. His story was that while passing through a narrow gorge he was suddenly attacked by robbers. Four of his yaks he managed to drive into a sheltered gully, while he made a show of defending them with the matchlock which Mantso had lent him. The remaining six were carried off, the animal entrusted with Lotzung's tent being one of them.

Philip had no alternative but to make the best of a bad business. There was little chance of his being able to buy a tent in the neighbouring village, which consisted of barely half a dozen houses. Besides, the fact that such a poorly dressed family should have money enough to buy a tent would only rouse suspicion. Nothing remained but to push along as quickly as possible and do without tents as well as they could.

Accordingly at dawn the following morning Philip once more resumed his journey to Lhasa. His small caravan of only twelve yaks attracted no special attention as it passed through the village. Lotzung had smeared her face again with the black paste, and in their homely clothing they were hardly likely to be taken for anything but Tibetan nomads. For this reason Philip decided to keep to the main road instead of following a by-path. Some time must still elapse before the lamas discovered they had been tricked, if indeed they ever discovered it at all. On the main road Philip could travel almost twice as fast as on the by-roads, and with good luck he might possibly reach Lhasa before the lamas between him and that city could be warned to intercept him.

Accordingly the young man pushed steadily on for the next six days. The weather grew worse, and the country through which he passed more bleak and inhospitable. The fact of having no shelter for meals or sleep beyond that afforded by rocks or boulders proved a severe test of endurance. Mantso, now recovered from his fall, stood the strain well; but Esa felt the hardship of the journey more than any one. He lost flesh rapidly, and the process had a weakening instead of a hardening effect upon him. Philip began to feel anxious about him.

On the seventh day they crossed the highest ridge they had yet encountered, and began the descent on the further side. After some two hours' journey Philip found to his surprise that their path ended abruptly in a glacier.

"You must have mistaken the road," he said to Mantso.

"No, Kushok, this is the proper way."

"But how are we going to cross a slippery expanse of ice like that?"

"We shall not cross it, but slide down it."

"And the animals?"

"They do the same. We generally send them first."

With these words Mantso drove the leading yak up to the edge of the glacier. The animal knew, but did not relish what lay before it, and stood hesitating on the brink, pouring clouds of steam from its nostrils and swishing nervously its long silken tail. A little forcible persuasion on Mantso's part made it place its fore feet tentatively on the slippery surface, and gradually work its way further on till only its hind feet remained on firm land. Then, summoning up its courage, the animal stepped briskly on to the ice with all four feet and shot away down the glacier, its legs stretched out wide, and turning, now head, now tail foremost, according as its fore or hind legs found the most slippery course. On arriving at the bottom, some two or three hundred feet below, it leapt into the soft snow which lay there and floundered on towards the road on the further side of the glacier.

Each of the twelve yaks performed the passage in this manner without mishap. Then came the men's turn. Mantso took the lead. Seating himself cautiously on the ice with his heels together, and using his ox goad to guide himself, he tobogganed down the glacier in the most skilful fashion. Phendi and Esa followed, the latter not steering so well as the other two. Then Philip turned to Lotzung.

"Will you go now, or shall I?"

"You go first, Khangsar," she answered, laughing, and without a trace of nervousness in her voice. "It is more fun to watch you from here than from below."

Philip felt that he would no doubt cut a ridiculous figure, but there was no help for it. Seating himself on the ice in the same manner as the others, and using his riding whip as a helm, he started off. But the whip did not prove strong enough, or he lacked the necessary skill, for he found himself gyrating like the yaks, and was finally shot head foremost into the snow at the bottom of the glacier. Mantso helped him out, a broad grin illuminating the muleteer's good-natured countenance, while Lotzung's merry peal of laughter could be heard coming down from the heights above.

If the young Englishman thought it would be his turn to laugh next he was mistaken. Lotzung seated herself confidently on the ice, and with the aid of a short stick as rudder shot swiftly and safely down the glacier. Champa was the last to come, and took the longest to make up his mind. After running to and fro on the edge of the glacier, alternately yelping and whining to show his desire to follow the others and the fear which held him back, he at length jumped vigorously on to the ice, his legs shot from under him, and he half rolled, half slid to the bottom, emerging from the snow in a very confused and angry state. No self-respecting dog likes to afford amusement to his mistress and his mistress's friends.

For the first few days it seemed as if they were descending one of nature's giant staircases. No sooner did they cover a piece of level ground than another descent appeared at the further end of it. The decreased altitude, however, failed to bring them a more temperate climate. A strong westerly wind blew in their faces, cutting their skin, inflaming their eyes, and seeming to pierce their thick sheepskin garments. During this part of the journey Philip lost three more yaks. Two died of exhaustion and the third fell down a precipice into a foaming torrent. The loss of this yak was all the more unfortunate as he carried a large supply of their two chief articles of food—tsamba and butter. The country through which they were now passing was almost entirely uninhabited, so that there was no chance of their being able to make good the loss. Philip began to think that the climate would bar his road to Lhasa more effectually than the lamas themselves.

At length they reached an undulating plain, across which a river ran. It was covered with a coat of ice, which Mantso considered strong enough to carry the laden yaks. Accordingly they were driven on to the ice one by one, a wide interval being left between each of them. Eight crossed safely in this manner, but the ninth, which carried Esa, who was now too weak to do a full day's march, suddenly disappeared, leaving its rider clinging to the ice at the edge of the hole it had made. Philip seized a rope, and, crawling along on his hands and knees, got near enough to throw a running noose over Esa's shoulders. He was then dragged out of the hole and brought safely to the bank.

But the immersion in the icy cold water proved a great shock to the weakened muleteer. His skin had taken a yellow tinge, there was a glassy look in his eyes, and the tears froze as they trickled down his cheeks.

"He is chilled to the bone, Kushok," said Mantso. "We must halt and make a large fire, or he will not live another day."

The camp was therefore pitched on the river bank, a big fire lighted, and Esa in dry clothes placed in front of it. Here his limbs were rubbed by his companions till the circulation was restored, and he at length fell into a peaceful sleep.

CHAPTER XIV

ALTHOUGH Esa was a good deal better on the following morning, he had not recovered sufficiently to be fit for travelling. Thus twenty-four hours were wasted and a proportionate amount of the caravan's rapidly diminishing stock of provisions consumed without getting any further. Next day, however, as Esa was strong enough to ride a yak, the journey was continued.

In two days three more yaks succumbed, leaving only a total of five. They were still a week's march from the nearest village, and had not come within shooting distance of any game, bird or beast, with which to replenish the larder. The rations for each person would now have to be considerably reduced, a serious matter in a climate where large quantities of food are required to maintain the normal heat of the body.

Pondering on this subject, Philip was passing through a narrow defile in Mantso's wake when a volley rang out in the silent air, and a score of bullets impigned against the cliff at the foot of which they marched. The first thought of a traveller in Tibet when attacked by chukpas is to protect his cattle, for they are always shot down first. Philip glanced at the opposite side of the ravine, from which the firing came, and saw that the enemy had plenty of cover behind the boulders with which it was strewn. It would be useless to return their fire or attempt to cross the torrent single-handed, in order to dislodge them from their posts. Nothing remained but to try and find some nook where the animals would be protected from the chukpas' fire.

Accordingly Philip told Phendi to drive the yaks forward as quickly as possible, while Mantso went on ahead to look for a place of shelter for them. Meanwhile the enemy continued to fire as quickly as they could load and discharge their matchlocks. Philip drove the first three yaks and Lotzung walked at his side, while Champa galloped up and down the line barking furiously, and with his hair standing up in a ridge down the centre of his back.

"You are not afraid, Lotzung?" said Philip, when he found that she did not scream or try to run for shelter.

The young girl's face was pale, but she answered, with a plucky little smile, "I should be afraid if you were not here with that wonderful gun you carry."

As she spoke the leading yak fell down on its knees and rolled on its side with a grunt, blocking with its body and load the whole of the narrow path. A shout of triumph came from the chukpas on the opposite side. The road was obstructed, and they could now shoot down the rest of the caravan at their leisure. Philip scrambled past the two intervening yaks, found the first yak quite dead, with a bullet through its heart. It had a valuable load of food, but it would be foolish to try and save it at the cost of the lives of the other yaks, if not of the human members of the caravan. He therefore dragged the animal and its pack to the edge of the cliff and pushed it over, so that the path was once more clear.

For the next two or three hundred yards no further casualties occurred, though they could not get out of range of the chukpas, who clambered along the face of the opposite cliff, firing as soon as they could reload and prime their matchlocks. Mantso now reappeared some distance ahead, making signals to show that he had found a suitable shelter. All might yet be well, and the four remaining yaks were urged forward at the best pace they could go.

Unfortunately at this moment Philip heard a cry behind him, and turning round saw that Phendi had fallen to the ground. Running back, he found that the muleteer had been shot in the shoulder. The only thing to be done was to mount him on the yak which Esa rode, and which was just behind Phendi at the tail of the caravan. Philip helped the man to his feet and tried to lift him on to the yak. But the firing had alarmed the animal, and it would not stand still. Phendi could never have been mounted if Lotzung had not run back and quieted the animal. When it had started with its double load Philip said—

"You ought to have gone on, Lotzung, and got under shelter instead of coming back here to expose yourself."

"I saw you wanted help," she answered.

"It is true, and I don't know what we could have done without you. I think we shall get under cover safely now."

Mantso had come back and was driving the first two yaks of the caravan; while Philip and Lotzung walked between the third and the last one, which Phendi and Esa rode. The shelter was close at hand when the second yak fell and rolled down the cliff, pack and all. Another cry of triumph came from the chukpas, who exposed themselves fearlessly to fire a parting volley. But they soon had cause to repent their rashness. Philip, now that port was in sight, took advantage of the opportunity at length afforded him. Discharging his magazine in quick succession, he had the satisfaction of seeing two of the enemy fall headlong down the ravine, while three more sank to the ground where they stood. The brief fusillade had a marvellous effect, every chukpa who had exposed himself speedily taking cover.

During the respite thus afforded Philip's sadly reduced caravan entered the retreat, the mouth of which was almost blocked by a huge mass of fallen rock. At the top of this rock there was a sheltered nook, in which Philip took up his position and fired at every puff of smoke he saw. Such an effective response quickly silenced the chukpas, who did not relish fighting with an enemy so well able to defend himself. More to their taste was collecting the loads from the yaks that had been killed, an occupation which Philip could not interrupt without exposing himself in the open. This would have been an act of useless bravado, and, feeling convinced that the chukpas would not attack him in his present retreat, he told Mantso to mount guard while he and Lotzung made a fire and dressed Phendi's wound, which fortunately was not of a serious character.

When this was done Philip took stock of the remnant of his caravan. Of the three yaks that remained two were so badly wounded that they would have to be killed. The baggage that remained consisted of rifle ammunition, Philip's personal belongings, and food sufficient for only two days. The nearest village was still six days distant. One yak could not carry Phendi and Esa as well as the baggage. What was to be done?

The young Englishman revolved the situation as he took his turn on guard that night. The wind whistled round the cliffs which formed his shelter, and the thermometer registered 10° of frost, but his physical discomforts were unheeded in face of the problem which confronted him. At length a possible but not very probable solution of his difficulties occurred to him, and when relieved by Mantso he fell into a sound sleep.

The following morning, after a frugal meal, Philip announced his plans. They had tried to eat a portion of the two yaks which had been killed the previous evening, but the flesh was so lean and tough that hardly any nourishment could be extracted from it. He had decided therefore to go in search of a nomad encampment, where he could buy food and yaks to carry their baggage. He would leave Mantso with one of the two remaining rifles in charge of the camp. The invalids were doing well, and would be all the better for a rest. Philip promised to return at latest by sunset on the following day. As he started off on his quest Lotzung came running after him.

"I want to go with you," she said.

"It would be a foolish thing to do," he answered. "We might be attacked by chukpas, and I could not defend you against them except in a sheltered spot like this camp."

"I shall be safer with you than remaining here."

"But I may have to make a long journey before I find any nomads. You would not be able to bear the fatigue."

"I can walk as well as any one in the caravan now."

The young girl had certainly gained in strength and endurance since the commencement of the journey.

"But it is absurd to undergo fatigue and danger when you can rest quietly in camp."

"If you will not let me walk with you I will follow at a distance. I am your wife till you reach Lhasa. Was it not agreed?"

In face of such determination it was useless to deny her any longer, and the two set out together, accompanied by Champa. Descending the further side of the narrow pass, they obtained an extensive view of the country beyond. Philip scanned it anxiously to see if there were any signs of nomad tents. He could detect nothing, but Lotzung, whose eyes were accustomed to this kind of work, pointed to the foot of a distant hill which lay to the south and said—

"I see some tents over there."

Philip looked in the direction indicated, and could just make out what appeared to be dark boulders at the foot of the hill. These might be nomad tents, which are made of black yak's hair, and they started off at once towards them.

Unfortunately it was a cross-country journey, without the vestige of a path. Loose stones covered the ground, and their course was frequently interrupted by patches of boulders. Lotzung clambered over them in the most determined fashion, and Philip purposely refrained from helping her, hoping she would soon get tired and decide to return to camp. But the daughter of Tibet seemed to gain strength by contending with the natural difficulties of her native soil, and followed vigorously in Philip's steps.

At noon they halted by a little stream and ate some of the balls of tsamba they had brought with them. In the clear air of Tibet distances are very deceptive, and the nomad tents seemed to be as far off as when they started for them. Accordingly, after barely an hour's rest, they set off on their way again. At three o'clock they found their course barred by a large river.

" You must stay here, Lotzung," Philip said. " Find a sheltered nook where you and Champa can spend the night, and I will be back at the latest by noon to-morrow."

Poor Lotzung's countenance fell at once.

" Why do you want to leave me behind ? " she said. " I shall be able to walk as far as you will."

" Your spirit is greater than your strength, Lotzung. Besides, how are you going to cross the river ? There are no yaks to help you now."

" I can swim across. I have often done it when herding my father's cattle at home. See ! "

And before Philip realized what she was going to do, Lotzung had run down the river bank, crashed through the fringe of ice, and plunged into the stream. The young man wasted no time in following her. The shock of the icy cold water took away his breath and almost numbed his limbs. He found himself unable to decrease the distance between Lotzung and himself, and at length saw the young girl reach the opposite side and scramble up the bank. She met him with a smile as he in his turn gained the land.

"I told you I could get across, Khangsar," she said.

Philip looked up stream to the spot on the opposite bank from which they started. They had been carried down at least a hundred yards.

"Yes, you can swim as well as I can," Philip admitted, "and you look as fresh and warm as you were before, while I feel chilled to the bone."

Lotzung said they must start off again so that exercise might restore his circulation. The water froze as it dripped from the edge of his heavy Mongol garment, and the icicles rang with every step he took like a fringe of glass beads. How it was he ever got warm again he could not tell, but after a time, in spite of the biting wind, a healthy glow pervaded his skin. Perhaps they would succeed in reaching the nomad encampment before sunset after all.

But Philip had not made due allowance for the capricious character of the climate. The sky became overcast with lowering clouds, and it began to snow with thickly falling flakes. The view of the hill for which they were making was entirely blotted out, and Philip could now only steer his way by compass. The rapidity with which the snow collected on the ground made walking very laborious. Now they would stumble against a huge hidden stone, now they sank into a drift which had collected on the lee side of a boulder. Lotzung, who had hitherto held out so pluckily, showed signs of fatigue, and as the daylight began to fade she came to a standstill.

"You were right, Khangsar," she said in a faint voice. "A girl cannot walk as far as a man. I ought to have stayed in the camp as you bade me. I will wait here till you come back."

What was to be done? How could he leave her here

alone in a blinding snowstorm? On the other hand, unless he pushed on he would not get back to the camp within the time he promised. Lotzung settled the question for him.

"Why do you wait?" she asked. "You want the daylight to find the nomad camp. Champa and I will spend the night here." She pointed to a little nook on the sheltered side of a large boulder. Philip saw that it was the only thing to do. Champa would be company, if not much protection to her. For the latter purpose he handed her one of his pistols with some rounds of ammunition. He had shown her how to use it, and she could shoot sufficiently well to keep off an enemy or wild beast at close quarters. Then, taking a careful note of the position, which was remarkable for a curiously jagged rock on the top of a small hillock, he bade her good-bye and set off by himself.

The journey was a trying one. Every few hundred yards he had to stop and take his bearings by the compass to make sure that he was travelling in the right direction. The heavy fall of snow made progress very difficult, and at times he began to doubt whether it was of any use to persevere. Fortunately at nightfall the snow ceased, and though there was no moon the stars gave sufficient light for him to pick his way. He struggled on more hopefully now that the storm had passed away.

But time crept on, and he seemed to get no nearer to the nomad encampment. His strength began to fail him, and he experienced the drowsy sensation of those who suffer from exposure to the cold. He might shortly have succumbed to the feeling had not the sight of a faint light in the distance put fresh energy into his weary limbs. The nomad encampment must be at hand and he would soon have food and warmth. Other lights appeared, but they were shortly hidden by his descending into a hollow between two hills. When he reached the summit of the second hill a bitter disappointment was in store for him. The lights were still there, but they only proceeded from the dying embers of camp fires, and the tents, with their owners, had disappeared.

Philip realized in a moment that he had not the strength to try and overtake them. This thought relaxed the little energy that still remained to him, and staggering to the nearest fire he sank upon the ground in front of it. He had touched nothing since his midday meal, and now drew forth from the folds of his sheepskin garment one of his two remaining tsamba balls. It was frozen into a solid mass. The embers of the fire sufficed to thaw it, and having eaten it, he lay upon the ground and fell asleep.

The following morning Philip awoke with the first faint streaks of dawn. He had taken the precaution to heap some argols on the dying fire, so that it was burning still. Having warmed and eaten his remaining tsamba ball, he took a draught of water at a small stream which ran past the camping ground and set out on his return.

The storm had passed away, and the sun shone brightly from a cloudless sky. Without his reason for anxiety such a morning would have raised his spirits high, but now it only seemed to emphasize the gravity of his situation. What would his muleteers think when they saw him return with neither yaks nor food? Unless these could be procured, death by starvation and exposure lay in store for all of them. It would be bad enough for the men, whose occupations called on them to run such risks. But it seemed too cruel that poor Lotzung, who was not inured to the hardships and perils of travel, should have to face such an awful death.

At seven o'clock there was another fall of snow, but it only lasted an hour, and towards nine o'clock he caught sight of the jagged rock near to which he had left Lotzung on the previous evening. Quickening his pace, he reached the top of the hill and came in view of the boulder under the shelter of which the young girl said she would spend the night. But neither Lotzung nor Champa were to be seen. A feeling of uncanniness took possession of Philip, so absolutely silent was the spot and so devoid of any sign of life, nothing but the glaring, remorseless rays of the sun upon the dazzling surface of the snow. The great orb of day seemed to be looking down with a mocking smile on his perplexity. What could have become of Lotzung ? Philip raised his eyes and saw not fifty yards distant a she-bear playing with a couple of cubs on the top of a small hillock. The sight made his blood run cold. Had he come too late ?

For a few moments Philip's power of will seemed paralysed. He could do nothing but stand and gaze at the she-bear and her cubs as they rolled with a playful but uncouth motion in the snow. What made the matter still more strange was that the she-bear did not run away when she became aware of his presence, but turned her bright yellow eyes upon him with a look of lazy indifference. Both animate and inanimate nature seemed to take no notice of him. Stung into action by the animal's irritating air of composure, he clubbed his rifle and strode towards her.

But the she-bear at length divined that there was trouble in store for her, and calling her cubs she shuffled away with them over the crest of the hillock and disappeared. No good purpose could be served by pursuing and killing her. It would never be known whether she was responsible for the disappearance of Lotzung and her dog, for the recent snow-fall would have obliterated any signs of a struggle. Philip searched the immediate neighbourhood of the jagged rock for an hour in vain, and then sank exhausted on the ground. If Lotzung and Champa had not been killed by the she-bear, it was impossible to say what had become of them.

CHAPTER XV

PHILIP lay for a long time on the ground, regardless alike of his bed of snow and of the pitiless rays of the Tibetan sun. His mind was full of Lotzung's fate. He now reproached himself for having left her the previous evening. If he had remained with her he might have been able to save her life, or at any rate he would have been spared the ignominy of surviving her. Now nothing could be done, and unless he committed the cowardly act of self-destruction he would have to face his followers not only without yaks and food, but also without the young girl in whose company he had left the camp.

There is no occasion to dwell on Philip's painful journey back to his caravan. That he should have been able to swim the river in his exhausted state, and then to walk all the intervening distance to his camp, seemed to him afterwards to be little short of marvellous. He did not, indeed, reach his destination till dawn the following morning, twelve hours later than the time he had mentioned for his return. He was then so feeble that Mantso, who met him, had to assist him to gain the camp, and refrained, of course, from asking questions about the success or failure of the expedition.

Although the young man was too tired to eat, his capacity for sleep had not yet deserted him, and he fell into a deep and breathless slumber. Then the vigour of his youthful constitution reasserted itself, and he awoke and asked for food. Mantso, who had anticipated the question, brought him some tea and tsamba. Philip ate with a ravenous appetite, and it was not till he had finished all that had been set before him that he remembered the circumstances in which they were placed.

" How much tsamba is there left, Mantso ? " he asked.

Mantso seemed somewhat confused.

" There is a good deal yet, Kushok," he answered.

Philip looked round him and saw Phendi and Esa squatting on the ground, the former with a marked abatement of his usual melancholy, and the latter with a cheery smile.

" The invalids are better, I see," continued Philip, " but they must have been living on something. Come, let me see the tsamba bag."

Thus bidden, Mantso reluctantly produced it, and Philip found that there remained only one more meal for each of them.

" I have eaten enough for three," said Philip. " Why did you not remind me, Mantso ? "

" The Kushok needed it most. Has he not been two days with scarcely any food ? "

Mantso's words suddenly recalled to Philip the fact of Lotzung's disappearance, and a shadow seemed to fall upon the camp.

" I have told you nothing about my journey yet," said Philip. " You can see for yourselves that I was unable to procure either yaks or food. In addition, I lost Lotzung."

Mantso, of course, had noticed Lotzung's absence, but had shrunk from making any comment to his master on the fact. Now, however, that Philip had introduced the subject, he said simply—

" How did it happen, Kushok ? "

Philip briefly related his experiences of the last two days, Mantso and Esa listening with rapt attention ; while even the melancholy Phendi displayed a fleeting interest in the story. A short silence followed its conclusion, and then Mantso said—

"What is to be done now, Kushok?"

Philip's first impulse was to say that it did not matter now what happened. But he remembered that three men still remained in his charge, and that he ought not to despair till every effort had been made to save them. Accordingly he answered—

"You, Mantso, had better go in the opposite direction to that in which I went, and see if you can find any nomads. I will remain in charge of the camp."

That same morning Mantso set out on his quest, and Philip mounted guard on the camp. He found it dreary work, lack of active occupation being conducive to gloomy thoughts. Apart from the distress he felt at Lotzung's disappearance, his present position filled him with anxiety. All the tsamba would be finished at their next meal, and they would have nothing but the yak meat, which was so tough that it was only fit for soup. One yak, indeed, still remained alive, but to judge from its emaciated appearance it would prove as tough as its fellow.

Mantso did not return that day, nor did any chukpas show themselves. A lovely dawn ushered in the following day, but fine weather will not fill an empty stomach. Phendi and Esa began to feel the want of proper food, and Philip's youthful constitution clamoured for something more substantial than tea and soup. He almost longed for the appearance of some chukpas, so as to relieve the dreary monotony of his vigil.

This half-formulated wish seemed destined to a speedy realization. At noon Mantso came hurrying back to camp with the news that a large party of brigands were approaching. He said that he had searched in vain for any signs of a nomad camp, and that when re-entering the narrow pass in which the caravan lay he found that he was being followed by a large number of armed men on horseback.

They must have hidden till he returned to the pass, where they reckoned on finding the caravan to which he must belong.

Philip experienced a sense of relief at Mantso's news. The suspense had become intolerable, and if they had to die it was better to do so fighting than by slow starvation. The young man gave Mantso the other rifle and Phendi and Esa a pistol each. They would account for as many of the enemy as possible before they themselves were killed. Then, covering the entrance to their retreat with his rifle, he calmly awaited the chukpa attack.

A quarter of an hour later the first horseman made his appearance along the main path at the place where the by-path from their hiding-place ran into it. Philip waited for him to turn down the by-path before firing at him. Strange to say he did not do so, but rode on past the entrance without even turning his head. Others followed, and although some of them glanced casually in Philip's direction, none of them looked as if they expected to see any one there. What could be the explanation of it? Did they fancy that Mantso had not yet left the main path, or had they merely mistaken the turning which he took?

After a score of fully armed men on horseback had passed by a number of baggage animals followed. Then came another set of horsemen, not so heavily armed as the first. As Philip watched them, a stout man, riding on a good horse, came into view, and he recognized his late fellow-traveller Purdung. His easy-going, contented appearance suggested an explanation of the affair to Philip. These were not chukpas, but an armed force which Purdung had persuaded to escort his caravan. The young man determined to make himself known at once.

Clambering down from his shelter he ran towards the main path, calling Purdung by his name. His sudden apparition caused a panic, and Purdung's companions galloped off as hard as they could go. Purdung's horse, however, became unmanageable, and, refusing to follow the others, curveted about on the path with his head towards Philip. The young man seized his bridle and brought him to a standstill. Purdung, who evidently thought he was attacked by chukpas, looked as if he expected to be killed forthwith.

"Do you not remember me, Purdung?" said Philip. "I am Khangsar, the Eastern Mongol, who travelled with you from Batang to Namcho."

The light of recognition gradually came into Purdung's eyes and the colour returned to his cheeks.

"I mistook you for a chukpa," he answered. "There are so many in this neighbourhood. But how is it you are here? I thought they sent you back from Namcho."

Philip briefly explained how he had eluded the lamas.

"They will not trouble you now," said Purdung. "You are more likely to be stopped by chukpas."

"I have already been attacked by them and lost all my baggage animals but one, besides having a muleteer wounded."

Purdung smiled the smile of a prophet justified.

"Your gun," he said, pointing to Philip's rifle, "is a good weapon, but it can be overcome by numbers. I had no such gun to help me, so I journeyed very slowly, and made long halts in different villages, till I was overtaken by a detachment of soldiers marching to Lhasa. I persuaded them to let me travel with them, and now I march with half of their number in front of my caravan and half behind it. Since I have been in their company no chukpas have dared to show themselves. You must join us. Between here and Lhasa no lamas will interfere with you. Where are my men?"

When Purdung's attendants, who had run away, saw that he was unharmed, they came back one by one. He abused them roundly, and told them to assist Philip's men in packing their baggage. Two yaks sufficed to carry it, the solitary yak that alone survived and one which Purdung lent. The Tibetan merchant made his cowardly servants give up their horses to Philip and his men, while they rode some of the spare yaks accompanying the caravan. The march was then resumed and the camp pitched at four o'clock in an excellent camping-ground. Purdung insisted on Philip sharing his tent, and it was not long before the young Englishman and his men were enjoying the first good meal they had tasted for many days.

During the rest of the journey Philip was treated with great kindness by his Tibetan friend, who was of a generous disposition and found pleasure in rendering assistance to one who was in need of it. They now began to descend to the lower country near Lhasa, and the nomad tents became more numerous. Owing to the plentiful provisions that could be purchased, and to the milder temperature, Phendi and Esa soon recovered their strength. A few huts, mostly of mud, soon made their appearance, proving that the climate admitted of people living in the district all the year round, instead of having to move like the nomads to warmer quarters for the winter. Then one or two straggling villages were passed, and, as cultivation became possible, well-made farm-houses and country residences. Some of these latter were substantial structures of stone, with carefully tended gardens round them.

Philip gained his first view of the Mecca of Buddhism on a lovely afternoon four months after leaving Ta-chien-lu. The sight impressed him deeply. He had seen more magnificent cities, but none which took such a strong hold on his imagination. There was something altogether unique in this citadel of Buddhism planted in the centre of a country in such striking contrast to the land which gave birth to the religion it upheld. It seemed at first glance as if the city had dropped from the heavens into the midst of a barren and inhospitable waste. Philip gazed with admiration at the gilded cupolas of the temples as they shone in the rays of the declining sun, and felt no wonder at the spell which the city exercised on all who saw it.

It was close on sunset as they entered Lhasa by the eastern gate. In spite of the guard stationed there Philip passed through without a challenge, as forming part of Purdung's caravan. Mantso led the way with head erect, a smile of satisfaction illuminating his good-natured countenance. He felt he had performed his task and brought his master safely to the sacred city. Even in Phendi's melancholy eyes a gleam of pleasure could be seen, while Esa, now fully recovered from his illness, was inflated with a sense of the triumph they had achieved.

Purdung had pressed Philip to put up at his house, but the young man, not wishing to impose upon his friend's good-nature, decided to seek quarters for himself in a secluded portion of the town. The Tibetan merchant, seeing that he was not to be shaken in this resolve, offered to find the lodgings he required. As the sun set the lamas blew their trumpets and conches from the gates of the various temples. This was the signal for everybody to cease from the occupation in which he was engaged and join in the evening prayer. Women mounted to the house-tops, and, burning juniper branches, began to chant the evensong in their clear, melodious voices. The men, standing at the doorways or in groups at the corners of the streets, added their deep tones to the women's trebles, making altogether a most impressive evening service. At its conclusion every one resumed his interrupted occupation, and Purdung's caravan, which had halted, moved on towards its destination.

A Wife from the Forbidden Land

It was not long before the Tibetan merchant found some comfortable quarters for his friend, and parted with him for the night, saying that he would come and show him something of the city on the following morning. Philip's two yaks were accommodated in the yard, and he was conducted by the owner of the house to a couple of rooms on the second floor, the first floor being already let, though the tenants were away. Mantso carried his master's goods up to his rooms, and soon managed not only to get things in order, but to cook a tempting supper as well. This was the first night they had spent under a roof since leaving the village in which Philip's marriage with Lotzung had taken place.

It was poor Lotzung's absence that alone detracted from Philip's satisfaction at having gained the goal of his long journey. Unfortunately he did not know the name of the uncle with whom she had told him she would reside on reaching Lhasa. Phala's friend Rashwa, however, to whom he had a letter of introduction, would perhaps be able to give him the name and address of this uncle. Accordingly, after breakfast on the following morning, Philip sent Mantso to find Rashwa's house, and to ask when he could grant him an interview. Mantso returned with the news that Rashwa was on a visit to some friends not far from Lhasa, but was expected back in the course of a week or ten days.

There was much to interest Philip till Rashwa's return. Purdung called for him about nine o'clock, and took him through the city. After walking along the principal streets they set out for the Potala or Dalai Lama's palace. Although about a mile from the town it could be seen from any part, being built on a rock rising sheer out of the ground to a height of some seven hundred feet. The structure was of stone, and so well whitewashed that when the sun shone upon it the effect was almost dazzling. Philip longed to have an audience with the Dalai Lama, but refrained from asking the good offices of Purdung for the purpose. Rashwa would probably be able to obtain an interview for him if any one could, and it would be foolish to imperil his chances by applying to a man who had not equal influence.

On returning to the city Purdung took Philip into the principal Buddhist temple. The resemblance between the Lamaist and Roman Catholic ritual was very striking—the chanting of the monks, the incense, and the gorgeous vestments. In one respect, however, there was a radical difference between the two services. Whereas in Roman Catholic churches women usually form the majority of the congregation, in this Buddhist temple there were no women to be seen at all. In the Buddhist religion men alone possess souls to be saved, and the gates of heaven are shut to women.

But if the fair sex were excluded from the temples there were plenty of them to be seen in the streets. Indeed, the population of Lhasa seems to consist chiefly of monks and women. The former pervaded every quarter of the city, swarming round the Potala, going in and out of the temples and lamaseries telling their beads, and twirling their prayer-cylinders in every street in the town. Their demeanour in public was certainly beyond reproach. On meeting women they turned away their heads or cast their eyes upon the ground. It is true that the temptation to do otherwise was not very great, for the majority of women daubed themselves with the black paste ordained, it is said, by a lamaist reformer, to prevent them luring the hearts of the monks away from their profession. A certain number of women disregarded the ordinance, but these belonged to the upper classes, who were not so much fettered by lamaist tyranny.

As Purdung and Philip were walking down the main street loud cries and the cracking of whips attracted their attention. Turning round they saw a long procession overtaking them from the direction of the Potala, and heard that the Senior Chinese Amban, escorted by the Regent, was returning from an audience with the Dalai Lama. The Senior Amban was, of course, Tuen Fang, the mandarin who had flogged Mantso at Ta-chien-lu, and whom Phala had treated so cavalierly at the village of Namcho. It was to Philip's interest to avoid encountering this mandarin, but he was curious to see the Regent of Tibet, and drew Purdung into a doorway, from which he could watch the procession without being at all conspicuous himself.

Half a dozen Tibetan policemen with long whips cleared the course, and were followed by a body of Tibetan cavalry. Then came the Regent, accompanied by a retinue of Tibetan noblemen. The Regent, a man of nearly sixty years of age, showed great power and determination in his face, and would have excited Philip's admiration but for a look of cruelty and cunning in his small black eyes. Behind the Regent rode a number of Chinese officials belonging to the Amban's staff, their gorgeous robes in strong contrast to their yellow faces and feeble frames. Next came the Senior Amban, Tuen Fang, carried in a palanquin with four bearers. He was leaning back on his cushions, and Philip only caught a momentary glimpse of his puffy, sensuous face.

The procession ended with a body of Chinese and Tibetan retainers of the Amban walking on foot. Amongst the latter there was a face which Philip knew. It was Jasi, the muleteer who had betrayed him. How had he entered the service of the Amban ? His former masters, the lamas, may have required him no more, and procured him a post in Tuen Fang's household. In any case it would not do for Philip to be seen by him, and the young Englishman shrank back into the shadow of the doorway till the group of retainers had passed by.

CHAPTER XVI

FOR the next few days Philip did not venture out in the daytime lest Jasi should chance to meet him and give information to the authorities. When Purdung came to see him and proposed a walk he complained of indisposition. It would have been unwise to tell the Tibetan merchant that he had seen the man who had in all probability denounced him to the lamas of Namcho and who had undoubtedly prepared a second trap for him. Purdung was a pleasant companion, but his friendship could hardly be expected to bear the strain of association with a man who might at any time be driven out of the city.

A week passed in this manner, but no action was taken against Philip. Jasi was evidently a member of Tuen Fang's household now, and as long as Philip did not approach the Amban's palace the risk of meeting the muleteer was not very great. He therefore began to go out in the daytime again, and resumed his walks with Purdung.

It was during one of these that Mantso, whom he had left in charge of his rooms, came running full speed after him.

"What is the matter, Mantso?" Philip asked.

Mantso glanced at Purdung and then said—

"May I speak to you alone, Kushok?"

Philip asked Purdung to excuse him, and went aside with Mantso.

As soon as Purdung was out of earshot Mantso said—

"The Khalons * have sent an official with two soldiers

* Magistrates.

to take you to them. When he found that you were not in he bade me go and find you."

Philip saw that Jasi must have caught sight of him and informed against him. It was fortunate that Purdung had not heard what Mantso said, for it would have alarmed him considerably. As it was, Philip merely told him that he had to go home, as some one wanted to see him, and they parted without the Tibetan merchant having any suspicion of the character of Philip's visitors.

When the young man reached his rooms he found the Khalons' official and his two soldiers in possession, awaiting his return. On seeing him the official produced a document and said—

"You are the Eastern Mongol who goes by the name of Khangsar?"

Philip acknowledged that this was so.

"I have a summons for you to appear at the Khalons' court."

"On what charge?" asked Philip.

"That of failing to report yourself to the authorities when you entered the city."

Philip saw that it would be useless to plead ignorance of the custom, and merely replied that he was ready. The two soldiers marched out of the room and drew up on either side of the door. Philip followed, accompanied by the official. As he left the room the young man told Mantso to take care of it till his return.

"The Khalons will want to see your servant also," said the official. "But do not be alarmed about your room. I have the key and will lock it up securely."

As soon as Mantso had crossed the threshold the key was turned and the party descended to the courtyard. On gaining the street one of the soldiers led the way, Philip and the official followed, and Mantso with the second soldier brought up the rear. As he went Philip speculated on the nature of the inquiry which was about to take place, and what penalty would be imposed if it were proved that he was the same man whom the lamas had ordered back from Namcho. He had always heard that suspected persons met with short shrift in Lhasa. If only Rashwa had returned and Philip could have handed him Phala's letter of introduction, he would have had some one to speak in his favour. As it was it would be very difficult to dispel any suspicions which attached to him.

Meanwhile a number of young children began to follow the procession which was wending its way to the Khalons' court, and notoriety of that kind was what Philip was particularly anxious to avoid. Fortunately it was the hour of the midday meal, so that the adults who followed were comparatively few. Philip was relieved when at length they reached the court-house, and he was conducted into an ante-room, whilst the official entered the court to announce the arrival of the suspect.

They did not keep him waiting long. The official reappeared, and, holding open the door, motioned for Philip and Mantso to enter the court. On doing so Philip found himself in a spacious apartment, the roof supported by handsome pillars and with a rectangular hole in the centre to admit the light and air. At the further end of the court the judges sat on cushions on a dais. Only three were present, an unoccupied pile of cushions being evidently the seat of the fourth Khalon. They were dressed in costumes of rich silk, and in front of each of them in the body of the court sat a secretary, with a roll of papers on the desk before him. Each Khalon had a tea bowl at his side, an attendant with a teapot refilling it when empty. No ceremony—social, legal, or religious—can be carried on in Tibet without the assistance of tea.

Philip did not know whether he was expected to prostrate himself before the magistrates as a Tibetan of the middle or lower class would have done. In his character of an Eastern Mongol he decided to forego a custom against which his English blood revolted. Mantso, however, made full amends for his master's remissness in this particular, and, falling on his knees, struck the floor with his forehead three times in obeisance to each of the Khalons. While he was doing so Philip scanned the faces of his judges. They appeared to be clever, capable men, far superior to the ordinary Chinese mandarin. The centre Khalon motioned him to take a seat on some cushions in the body of the court, and began the examination.

"How long have you been in Lhasa?" he asked.

"A little over fourteen days," replied Philip.

"Then why have you not reported yourself to us earlier?"

"I am a stranger to your city and did not know the custom."

"We do not welcome strangers in this country," said the Khalon on the left. "You cannot have travelled through it without learning that."

The Khalon looked at him sternly as he spoke. Perhaps Jasi had betrayed him to this man. Philip felt that he must be careful how he answered, for the Ladaki might be produced at any moment to contradict his statements. Accordingly he said—

"Any one who visits Tibet sees that your countrymen will not brook interference on the part of foreigners."

The Khalon on the right, who had hitherto made no remark, now nodded approvingly and said—

"This man has not misread our national character, it seems."

"But that is not the point," rejoined the Khalon on the left. "It is not a question whether we allow foreigners to interfere with our affairs, but whether they are to be admitted into this country at all without a proper permit. Where is your passport ?" he added, turning to Philip.

It was an awkward question, and one which Philip had feared might be asked at any moment.

"I have no passport," he answered. "I did not know that it was necessary."

The Khalon who spoke gave his brother judges a significant look, as much as to say that this statement only confirmed the suspicions which he entertained.

"It is strange that you should have come all this distance through Tibet," he continued, "and not have heard that foreigners who travel without passports are regarded with suspicion. Very few succeed in reaching Lhasa. Our lamas in the distant provinces keep a careful watch, and refuse to let those whom they suspect proceed. Did you not find it so ?"

It seemed almost certain that this Khalon had received information from Jasi. Was it worth while fencing any longer, or should he give the struggle up ? Philip decided on the bolder course and answered—

"I found that the suspicions of your lamas were easily aroused, but I did nothing to deserve them, having no wish to do your country harm. One of your own citizens, who holds a high position in Lhasa, can speak for me."

"Is he in court now ?"

"Unfortunately he is absent from Lhasa at the present time."

The hostile Khalon gave his brothers another glance expressive of the confirmation of his views, and then continued—

"We have reason to believe that you are the same man whom the lamas at Namcho ordered to return to China. Is that so ?"

It was useless to maintain the struggle any longer. The Khalon knew everything, and if Philip denied his identity with the man whom the Namcho lamas had sent back, Jasi would be called in to disprove his statement. But a diversion was now created by the entrance of the fourth Khalon. As soon as he had taken his seat the Khalon who was examining Philip turned to explain the case to the new arrival.

"We have a foreigner here," he said, "whom we have good reason to believe was ordered to leave the country by the lamas of Namcho, but he disobeyed the order. It is a serious matter, and his punishment should be severe."

Philip watched the fourth Khalon keenly whilst these words were being spoken. He had a clever, well-shaped head, clear dark eyes, and a very pleasant expression.

"I suppose you have ample proof that he is the man you take him to be. What have you got to say in your defence?" he continued, turning to Philip.

"I have nothing to say in my defence," answered Philip, "because I have done nothing wrong. The writer of this letter will no doubt bear witness to my character, though the person to whom it is addressed, being absent from Lhasa, cannot vouch for me himself."

With these words Philip rose from his seat and handed Phala's letter of introduction to the new-comer. The latter glanced at the name on the outside, fixed his keen gaze for a few seconds on Philip, and then, opening the letter, ran his eye quickly over the contents. When he had read them he turned to the other Khalons and said—

"This man may possibly be as honest as he says. I know the person to whom the letter is addressed and will hand it to him on his return to Lhasa. Meanwhile I think we might let the foreigner go, merely keeping a watch upon his movements so that we can have him brought before us again when we require him."

The hostile Khalon seemed to demur to this proposal, but the other two agreed to it, and Philip was told that he and his servant might go. At this announcement Mantso fell upon his knees and kow-towed to the four Khalons with much fervour, being particularly demonstrative in his obeisance to the last arrival.

Having reached his rooms Philip reviewed the situation at his leisure. Things had certainly looked unpleasant for him at one time, and if Jasi had been sent for the verdict would have almost certainly gone against him. But the fourth Khalon had just appeared at the right moment and relieved the threatening atmosphere. It was certainly curious that, having opened and read the letter himself, he did not divulge its contents to his brother judges. In any case Philip had obtained a reprieve, and was inclined to regard the future hopefully, as he had been much struck by the noble bearing and kindly expression of the Khalon who had taken up his case.

That evening, as Mantso was laying his master's supper, he could not refrain from alluding to the proceedings in the Khalons' court.

"I marvelled at the Kushok's calm," he said. "I was trembling all the time."

"What was there to be afraid of?" Philip asked.

"The Kushok does not know how powerful these Khalons are and what punishments they can mete out."

"They could not punish me for merely coming to Lhasa; and as for you, it is your own country, and you can go where you like in it."

"Yes, but if a man displeases the lamas, they persuade the Khalons to punish him. I know the Khalon who asked so many questions, and he is a harsh man. The Khalon who came last I do not know, but I think he will take the Kushok's part."

"I hope he will, Mantso," replied Philip cheerfully. "But make haste and get my supper served. A visit to your Tibetan courts has made me hungry."

For a suspect in the town of Lhasa Philip made a capital meal. Food was good, though dear in the town, and Mantso with practice was becoming a capital cook. After dinner the young man was settling down to read a Tibetan book in order to improve his knowledge of the language, when he heard some one ascending the stairs. There was a brief exchange of words with Mantso and then the latter, opening the door, ushered the visitor in with these words—

"This man says he has a message for you from Rashwa."

So Rashwa had at last returned, and the friendly Khalon must have given him Philip's letter as well as Philip's address.

"What is your message?" the young man asked.

"My master, Rashwa, has sent me to conduct you to his house."

The invitation was a welcome one, and, laying aside his book, Philip rose and accompanied the messenger. Rashwa would no doubt soon put matters all right with the Khalons. He would also in all probability give the name and address of the uncle with whom Lotzung had said she would stay in Lhasa, so that he could tell him of her disappearance, and get information as to the best means of letting her parents know the fact.

On reaching the house Philip was conducted by an attendant through an ante-room into a fine apartment. The attendant, after placing cushions for him to sit upon, withdrew, and the young man was left alone to inspect his surroundings at his leisure. The room was lighted with butter lamps, and a desk with writing materials stood at the further end of it. The thick carpet and rich silk hangings showed that the owner of the house was a man of considerable means.

Whilst he was engaged in this inspection a side door opened and, to Philip's surprise, there appeared not Rashwa, but the friendly Khalon. He advanced with a pleasant smile, and, motioning Philip to a seat at the end of the room where the desk stood, sat down beside him. Then, as his visitor was too much surprised to speak, he said—

"What is it that you wish me to do for you?"

"I have no request to make of you," answered Philip. "I came here because I was told that Rashwa wished to see me. Is he in the house?"

The Khalon smiled quietly.

"Yes, he is in the house and is talking to you now."

Philip looked at him in astonishment.

"Then the letter which I handed you in court to-day was for yourself."

"I saw that you did not know who I was, and there was no occasion to tell you then. Neither had I any reason to divulge the contents of the letter to the other Khalons. The truth is that Phala was at variance with the authorities here in the matter of politics, and it would be unwise to make it known that he is corresponding with any one resident in Lhasa."

"The Deba hinted to me that he had been driven from the town by the action of his political opponents, and I now understand why you kept the letter secret. You are still his friend?"

"I am, and I will do all I can for you if you will be candid with me. In the first place, is it true that the lamas of Namcho ordered you to return to China?"

"Quite true."

"Does any one in Lhasa know this?"

" A Ladaki, named Jasi, who was in my employment as a muleteer and who afterwards deserted, is aware of it. I think he must have informed the Khalons."

" What is he doing now ? "

" I have only seen him once since I have been in Lhasa. He was then amongst the attendants of the Senior Chinese Amban."

" The probability that he has already given information against you to my brother Khalons makes it a difficult matter to deal with. However, as he is a Tibetan, I dare say I shall find a means of making him hold his tongue, in spite of his being in the service of the Chinese Amban. Is there anything more that I can do for you ? "

Philip remembered Lotzung's uncle.

" There is one more favour I have to ask you," he said. " You are probably aware that the Deba of Namcho had a daughter called Lotzung ? "

" I know her well," replied Rashwa.

" She set out to accompany me on my journey to Lhasa."

" There is no mention of the fact in Phala's letter to me."

" The letter was written before he heard that she had made up her mind to come to Lhasa. She was anxious to see her brother, who resides here."

" Has she told you all about this brother ? "

" Nothing except that he lives in Lhasa. She said she had an uncle here with whom she could stay. Her plan for getting to Lhasa was to come as somebody's wife."

The Khalon smiled.

" Whom did she select for her husband ? "

" Well, her choice fell on me," replied Philip, somewhat embarrassed at having to make the avowal. " A number of young girls married me to her in a grove outside a small village on the road. I informed her father of the fact, but he said that as the marriage had been duly celebrated he could do nothing in the matter. I was on the point of repudiating the contract when Lotzung begged me to take her as my wife to Lhasa, after which she promised to release me from my bond with regard to her. Do you know her uncle ? "

" I know him very well. You wish, I suppose, to put Lotzung under his care ? "

" Unfortunately, no. During the journey the young girl disappeared, killed, I am afraid, by bears." And Philip gave Rashwa an account of the circumstances under which she had been lost.

" Well, there will be time enough to attend to this matter to-morrow," said the Khalon, who seemed to regard the affair very lightly. " Meanwhile you must come and see my wife and family," and he led the way to the door by which he had entered the room. Throwing it open, he stood aside for Philip to pass through. But the young man came to a standstill on the threshold, for with Rashwa's family sat Lotzung, bending over a hand-loom at which she worked, while Champa lay full length on the floor at her feet.

CHAPTER XVII

LOTZUNG made a charming picture as she turned her loom, the light pink costume of rich silk, in which she was dressed, throwing into relief her dark hair and eyes. Her complexion was less sunburnt than when Philip saw her last, and her expression was a shade more thoughtful. But these changes did not detract from her appearance, and the young man found himself wondering how he had hitherto failed to realize what a pretty girl she was.

There was no time, however, for reflection on the subject, as the opening of the door caused Lotzung to look up. On seeing Philip her expression was one of the utmost astonishment, but when she realized who it was, she ran up to him with the natural impulse of a child, and taking both his hands in hers she said—

"So it is really you, Khangsar? I feared that you were dead."

"And I, for my part, had given you up as lost. So then," he continued, turning to Rashwa, who had followed him into the room, "you are the uncle of whom Lotzung spoke to me?"

Rashwa smiled at the success of the surprise he had planned for Philip.

"Yes, I am the uncle," he answered, "and this is my wife, Gyung."

Philip exchanged greetings with Gyung, a handsome woman with a boy on either side of her.

"You had a letter to my husband from my brother

Phala, the Deba of Namcho," she said. " My brother's friends are my friends, and you have been kind to my niece Lotzung. She has told me that you agreed to let her travel with you as your wife till she should reach Lhasa in safety. She is a good girl and very useful in the house. You have not come to take her away ? "

" No, he does not want me as his wife," interposed Lotzung. " I only persuaded him to let me be called so till we should get to the end of the journey. Was it not so ? " she added, turning to Philip.

" That is what we agreed upon," replied the young man, a little piqued at Lotzung's ready renunciation of her marriage ties. " But tell me how you got here, Lotzung ? " he continued. " When I returned to the place where I left you I could find no trace of you, and seeing some bears close to the spot I thought they must have killed you."

In reply to Philip's question the young girl gave the following account of what had happened to her since they parted. When she awoke the morning after Philip had left her she went to the top of a neighbouring hill, and was surprised to see no traces of the nomad encampment. She wondered if it had disappeared before Philip reached the spot or whether its members had carried him off with them. The distance to the spot where the encampment had been was not great, and Philip could easily have got back by dawn as he promised, unless something had happened to him.

When eight o'clock came she was making up her mind to go in search of him when she saw some figures approaching from a point to the eastward of the site of the nomad encampment. Thinking that Philip had overtaken the nomads and was returning with some yaks, which the men were driving for him, she set out to meet him. To her great disappointment Philip was not amongst them, but she recognized in the chief of the caravan a lama who came from a monastery not far from her father's house.

This lama knew her at once and asked her how she came to be there all by herself, so far from her home. She replied that she had been travelling with a caravan bound for Lhasa, but that it had been robbed by chukpas, and the chief had gone in search of a nomad encampment from which to buy more food and cattle. There were no nomads in sight, and the lama, evidently not believing her story, said that she must join his caravan, as he, too, was bound for Lhasa. On her replying that she preferred to wait for the chief of her caravan, one of the lama's companions asked what he was like and how he was dressed. As soon as he heard Lotzung's description he declared they had seen such a man being driven along by a party of nomads with his hands tied behind him. He gave such a minute account of the affair, and was so unanimously supported by the others, that Lotzung had no alternative but to believe the story and accompany the lama's caravan. They had good cattle and carried very little baggage, so that the journey was accomplished quickly.

By the time that Philip had in his turn given an account of his adventures after parting with Lotzung it was quite late, and the young man rose to go.

"You must often come and see us," said Rashwa, as he bade his guest good-bye. "The evening is the best time. There are many questions I should like to ask a man who has stayed so lately with my wife's brother, the Deba of Namcho."

Philip had plenty to occupy his thoughts when he returned to his lodging that night. He remembered that Lotzung had never mentioned her uncle's name to him, or he would have known that Phala's friend and the young girl's uncle were the same person. Rashwa was evidently an influential man, to whom it was fortunate to have an introduction. The Khalons came next in authority to the Regent, and Rashwa seemed to be the most powerful of the four. If a way were found to shut Jasi's mouth Philip might reside in Lhasa with little likelihood of interference.

The young man's chief desire now was to obtain an audience with the Dalai Lama, and Rashwa was the person whom he thought most likely to assist him in the matter. Accordingly a few days later he called on the chief Khalon, which he now found was Rashwa's proper title.

" I want to have an audience with the Dalai Lama," he said, " and thought you might, perhaps, be able to arrange it for me."

Rashwa looked grave.

" This is a matter for the Regent," he replied. " The list of those who wish to see the Dalai Lama must be submitted to him."

" I am glad of that," said Philip. " The Regent knows nothing against me and would have no reason to refuse my application. It would have been otherwise with the Chinese Amban. I interfered with Tuen Fang in Ta-chien-lu, when he was flogging a man, who afterwards became my servant. Though he would not know my name he would probably recognize my face."

" But it is because the Regent has to be consulted when seeking an audience with the Dalai Lama that I cannot undertake this service for you."

Philip's hopes fell at once to zero. His powerful friend, the chief Khalon, failed him in just the very matter in which he had felt sure of his assistance. Of course, the young man could not ask the reason for his refusal, and a silence ensued which Rashwa broke at length.

" But because I can do nothing for you in this matter

there is no reason why you should not get some one else to help you. Have you no other acquaintance in Lhasa ?"

Philip remembered Purdung.

"There is a merchant named Purdung with whom I travelled part of the way to Lhasa."

"I know him well. He will be able to do what you want. It is not a difficult matter."

There the subject dropped, and a little later they joined the family circle, playing games and singing to the accompaniment of various instruments. Champa alone did not seem to enjoy the music, and as he lay stretched full length upon the floor, his muzzle between his two fore feet, he would now and again cast a distressful eye upon the performers, emitting a whine of expostulation when the crescendo parts were rendered with more vehemence than he could bear.

Once during the evening, when Rashwa and Gyung were playing a duet, the former with a flute and the latter with a stringed instrument, Philip found an opportunity of speaking a few words with Lotzung which the others could could not hear.

"Have you accomplished the object, Lotzung, for which you were so anxious to come to Lhasa ?" he asked.

"What object do you mean ?" she answered.

"Have you forgotten that you told me that your reason for wishing to come here was to see your brother ?"

Lotzung put her finger to her lips to silence him, and glanced quickly at her uncle and aunt. They were both too intent upon their performance to notice what was going on around them, Rashwa staring straight ahead of him as he puffed out his cheeks and produced strange noises from his flute, while Gyung's attention was fully engaged with the fingering of the stringed instrument she played.

"You must not let them hear you mention him," said Lotzung in a low voice, nodding her head in their direction.

This brother seemed to have a bad name everywhere, thought Philip. Not only had his parents disowned him, but his uncle and aunt would have nothing to do with him. What had this lad of fourteen done to make his relations refrain from speaking of him? Philip's interest in the family scapegrace grew deeper still.

"So you have not seen him, after all?"

"Yes, I have seen him, but only once. It is very difficult to arrange a meeting."

"How is he getting on?"

Lotzung shook her head.

"The future is clouded for him. I see no chance——"

But at this moment the music ceased abruptly, cutting short Lotzung's sentence, and Philip did not get another opportunity that night of a private conversation with her. The youthful brother, however, continued to engage his thoughts after leaving Rashwa's house. Why should it be so difficult for Lotzung to arrange a meeting with him, considering the liberty allowed to Tibetan girls, and the fact that she could go out unattended any hour of the day up to nine or ten o'clock at night? Why, too, did she speak so gloomily of his future? Was he already, at the tender age of fourteen, so hardened a reprobate that even an affectionate sister saw no chance of his reformation? Philip's curiosity was aroused, though there was little prospect of its being gratified unless Lotzung herself should volunteer the information.

The following day, anxious to lose no time in visiting the Potala, Philip called on Purdung. The Tibetan merchant received him with his customary warmth, and when they had sat down with a supply of "chang" (the beer of the country) between them, Philip referred to the object of his call.

"I have come to ask you to obtain for me an audience with the Dalai Lama."

Purdung became thoughtful.

"I suppose you have not roused the suspicions of the lamas since you have been in Lhasa?" he asked at length.

Philip determined to be open with him.

"I have had no dealings with the lamas; but a few days ago the Khalons summoned me to their court."

"Ah!" exclaimed Purdung, in a tone which made it clear that he thought it a serious matter. "And what did they say to you?"

"There were only three of them present at first, and they were inclined to be unfriendly, but when the chief Khalon came he took my part."

Purdung seemed considerably relieved.

"If Rashwa is on your side you are not likely to meet with interference. He has a great deal of influence amongst the citizens of Lhasa. But why do you not ask him to obtain the audience for you?"

"I have asked him, and he said he would rather not do so."

There was a short silence, and then Purdung said—

"I suppose it is because application has to be made to Tsering, the Regent. Rashwa is the only man in Lhasa who has had the courage to openly oppose him, and that is why he does not care to ask any favour of him."

"In what respect does he oppose the Regent?"

"As this is your first visit to Lhasa you are of course unacquainted with our political affairs. I will give you a little information about them, which may perhaps be useful to you. In the first place, the present Dalai Lama is the third for whom Tsering has acted as Regent."

" Is that against the law ? " asked Philip.

" No, but it seems that both the previous Dalai Lamas died before they came of age."

" It was a mere matter of chance, I suppose."

" That is the question. It was of course to Tsering's interest that they should die before they came of age, so that he might become Regent to the successor."

" Is it suggested then that he did away with them ? "

Purdung nodded his head.

The possibility of such an infamous crime gave Philip pause. To find a European parallel it would be necessary to go back at least to the Middle Ages.

" Do Tibetans then allow," he asked at length, " the Head of their Church to be sacrificed to the ambitions of a wicked Regent ? "

" Tsering's connection with the crime would be difficult to prove. The Regent has sole charge of the Dalai Lama, and all the attendants are chosen by him. He is the most powerful man in the state."

" Yet Rashwa is both popular and influential, you say ? "

" Amongst the laymen ; but Tsering has at his back the ten thousand lamas of Sera Monastery, of which he was Abbot before becoming Regent. He favours them in every possible way, and they would not let him be deposed."

" Are not the citizens of Lhasa, led by the chief Khalon, a match for the Regent and his monks ? "

Purdung shook his head.

" The Monastery of Sera possesses as much wealth as all the merchants of Lhasa together. Besides, they are prepared to fight in person for their rights. The majority of them are young men who entered the monastery because they were incapable of supporting themselves as laymen, or because they fled to it as a sanctuary to escape the consequences of some crime. The Regent has also taken care to have the Senior Chinese Amban on his side. The Amban commands the Chinese troops in Lhasa and Tsering the Tibetan troops. A rising of citizens could do nothing against these soldiers supported by the Sera Monastery."

"Has Tsering always won over the Chinese Amban?"

"Hitherto he has done so. In fact, the last Amban was so much under his influence that the Chinese Emperor recalled him. Tuen Fang is more careful at present, but he is not likely to prove any better in the end."

From Philip's own experience of him it certainly seemed improbable, but the young man made no reference to his encounter with the mandarin at Ta-chien-lu for fear of making Purdung uneasy. He merely inquired if, under the circumstances, it was useless to ask the merchant to obtain for him an audience with the Dalai Lama.

"I will do my best," replied Purdung. "The Regent has no reason to think that I should wish to present a suspicious character. I will submit your name to him, and will let you know if the interview is granted."

Philip thanked the good-natured merchant, and went off in high spirits. What he had heard about the Regent made him all the more anxious to see his charge. If only half what Purdung had said was true Tsering must be a bloodthirsty and unscrupulous scoundrel, while Rashwa excited the young man's admiration for having the courage to oppose the tyrant.

In the absence of news from Purdung Philip spent the next two days in a state of great restlessness, now buoyed up with the hope of obtaining his object, now despairing of it altogether. On the third day, however, Purdung came to his rooms and announced that he had arranged an interview for the following morning at eleven o'clock. Philip was much gratified by the news, and, as soon as Purdung had gone, hunted amongst his property for some suitable presents to give the Grand Lama. Fortunately some of the most valuable articles which he had brought from China for this purpose were still in his possession, and he selected a pair of handsome silver drinking cups and three cloaks of the richest Chinese silk.

That evening he went round to Rashwa's house and informed him of the approaching interview.

" I am very pleased to hear that Purdung has arranged it," said the Khalon. " I have only one thing to ask, do not mention my name to any one at the Potala, nor let it be seen that you know me if you happen to meet me there."

Philip promised to do as he wished, and then the conversation, which had taken place in the family circle, turned on general topics. Lotzung, however, remained unusually silent, and after a short time rose and left the room. She was still absent when Philip took his leave about an hour later, and he came to the conclusion that she had retired for the night.

But the young man had not gone many paces from the house when he heard a light step hurrying after him, and a girl's voice calling softly, " Khangsar, Khangsar ! " He turned to find that it was Lotzung.

" You, Lotzung ! " he exclaimed. " I thought you had gone to bed a long time ago ! "

" No, I did not go to bed," she answered. " I stayed up because I wanted to ask you if you would do something for me."

" I will do what I can for you, Lotzung," he answered.

" I heard you tell my uncle," she continued, " that you were going to have an audience with the Dalai Lama tomorrow."

" Yes, that is so," said Philip.

" We women are not allowed to enter the Potala, any more than we can gain admittance to the temples."

Philip nodded to show that he was aware of the fact.

"But although we cannot join in public prayers, nor ever see the head of our Church, we may still be devoted to the religion of our country."

Philip again silently acquiesced, wondering at a faith which shut the gates of heaven to an innocent young girl like Lotzung, while the most depraved and dissolute lama could walk in without a word of protest from the door-keeper. But Lotzung resumed—

"One of the ways in which we can show our devotion is by giving offerings to the Dalai Lama. This we do through those who are privileged to have an audience with him. Will you take a small offering from me to the Dalai Lama to-morrow?"

She looked up to him with an earnest appeal in her dark eyes.

"Of course I will, Lotzung," he answered. "Have you got it with you?"

Lotzung produced a small parcel, very neatly done up in paper.

"I have hardly any money of my own," she continued, "and my offering has no value. In fact, it is only a little khata. Still, it is all I can give, and you will make me very happy if you will place it amongst your richer gifts to the Dalai Lama."

"I will present it with them."

A pretty smile lit up the young girl's face.

"You are very good to me, Khangsar. Of course, you will not say from whom it comes, but merely present it with your own khata when you are in the presence of the Grand Lama. Keep it packed up in the paper as long as possible to prevent it being soiled. Good night, dear Khangsar," and with a farewell smile she turned and hurried back to the house.

CHAPTER XVIII

AS Philip walked back to his rooms that night his recent interview with Lotzung engaged his thoughts. During the time that she was with him on his journey to Lhasa he had not realized that she was such a devoted follower of Buddha. He remembered, of course, that she had persuaded him to kneel at the cairn on the top of the first pass they had crossed together, and on subsequent occasions she had placed a stone upon the pile, and attached lung-ta to the prayer poles like an orthodox believer in Gautama. But he had not suspected her of such deep religious convictions as to wish to spend the little money she had in making presents to the Dalai Lama, whom she could never see, and who would not even be aware that she was the donor of the gifts.

Philip rose early the following morning and got ready the presents which he had set aside to take to the Potala. The silver cups received a final polish, and the silk cloaks were shaken and carefully folded. Lotzung's khata, still in its paper covering, was placed with his own on the top. The presents were then done up in a parcel for Mantso to carry to the Potala.

Although the palace lay barely a mile from the town it was customary for all but the very poorest to ride there on horseback. Philip did not possess any horses, but he found no difficulty in hiring a couple of ponies for the purpose. At half-past ten he started from his lodgings, Mantso carrying in addition to the presents a bundle of incense sticks for presentation at the entrance hall of the Potala. As they rode out of the courtyard the muleteer pointed with evident satisfaction to a woman carrying a bucket of water.

"It is a very lucky omen," he said, "when the first person you see on leaving the house in the morning is a woman carrying water."

Philip smiled and said that he was glad to begin the day in such an auspicious manner. It would indeed be unfortunate if anything should occur at the last moment to prevent the interview to which he had looked forward with such curiosity. On nearing the Potala the numbers of lamas passing in and out seemed larger than usual, and pilgrims, bound for an audience like himself, were riding towards it. The sun shone brightly on the building, the nine stories of which stood out boldly in the clear atmosphere.

Arrived at the eastern gate, Philip and his servant were received by three lamas, who bade them dismount and follow them with their ponies. The monks led the way into a fine entrance hall, with a row of prayer cylinders on either side. Philip rotated those on the side along which he passed, following the example set him by the lamas. Leaving the hall they ascended a flight of stone steps, still leading the ponies. After two more flights had been surmounted the lamas said that the ponies must be left behind. Mantso remained in charge of them, and one of the lamas carried Philip's bundle of presents.

The reason for leaving the ponies at this point now became evident, for the next ascent was made by a ladder. Then four terraces connected by ladders brought them to a building called the Red Palace. Here the party rested to take breath, and Philip gazed on the magnificent panorama which lay stretched before him, including the whole of the city and the rolling expanse of plain beyond up to the foot of the distant hills. Six more ladders followed, and the reception hall was gained at length. The lamas ushered Philip within. Three or four score pilgrims were already assembled in this chamber, which was hung with rich brocades and cloth of gold, while the walls were ornamented with gorgeous frescoes. The floor was made of Tibetan polished cement, which by frequent rubbing acquires a surface as glossy as the finest marble.

The chamberlain now entered and inspected the tickets of admission with which each of the visitors had to be provided. Philip spoke to the official in Tibetan, and was glad to find that neither his speech nor his outward appearance seemed to arrest the man's attention. Meanwhile the pilgrims were busy getting ready their presents, and the young Englishman followed their example. The silver cups he placed on the top of the rich silk cloaks. He then unwrapped Lotzung's khata, and was struck at once by its colour, which was a darker shade of blue than the kind most frequently used. As he turned it over he noticed some Tibetan characters in needlework in one corner of it. They formed, no doubt, the universal text, "Om mani padme hum," but before he could assure himself of the fact the door into the audience chamber opened and the pilgrims were summoned into the presence.

Wishing to be neither in the front nor in the rear, Philip took up his position about midway in the line, and soon entered the audience chamber. He found it to be smaller than the reception hall, but, if possible, still more lavishly adorned with costly hangings and bright-coloured frescoes. In the centre at the further end, on a pile of cushions arranged on the top of a small raised platform, sat the Dalai Lama, in the cross-legged attitude in which Buddha is almost always represented. On his right, on a lower platform, the Regent was seated, the four Khalons being also present, two on either side. Philip saw Rashwa at once, but in deference to his wishes gave no sign of recognition. Each end of the central row was flanked by a large number of lamas.

The pilgrims approached the Dalai Lama in turn, placed their gifts on the fore part of the throne, answered any questions addressed to them, and then knelt down to receive his blessing. When a pilgrim retired an attendant removed his presents and the next approached. The scene was full of interest to one who had not witnessed it before, but the chief figure in it engrossed the whole of Philip's attention. The Head of the Buddhist Church and the living embodiment of the being worshipped by it, was a young boy of princely bearing and strikingly beautiful face. The features, but for the eyes, showed no trace of Mongolian extraction, and the complexion was clear and fresh, though there was an appearance of delicacy induced by too constant attendance at the religious ceremonials of the Buddhist faith. The Grand Lama spoke to each pilgrim in turn, but in such a low voice that Philip could not hear what he said until he approached quite close to the daïs.

At length it was the young man's turn, and, advancing, he placed his presents on the Dalai Lama's throne. The boy's attention had been distracted for a moment, but when his eyes fell upon Lotzung's dark blue khata, which lay on the top of Philip's present, his interest seemed to be aroused at once. Taking up the khata—it was the first that he had touched—he opened it out, and Philip thought that his eyes rested for a second on the worked characters in the corner. Then a harsh voice exclaimed—

"Does not the Gesub Rimpoche" (one of the Dalai Lama's titles) "see the pilgrim who awaits his blessing?"

The speaker was the Regent. At the sound of his voice the Grand Lama dropped the khata hastily. Then, with the blood suffusing his delicate skin, he bent forward and laid his hand on Philip's head.

"May Buddha, whose glance explores the infinite, give you peace," he murmured; and Philip was motioned to withdraw.

In the centre of the chamber cushions were provided to seat the visitors, and when all the offerings had been presented tea was served. Some of the more devout pilgrims instead of drinking the tea poured it over their heads, but Philip did not follow their example, for it was the most fragrant he had ever tasted. He allowed the attendant to fill his cup three times, and would have drunk as much again if the cups had not been now collected and an old lama commenced an address to the pilgrims on the Buddhist faith. This was followed by a chant, in which the Dalai Lama, with his boyish treble, took the solo, while the bass voices of lamas joined at regular intervals in the refrain.

The religious fervour and apparent sincerity of the lamas would have made a deep impression on Philip if the two principal actors in the scene had not attracted his whole attention. It would be hard to find a greater contrast than that which existed between the countenances of the Dalai Lama and the man who acted as his Regent. The former was full of refinement and purity, while the latter had a sensuous look about the mouth and a mixture of cunning and cruelty in the small black eyes which made Philip inclined to believe all the stories which were told about him. What if they were really true, and the beautiful youth who combined the best qualities of a high-born prince and a saintly priest, were indeed destined to fall a victim to the Regent's greed for power?

The question haunted Philip after he had left the Potala and returned to the seclusion of his rooms. The tragedy of the Dalai Lama's life seemed gradually to reveal itself to him. Chosen by the lamas from amongst the infants born at the time of his predecessor's death, he was devoted from his earliest days to the service of the Church. At the age of three he would already be receiving audiences, and beginning to learn by heart the hundred and eight volumes of the Lamaist sacred writ. The Regent would arrange his hours of study, his meals, his rest, just as he pleased, without being responsible to any one in connection with them. The boy's delicate appearance resulted from too close an application to the sacred books, too much fasting, and too little repose. If the Regent continued this regime a little further he would gain his end without recourse to violence or poison.

One evening, about a week later, Philip was sitting reading alone in his room. It was ten o'clock, a late hour for Tibetans. The landlord and his family had retired to rest and Mantso was asleep in the next room. But on the first floor immediately beneath him Philip fancied he heard voices. The tenants who had been away so long had evidently returned, though it was curious that they should have come back at that late hour of the night. This fact distracted Philip's attention from his book, and he found himself listening to the voices beneath.

Presently he caught the sound of a faint moan, and the voices ceased. What could be going on? Philip's curiosity was now thoroughly aroused, and he strained his ears to catch the slightest sound. At this moment some one opened the door of the room below and, stepping out on to the landing, stood still, as though listening. Then the young man heard footsteps ascending the staircase to his floor. They reached his door, and, after a momentary hesitation, there came a knock and the door opened. Philip sat gazing at his visitor in blank astonishment, for there before him, with pale cheek and anxious eyes, stood

Lotzung. She started on seeing who it was, and then with a look of intense relief exclaimed—

"So it is you, Khangsar! How glad I am. Quick! Come and help me; my brother has fainted."

Philip understood the situation at a glance. Unable to meet at their uncle's house, the brother and sister had hired rooms in an out-of-the-way quarter of the town, where they could see each other without the knowledge of their relatives. He was curious to see this brother of whom Lotzung was so fond, and, taking a restorative from his medicine chest, he followed her to the room below.

Here a still greater surprise awaited him. For in the senseless form of a boy who lay on some cushions in the centre of the room, guarded by the faithful Champa, he recognized the Dalai Lama. Everything was now clear to him. This explained why Lotzung was so anxious for Philip to present to the Grand Lama her khata with the characters in one corner of it, doubtless arranging for their meeting to-night. No wonder the boy had scanned the letters so intently, till interrupted by the harsh accents of the Regent.

But the patient required immediate attention. As he lay back motionless amongst the cushions the unsteady light from a pair of flickering butter lamps intensified the pallor of his delicate but handsome countenance. Philip knelt down at his side, and, applying the restorative which he had brought with him, soon had the satisfaction of seeing the colour return to his cheeks and his beautiful dark eyes open.

"Om mani padme hum!" he said, trying to raise his hand as he pronounced the sacred formula, though it fell helpless to his side again.

"Poor Pantchen!" * murmured Lotzung, bending over

* One of the Dalai Lama's numerous titles.

him with moist eyes. " He fancies he is still on his throne saying the benediction. Look at me, Pantchen ! " she continued, raising her voice. " Do you not know me ? It is Lotzung—your only sister, Lotzung."

The boy turned his gaze towards her and a look of recognition came into his eyes.

" Is it really you, Lotzung ? " he said, looking at her earnestly. " I thought I was in the audience chamber receiving pilgrims. Then I heard your voice and was amazed, for no woman ever enters the Potala. Now I see that I am back again in the little room in which you had arranged that we should meet. I suppose I must have fallen asleep. What would Tsering say if he saw me lying thus ? Even at night-time I am not allowed to rest, except in a sitting posture." Then, catching sight of Philip, who had risen and was standing behind Lotzung, he exclaimed in an accent of alarm, " But who is that man who stands behind you ? "

Lotzung took Philip's hand and presented him to the Dalai Lama.

" This is my kind friend, Khangsar, the Eastern Mongol," she said, " of whom I told you, and who accompanied me the greater part of the journey from Namcho to Lhasa. I owe him many thanks for that ; but he has done me a still further kindness, for it was he who presented you with the khata by which I sent you my last message."

The Pantchen made an effort to rise from his cushions, but sank back into them again.

" I cannot sit up to talk with you as I should like to do, for I still feel very weak," the boy replied, turning to Philip ; " but I must thank you for your kindness to my sister. Yes, I recognize you now, though I was too busy with the khata that you brought me to do more than glance at you. I can see by your face that I can trust you to say nothing of my visit to this house to-night. But how is it that you are here ?"

Lotzung explained that when the Pantchen fainted she had gone for help and found, quite accidentally, that Khangsar was occupying a room in the same house.

"Yes, I suppose I must have fainted," rejoined the boy thoughtfully. "But I am well now, and must be returning."

If Philip had not been acting the part of a faithful follower of Buddha he would have settled the matter out of hand for the young boy. As it was he had to show some deference to the Head of the Buddhist Church. After glancing hastily round the room he said—

"But the Pantchen has had nothing to eat. He must take some tea before going out into the cold night air."

The boy gave a wan smile and shook his head.

"I had my last meal at five this afternoon, and can touch nothing till eight o'clock to-morrow morning."

"Not under ordinary circumstances, of course," replied Philip. "But this is a special occasion, for the Pantchen is not well. I know something of the healing art, and see that a little food and drink is necessary for you."

The Pantchen again shook his head, but Lotzung said—

"It is quite true what Khangsar says. He is a wonderful physician, and cured many ailments at our castle. Unfortunately I have neither food nor drink in this house," she added regretfully. "I did not think of it when I arranged the meeting here."

"That can soon be put right," said Philip. "I have plenty of meat in my larder, and will go and rouse my servant."

"Your labour will be vain," rejoined the Pantchen. "It is the season of the fasts, and I may not touch meat.'

"I have other things in my larder besides meat. A light meal shall be prepared at once."

Mantso was much surprised when Philip woke him with the order to cook supper. His master was not particular about his meals, and had never asked for one at that time of night. But the faithful muleteer obeyed the order without a murmur. The stove was soon burning brightly and water boiling for the tea. Meanwhile Philip, disregarding the Dalai Lama's remark about the fasting season, began to chop up some cooked meat. When this was very finely cut up he mixed it with some tsamba and a couple of raw eggs, making the whole, in Tibetan fashion, into a fairly thick paste. Then, bidding Mantso stay where he was, he carried the meal down to the floor beneath. The poor Pantchen's eyes glistened when he saw the steaming teapot and the tsamba paste.

"It is very wrong of me to eat now," he said, "but Khangsar, the clever physician, orders it, and I really feel the need of food."

The boy ate heartily, almost ravenously, of the tsamba paste, and gulped down the buttered tea with the most evident satisfaction. It seemed as if he were almost starved. Lotzung's eyes filled with tears as she watched him eat, and Philip burnt with anger and indignation against the unscrupulous Regent who had reduced his ward to such a state. To relieve the Pantchen of the embarrassment of eating alone Philip poured out a cup of tea for Lotzung and took one himself.

"This tsamba paste is very good," said the Pantchen. "If I had not reminded Khangsar that it was the season of the fasts I should have thought that both meat and eggs were in the mixture."

"Let not the Pantchen be afraid," replied Philip. "Khangsar knows well that it is the fasting season, and that a lama may eat neither meat nor eggs while the season lasts."

Reassured by Philip's words the Dalai Lama applied himself again to the paste, and ended by disposing of the whole of it. This done, he lay back on the cushions with already a stronger look in his delicate face.

"Khangsar must indeed be a great physician," he said, smiling. "After taking his prescription once I feel better than after a dozen doses of the medicine they give me at the Potala."

"He healed a wound which Maru received from a fall on horseback," said Lotzung, "and he prescribed for both father and mother when they were unwell. But he would not give me any medicine," she added with laughing eyes. "That is, not till I had begged him for it."

The Pantchen looked inquiringly from one to the other, trying in vain to read the explanation of his sister's words in their faces.

"How was that, Khangsar?" he asked at length. "You who were so kind to her in other respects, why did you refuse her medicine?"

"That is easily answered. She was not in need of any."

The boy gave utterance to a merry peal of laughter.

"So you ask for medicine, Lotzung, when you do not require it?" he said. "You evidently do not know what it is like. If you had to take all the medicine I am given you would soon cease asking for it."

These words banished the smile from Philip's face and made him grave again. Not content with starving, was the Regent also trying to poison the boy?

"Yes, Pantchen," he answered, "it is possible to take too much medicine, not only for one's inclination but for one's health. It seems to me that the Pantchen is given more medicine than is good for him."

The Pantchen shook his head.

" The doses have been sanctioned by long custom at the Potala, and have been administered to all my predecessors."

Philip saw that it would be useless to carry his protest any further, and the conversation turned on general topics. Lotzung and her brother were in the best of spirits. It was a pleasure to see the Pantchen give rein to his mirth, and, laying aside the restraining influence of his exalted station, act his natural part as a merry, light-hearted boy. The gaiety of the party was at its height when the blare of horns and trumpets burst forth from a neighbouring temple and reminded the Pantchen of the routine imposed upon him by his Church.

" That is the summons for midnight prayer, and I should have returned to the Potala by this time. I must not stay another moment, or my private chamberlain, who aided me to get away unseen, will be alarmed."

As he rose to his feet Lotzung threw a long cloak over him, covering him from head to foot. Then, similarly arraying herself, she led the way out of the room.

" How does the Pantchen get home ? " Philip asked Lotzung in low tones.

" A palanquin awaits him below.'

" And you ? "

" I walk."

" Then I accompany you. But before you part with the Pantchen, make another appointment with him here."

Lotzung nodded, and they groped their way slowly down the staircase in the light of a butter lamp held by Philip. In the yard a palanquin, with an attendant and two bearers, was waiting for the Dalai Lama. The young boy bade his companions a hasty farewell, and, entering the palanquin, was carried swiftly and silently out of the yard. Philip and Lotzung followed, and Champa, glad to be in the open air again, began to dance round his mistress, emitting whines of delight, which would soon have developed into ringing barks, if Lotzung had not prevented it.

"Silence, Champa!" she said. "It is midnight, and all except the priests are asleep." Then, turning to Philip, she continued, "But why are you coming with me? I can go quite well by myself."

"I do not mean to leave you unprotected."

Lotzung laughed softly.

"Unprotected against whom? Lhasa is not full of bad men, and no one would touch me. Besides, have I not Champa?"

All the same, Philip persisted in accompanying her, and as they went he talked to her of the Pantchen. As far as he could do so without alarming her too much he pointed out that her brother should have more to eat and drink, and fewer drugs to swallow. This conversation made Lotzung very grave, and on bidding Philip farewell at her uncle's house she said—

"I am glad that you now know who my brother is, and that there exists no longer any secret between us. From what you say I must keep a careful watch over him, and you will help me do so, kind Khangsar, will you not?"

CHAPTER XIX

LOTZUNG did not fail to arrange another meeting with her brother at Philip's lodging-house, and afterwards they took place at least once a week, and sometimes oftener. With the aid of the good food which he then obtained, his health improved and he looked more robust. But in the matter of the medicine Lotzung was not so successful. The young lama, who had known only one preceptor from his earliest days, possessed the most absolute faith in all that Tsering told him. Moreover, the Regent's instructions were supported by the authority of precedent. The routine of a Dalai Lama's life had been mapped out down to the minutest details—what he should eat and drink, the hours he should devote to rest, and even the medicines he should take. A certain amount of discretion, of course, was left to the Regent, and by administering the drugs at improper hours or in undue quantities he could render their effect harmful instead of beneficial. But Tsering had acquired such an ascendancy over his ward that the boy would never believe him capable of wishing to do him any ill, and Lotzung saw that in speaking against the Regent she would only make her brother unhappy without convincing him.

Philip had now got into the habit of walking about Lhasa at all hours of the day without any fear of attracting attention. The representatives of many diverse nationalities were to be seen in the sacred city. The fact that they had passed the cordon of lamas on watch at the outskirts of the country was considered by those in authority as a proof that their character was satisfactory. Since Rashwa had befriended Philip the other Khalons had left him alone. As for Jasi, the young Englishman came to the conclusion that he had been effectually silenced, for he had neither heard nor seen anything of him since his summons to the Khalons' court. But Philip did not neglect to take every precaution possible. As the tan began to fade from his skin, now that he no longer lived in the open air, he had recourse to artificial pigments. In this way he maintained a dark complexion, which prevented him from being taken for a European, and secured him from any annoyance on this account.

Philip, with Mantso in attendance, was making some purchases in a Lhasa store one morning, when the cracking of whips and shouts of those who cleared the way showed that some one in high office was coming down the street. Mantso went to the door, and returned with the intelligence that the Senior Amban, Tuen Fang, was taking an airing.

"Is he on horseback or in his palanquin ?" asked Philip.

"He is on foot, Kushok," Mantso replied.

"We must stay in the store till he has gone by, and take care not to show ourselves. He may have a good memory for faces and recollect having you flogged in Ta-chien-lu."

"I shall not forget it, at any rate, Kushok," replied Mantso.

The tramp of feet drew nearer, and Philip and his servant stepped into the shadow of the doorway to watch the procession go by, whilst free from observation themselves. The Amban was preceded by a couple of attendants armed with whips to keep the course clear, though there was no occasion to use them, as the inhabitants were now familiar enough with the appearance of Tuen Fang not to feel any curiosity with regard to him when he went abroad. Half a dozen

Chinese soldiers came next, and then the Amban, followed by a group of gorgeously attired retainers.

From the obscurity of his retreat Philip watched Tuen Fang as he came slowly down the street. Self-indulgence had made his cheeks more white and puffy, and the rings beneath his eyes more dark. When Philip first caught sight of him his face was absolutely void of expression. But presently he must have seen something which attracted his attention, for his dull eyes grew brighter and his flabby cheeks became agitated with an effort to smile. On reaching the door which sheltered Philip, Tuen Fang stopped and made a profound bow to some one who was evidently approaching him.

"All hail, fair maiden!" he said, with a ludicrous attempt at gallantry. "Has the heaven-born slept well?"

"No better than usual!" replied the maiden, whom, as she appeared in front of the doorway, Philip recognized as Lotzung, with Champa at her heels.

"I should have thought you had slept better, for you cannot be as lovely every day as you are this morning."

Lotzung tossed her head and endeavoured to pass on, but Tuen Fang placed himself in front of her.

"Nay, be not in such a hurry to run away; stay and talk a little longer. Perhaps you do not know who I am?"

"Yes, you are Tuen Fang, the Chinese Amban. I have seen you in the streets of Lhasa and I have heard my father speak of you. Please let me pass."

But Tuen Fang was rather pleased by a show of opposition, such as he seldom met with, and putting out his hand with a fatuous smile, he placed it on the young girl's arm. A savage growl from Champa, however, made him loose his hold, and the young girl slipped past him. The colour rose to Tuen Fang's pale face as Lotzung thus escaped him. Turning to an attendant, whom Philip did not see, and telling him to follow the girl and find out where she lived, he passed on down the street.

Philip's first impulse, as soon as the Amban had disappeared, was to hurry after Lotzung and warn her that she was being followed. A moment's reflection, however, showed him that it would be a useless errand. Although she might lead her follower astray by going into the house of a friend, such a course would only delay the discovery of her real home by a few hours. No servant of the Senior Amban's would dare to abandon a search till he had obtained from a reliable source the information which his master desired. Besides, there was no reason why Lotzung should conceal her identity. She had done no wrong, and even the Senior Amban could not punish a niece of the chief Khalon merely because she did not wish to stand talking with him in the street.

Accordingly Philip completed his purchases and returned home, while Lotzung went on to her uncle's house, unconscious that she was being tracked. As to Tuen Fang, the incident left by no means an unpleasant impression upon him. Senior Ambans are not exempt from the law which forbids Chinamen to bring their wives into Tibet. At his former posts Tuen Fang had his wife with him, or at any rate a Chinese woman who passed for his wife. Although he had only been in Tibet a short time he began to feel the lack of female society. He knew, of course, that his countrymen were in the habit of contracting temporary marriages with Tibetan women during their stay in the country, but such women as he had hitherto seen in Lhasa possessed no attraction for him.

At last, however, the mandarin had met a girl of the country whom he considered really pretty. From her dress and bearing he could see that she was of high rank, so that she would be suitable for the position of his wife as long as he remained in Lhasa. He never doubted that her parents would consent to the match. The majority of Tibetans were quite willing to exchange their daughters for a handsome present, especially when the rank of the prospective bridegroom proved a further attraction. As for the girl's views on the subject he had not given them a thought. In his own country marriages were arranged by the parents without the engaged couple in many cases even seeing each other. The independence which Lotzung had shown, so far from being an obstacle to the match, only seemed an additional charm, after the tame submission of Chinese women.

Tuen Fang's thoughts were busy with the subject as he reclined at ease on a divan that same evening after supper. A brázier was burning in the centre of the room, maintaining it at an agreeable temperature. The apartment was furnished with the best Chinese upholstery, and costly silks adorned the walls. A cup of tea had just been served, when an attendant entered and announced the Regent. The familiar terms on which the two men stood with regard to each other was plain from the manner in which Tuen Fang without rising motioned his guest to take the opposite divan. Nothing more than commonplaces passed between them whilst the attendant was pouring out a cup of tea for Tsering, but as soon as they were left alone Tuen Fang said—

" I was glad to get your message saying you would pay me a visit this evening."

Tsering's small black eyes emitted a fiery glint, and his brows contracted angrily. He was tired of Chinese fine phrases, such as he took the one uttered to be, and he wished to get to business at once.

" It is well that you are glad to see me, for I have matters of importance to discuss with you."

Tuen Fang was in much too comfortable a frame of mind to be annoyed by curt words. He had made an excellent supper, washed down with very good wine. The cup of tea which he now sipped just suited his palate, while his opium pipe and tray stood within reach, ready for use as soon as he had finished his tea. This was the first night in which he had felt really at home since he had been in Lhasa.

"I have also something to discuss with you," he said to his guest. "But it is only a trifling personal affair. Yours, no doubt, is a matter of state, so let us do business first and pleasure afterwards."

He concluded these words with a leering smile, which made Tsering still more angry, as it seemed that the Amban must be mocking him.

"Let it be business at once then," he answered sharply. "I am not in the mood for trifles. It is about the Dalai Lama that I wish to talk."

"Ah!" exclaimed the Amban, laying down the cup of tea which he had just drained and drawing the opium tray towards him. "That is always a serious subject with you, I know. I wish I could teach you to smoke opium, you would not take life so grimly then. Make a beginning to-night," he added, holding out a pipe towards his guest.

The Regent waved it impatiently aside.

"It will be time for me to learn opium smoking when I am good for nothing else," he said. "At present the government of this country sits upon my shoulders, and its welfare is my sole concern. It is the Dalai Lama who causes me uneasiness."

Tuen Fang put his opium dipper into a small bowl and pulled it out again with a string of sticky substance adhering to it, which he retained by twirling the dipper round, as one does with treacle. Then, as he heated the mass over the flame of a lamp, he replied—

"What is the reason of your uneasiness? Is he not well?"

"A Dalai Lama should be above such a consideration as mere health. What alarms me about him is that he is losing that delicacy of feature which is essential to the Head of our Church, if he is to retain his hold upon the people."

"You mean that he is looking stronger and more robust than you like to see him," rejoined Tuen Fang, transferring the roasted opium from the end of the dipper to the bowl of his pipe, and heating the latter over the lamp preparatory to smoking it. "Yes, I was forgetting. It does not, of course, suit your plans that he should enjoy good health."

The Regent made a gesture of irritation.

"I am thinking only of my country's good. It is necessary that a strong man should be at the head of affairs and one who knows by experience how to govern."

"You have certainly had experience," rejoined Tuen Fang. "Regent to the two former Dalai Lamas, whom you were unfortunately unable to keep alive, you are most fitted to be Regent to the third."

"What will happen if the present Grand Lama grows up strong and worldly-minded?" continued Tsering, disregarding the Amban's innuendo. "The Buddhist pilgrims will not recognize a Dalai Lama who no longer looks the part he acts. Evil counsellors will soon surround him and the country will be badly governed."

But at this moment the heated opium began to fizzle in the bowl of the Amban's pipe, and, with a sigh of contentment after the lengthened preparation, Tuen Fang put the stem in his mouth and commenced to smoke. The sensation was too precious to interrupt with words, but when, after some thirty seconds, all the opium had been consumed, the Amban took the pipe from his mouth and said—

"I quite understand. If this boy is allowed to live he may develop a will of his own, which will interfere with the plans of his indulgent Regent. But there is one thing I must say. If it is time to do away with the boy, let it be done in such a manner that there is no scandal about it. I should get into trouble if the story should happen to reach Pekin."

"That is my difficulty. The two other boys died after a course of fasting, accompanied by suitable drugs. This boy seems to thrive on the treatment. If I did not watch him so carefully I should think that he was obtaining food without my knowledge. That, however, can hardly be the case, as I am constantly in his apartment, and rarely leave the Potala except for an hour or two in the evening, when he has retired to rest."

"You think the matter urgent ?" inquired Tuen Fang.

"Very urgent. As long as this boy is alive I am less secure than I was with either of the other two. You must remember that I have banished his father from the holy city. It was a dangerous step, but I had no alternative. Hitherto the parents of the Dalai Lama have lived in Lhasa in a palace specially set apart for them, and although neither the father nor any of the family were allowed to hold a public appointment, they still possessed considerable influence. Phala nurses this grievance against me, and he is a powerful man."

"I know him," replied Tuen Fang, his brow clouding for the first time that evening. "I shall not readily forget the way he treated me at Namcho."

"I am glad we are both of a mind with regard to him. As long as his son is the Dalai Lama it is always possible that he may create a disturbance. He has influential friends. The chief Khalon is his brother-in-law, and although I have not been able to detect him plotting against my power, I have little doubt that he would join any conspiracy which might be hatched to destroy me."

There was a pause, while Tuen Fang began preparations for another pipe of opium. At length he said—

"I suppose you came here to ask me to take some action in the matter. What is it you wish me to do?"

"Write to Pekin saying that you have very bad accounts of the Dalai Lama's health."

"Though everybody can see that he is looking better than ever?"

"I shall spread a report that he has taken a chill, suspend the audiences, and take care that no one sees him."

"His illness will end fatally?"

The Regent nodded. Another pause followed, during which Tuen Fang completed his preparations for a second pipe and smoked it. Then he said—

"If I assist you in this matter I shall expect your cooperation in another."

"Name it," answered Tsering.

"To-day I met the first pretty girl that I have seen in Lhasa."

"That is hardly a compliment to the capital of my country," rejoined Tsering grimly. "But please go on."

"I should like to contract a temporary marriage with her."

The Regent looked up inquiringly.

"It could, of course, be easily arranged," he said at length. "If she is unmarried her parents will gladly consent to such a match. If she is married, well—I dare say I could settle the matter with the husband, one way or another. Have you found out who she is?"

"Yes, that is where the difficulty comes. I caused her to be followed, and hear that she is the chief Khalon's niece and Phala's daughter."

The Regent looked grave.

"That would be a very difficult matter to arrange; in fact, I doubt if it could be done at all. I should advise you to give up the idea altogether. There are plenty of other pretty girls in Lhasa if you know where to look for them."

But the opium fumes had mounted to the Amban's brain, conjuring up an entrancing vision of the girl he had seen that morning. He was in no mood to let this vision be chased away by the cold logic of prudence, and replied—

"Those to whom the other pretty girls belong may keep possession of them. I want none but the Khalon's niece."

Tsering found the Amban's persistence distinctly annoying. "Don't you see," he rejoined, "that if you press the matter you will only arouse opposition, if not actual revolt? The consent of the girl's parents must be obtained, and you do not think that Phala, who openly flouted you, and whose hatred of the Chinese is known to everybody, will allow his daughter to marry one?"

But Tuen Fang was in an obstinate mood, and he replied—

"I mean to have her all the same. Of course, you need not help me unless you like. I dare say I shall get on very well without your assistance. Meanwhile, you will not expect any help from me in your affair."

The Regent's small eyes gleamed with irritation. What a pernicious habit this opium smoking was, he said to himself, if it made a man rush thus blindly into danger. Tsering was particularly anxious to get the Amban to write to Pekin about the Dalai Lama, but this other foolish matter had intervened. Well, if persuasion had no effect, he would try if threats would produce the desired result.

"You can please yourself in the matter, Tuen Fang," the Regent answered coldly. "I can do very well without your help, and you, no doubt, can do without mine. You have not made yourself so popular with the inhabitants of this city to be sure of their support when you wish to override the laws of our country. I have on my side the ten thousand lamas of Sera, who once rose up and put to death both the Chinese Ambans."

In spite of the opium Tuen Fang's jaw fell at these words. It was only twenty years ago, as he knew, that this occurred. The monks of Sera were bound in their own interests to support Tsering, for he had been nominated by them to the regency, and in return granted them special privileges over other monasteries. As for the laity of Lhasa, Tuen Fang knew very well that, if he had not actually roused their animosity, he had done nothing to gain their admiration or respect. Even his own Chinese troops were not to be relied upon. He was aware, of course, that if he were killed by a rising of the Tibetans, the Emperor of China would avenge his death, but this would give more satisfaction to his relatives than to himself. All this Tuen Fang saw clearly enough, but, buoyed up by the stimulus of the drug he was smoking, he determined to face the matter out.

"As Chinese Amban," he said, "I may not be popular with the people of Lhasa, but then I am told that the Regent, who has done away with two Dalai Lamas and is suspected of compassing the death of the third, is in no better favour with them."

Tsering rose from his couch. It was evidently useless to try and persuade Tuen Fang to do anything for him in his present perverse mood.

"I must return to the Potala," the Regent said. "Perhaps we shall come to a better understanding next time we meet. Till then, farewell."

Tuen Fang, either from a desire to show his independence, or because the opium had caused him to lose the use of his limbs, contented himself with merely waving an adieu to his guest. As soon as the door was shut the Amban gave an empty laugh, and, as he began preparations for another pipe, murmured to himself—

"So the Regent is trying to frighten me, is he? He comes here to ask my help in getting rid of the Dalai Lama, and then, when I want him to assist me in a much more simple matter, he advises me to give up all idea of it. He does not know Tuen Fang. When I give my services I expect something in return for them. My help goes to the highest bidder. As for his precious monks of Sera, let them do their worst. They will not face my Pekin soldiers nor dare the wrath of the Chinese Emperor!" and the old roué, with another hollow laugh, put his opium pipe to his lips, and, leaning back on his divan, gave himself up to the enjoyment of his cherished narcotic.

CHAPTER XX

AT the same hour that the Regent and Senior Amban were talking of them, the Dalai Lama and Lotzung were enjoying each other's society at Philip's lodgings. Meetings had been more difficult to arrange of late, for the Pantchen observed that a stricter watch had been kept upon his movements. On this occasion, however, his private chamberlain, who, with his three faithful attendants, alone knew of his secret visits, learnt that the Regent would be away from the Potala that evening, and the Dalai Lama contrived to let his sister know.

Philip joined them, and they spent a happy evening together. The Pantchen had much improved in health, his spirits being proportionately higher. Lotzung was delighted at the change which had taken place in him. It would have been hard to find a merrier trio in Lhasa that night.

" What do you think, Lotzung, of your elderly admirer, the Chinese Amban ? " asked Philip.

Lotzung laughed.

" So you know about his stopping me this morning ? "

" I was in a shop close to where he met you, and I heard all that passed."

" I do not like the Senior Amban," observed the Dalai Lama. " What did he say to you, Lotzung ? "

" He said some foolish things about my looks, but I would not listen to him."

" You have not heard the last of him yet," said Philip. " Do you know that he sent some one to follow you ? "

"He would only learn that I was the chief Khalon's niece, and then he would not trouble me again. He knows that my uncle likes the Chinese as little as my father does."

"Do not be too sure that the affair is finished, Lotzung," rejoined Philip in a spirit of raillery. "I should not wonder if he sent you an offer of marriage."

Lotzung dismissed the suggestion with a shake of the head, but she would not have regarded the matter so lightly if she had heard the conversation between Tsering and Tuen Fang that evening. It was true that the Regent did not give Tuen Fang any prospect of success in his suit, and that they parted without coming to an understanding with regard to it. But as the two men were in need of each other's support, a compact might be arranged at any time between them.

Tuen Fang lay in the drunken stupor induced by opium all through the night and late into the following day. Shortly after three o'clock, however, he awoke with the throbbing headache which usually accompanies a debauch of this kind. At first he could hardly move or speak, but his attendant brought him some strong tea, and after drinking two or three cups he was able to sit up and collect his thoughts.

These were of the most depressing character. The reaction from which an opium smoker suffers on awakening from his artificial sleep is most severe. The nerves are thoroughly relaxed and the most acute depression sets in. As the conversation of the previous evening gradually came back to him Tuen Fang began to feel that he had hopelessly estranged the Regent. Never very self-reliant, he now believed that he had set not only the Tibetan laity but the lamas against him. Why had he been so foolish as to quarrel with Tsering, by whose help alone he could maintain a secure position in Lhasa? He recalled the Regent's satirical allusion to his popularity amongst the townsfolk and his reference to the ten thousand monks of Sera, who had once put to death the two Chinese Ambans. In the pitiable state of collapse in which he found himself, Tuen Fang fancied that he heard these redoubtable lamas already marching on his palace. What could his Chinese soldiers do against them ? He had himself reduced their numbers by one third, and spent the money thus saved on his pleasures. Those who remained were poorly armed, and the Sera lamas could rout them with the greatest ease.

In his nervous condition these thoughts worked the Amban up into such a state of terror that he could no longer remain in the house. He felt that he would not be safe till he had apologized to the Regent for his rudeness of the previous evening, and offered to do what he desired in connection with the Dalai Lama. Accordingly he ordered his palanquin and, scrambling hurriedly into it, told his bearers to take him to the Potala.

Tuen Fang found the Regent busy looking through dispatches. The smile of welcome with which he greeted his visitor lifted a load off the Amban's mind. He had half expected to be denounced. Tsering pointed to a couch, and Tuen Fang sank into it with a sigh of relief, for his tottering legs were hardly equal to the weight of his body.

" I hope I am not interrupting you in the midst of important buisness ? " he began apologetically.

" I have no business so important that it cannot be laid aside to receive the Chinese Amban," replied Tsering.

The Regent evidently wished to be conciliatory, and the fact encouraged Tuen Fang.

" I have been thinking over our conversation last night," he began.

" Ah, yes, our conversation last night," repeated Tsering, anxious to hear what the Amban had come to say.

" You were talking of the Dalai Lama's indisposition, and saying that the Emperor ought to hear of it."

" I certainly think that he should be informed of the fact."

" In writing to him, what shall I say is the nature of the illness ? "

Tsering with difficulty restrained a smile, the Amban's *volte-face* was so complete.

" I think we had better call it nervous prostration, arising from a too zealous observance of the discipline to which Dalai Lamas are accustomed to subject themselves. You can, of course, point out that I do all in my power to prevent him sacrificing his health to such high ideals of duty, but that hitherto my powers of persuasion have been used without effect."

" Is the illness to be regarded as critical ? "

" Not at present, though I cannot say how soon it may become so. Meanwhile I shall suspend the Dalai Lama's audiences, and cancel all his engagements."

" A dispatch to the Emperor shall be prepared at once," said Tuen Fang, rising. " And with regard to the way in which I spoke to you last night, is it agreed that we forget all about it ? A man is not responsible for everything he says when smoking opium."

" Agreed ! we will work together in our own and each other's interests. That reminds me. What can we do about the chief Khalon's niece ? I do not see that there would be any objection to your submitting to him a formal offer for the girl's hand. If not welcomed as an honour, it must at any rate be regarded as a compliment. If he refuses we must think of some other plan."

" I will do as you propose," replied the Amban, " and between us we shall doubtless find some way to forward both your interests and mine."

As soon as Tuen Fang got home he sat down and wrote a dispatch to the Emperor, in which he alluded to the illness of the Dalai Lama, and hinted that though not immediately serious it might take a turn for the worse at any moment. With regard, however, to Tsering's proposal that he should write to Rashwa, making a formal proposal for Lotzung's hand, the Amban's nerves were not yet sufficiently steady to take such a step. Even supposing he applied to her uncle, it was very unlikely that the Khalon would be able to act without consulting her father. If Phala were consulted there would be an end of the matter at once. Tuen Fang had not forgotten the independent tone which the Deba had adopted towards him. He preferred to leave things as they were till he should feel in a better humour for dealing with them.

A week passed, and Tuen Fang might have forgotten all about Lotzung if fate had not once more put her in his path. This time he happened to enter a store where the young girl was making purchases. On seeing the Senior Amban the storekeeper left Lotzung and, prostrating himself before the mandarin, asked what were his commands. Tuen Fang, in the most affable tones, replied that he was in no hurry, and that the storekeeper must first supply the wants of the young girl who had entered the store before himself. This was a most unusual act of condescension on the part of a mandarin, and Lotzung could not do less than thank him for it. As she concluded her purchases Tuen Fang talked to her in a pleasant, unassertive manner, and when she had finished he bade his retinue in loud tones to make way for her, taking leave of her himself with a ceremonious bow. Lotzung left the shop with the feeling that she had met many more objectionable people than the Senior Amban.

As for Tuen Fang, this interview revived in its full force

his admiration for the chief Khalon's niece. Her cheeks had a more beautiful bloom, her dark eyes a brighter lustre, and her voice a sweeter tone than ever. Still more welcome was the absence of that freedom, he might almost call it insolence, with which she had treated him at their previous meeting, and which he never thought of attributing to his own conduct on that occasion. Since his last interview with Tsering he had refrained from opium smoking. His nerves were consequently in a better state, and he decided to send a formal offer for Lotzung's hand to her uncle and present guardian, Rashwa.

The composing of the letter took him some time, as he wished to embellish it with ornate phraseology and poetical conceits. At length the epistle took the following form, which, though not as beautiful as he would have wished, was the best his powers of invention could supply.

"To the most potent nobleman, Rashwa, Chief Khalon of the Holy City of Lhasa, greeting.

"Your contemptible servant, Tuen Fang, Senior Amban, and representative in Tibet of His Majesty the Emperor of China, hereby humbly offers himself as a suitor for the hand of the Khalon's niece. Although a person of such mean extraction is not worthy to make an alliance with this heaven-born lady, yet he trusts that the Khalon will lend a favourable ear to his petition. The lady is in the spring of youth, while the Amban is in the autumn of his years. Nevertheless, as like is often better yoked to unlike than like to like, so may the Khalon not deem it unfitting that her tender age should consort with his full maturity. Such is the prayer of Tuen Fang, Chinese Ambassador."

This letter, enclosed in an enormous Chinese envelope, was dispatched by special messenger to the chief Khalon's house. Rashwa happened to be in, and, after reading the effusion, sent back an acknowledgment by the same messenger, saying that the Senior Amban's illustrious communication had been duly received and was having his immediate attention. The matter did, in fact, occupy Rashwa's thoughts for some little time after the answer had been sent. He recognized that in several ways such a marriage would advance his interests. Tuen Fang had no wife, legal or otherwise, living with him in Lhasa, and Lotzung's position would be an influential one, as long as he remained ambassador there. She might even release him from Tsering's toils and assist in the discomfiture and final overthrow of the autocratic Regent.

On the other hand Rashwa, who was not inclined on every occasion to subordinate his private feelings to the exigencies of politics, shrank from allowing his niece to be sacrificed to such an undesirable specimen of the Chinese nation as Tuen Fang. The Amban might get tired of her in a few months, and then her position would be little better than one of his servants. It was even possible that he might use her as a means of extracting concessions from her relations by threatening to ill-treat her if they refused to grant them. In any case, the two people principally concerned, Lotzung and her father, should first be consulted in the matter. It would take some time to communicate with Phala, but Lotzung could be seen at once. She soon appeared in response to her uncle's summons.

"I have just received a letter from the Senior Amban, which concerns you," he began.

"Concerns me?" exclaimed Lotzung in surprise. "I have only met him twice. The first time was in the street, when he behaved in a foolish fashion; the second time was in a store, and he made some amends for his conduct."

"He wishes to make still further amends," said Rashwa. "In fact, he has sent you an offer of marriage."

" But I do not want to marry him. He is a Chinaman, and I dislike Chinamen."

" Yet he is a most important person, and if he chose to exercise his rights more powerful than the Regent himself. You would be a great lady, with garments of the finest silk, and a number of servants to do your bidding."

" All that is nothing if I did not like my husband. I would rather work in your house than be Tuen Fang's wife and have all the luxuries you speak of."

Rashwa was pleased with Lotzung's reply.

" You are a good girl, Lotzung," he said, " and I am glad that you do not want to leave me, for I should miss you very much. I shall tell the Amban that this is a matter which your parents alone can decide."

Accordingly that same evening Rashwa sat down to compose a reply to the Senior Amban's letter. It required some thought, for he was anxious not to make an enemy of Tuen Fang. He began, therefore, by declaring how sensible he was of the great honour which the Senior Amban was willing to confer upon his niece ; that he would be very proud of being connected by marriage with the chief ambassador of the Chinese Emperor in Tibet ; but that he was obliged to conform to the customs of his country, and, being only the uncle of the girl in question, he would have to refer the matter to her parents. Rashwa then added, as though Tuen Fang would probably be ignorant of the fact, that Lotzung's father was Phala, Deba of the Namcho district.

Although the Senior Amban had not expected any other answer, yet he was very much annoyed when he received it. Of course, it would be useless for him to apply to Phala, even if he could have subjected his pride to so humiliating a course.

The letter, however, required an answer, and he replied, thanking the chief Khalon for giving the name and address of Lotzung's father, and saying that he would take the first opportunity of laying his suit before him. This done, the question arose, what should his next step be? He was more than ever confirmed in his desire to possess Lotzung, though he could think of no plan for compassing that end. All he could do would be to call on Tsering, who had advised him to make the application to Rashwa, and who, now that it had failed, should suggest the next best course to take.

Tsering received the Senior Amban with much cordiality. Things had been going very well for him during the past week. Tuen Fang had written the letter to the Emperor of China which was so necessary to the furtherance of his plans. If the Chinese Ambassador, as well as the lamas of Sera, were on his side, the laymen of Lhasa could effect little against him. He saw that the chief Khalon recognized this, for he had kept in the background of late, asking no explanations when the Dalai Lama was withheld from the public and his audiences cancelled. The report that the latter was in delicate health seemed to be generally believed. His death in two or three weeks' time might consequently cause but little surprise. That the end could not be delayed much longer the Regent had already decided. The boy had shown for the first time that he possessed, if not a will, at any rate opinions of his own. When he was told that he must hold no more audiences till his health improved, he replied that he was quite well enough to hold such functions, and that it was his wish for them to be continued. Only after much time and recourse on the Regent's part to strong measures had the boy ceased from his protestations. Tsering had always found this trouble with the Grand Lamas as they grew up. How could it be in the interests of the country that it should be governed by a headstrong child, with no experience of the world, instead of by a man with thirty years' schooling in statecraft? By such arguments did Tsering attempt to quiet his conscience for his contemplated crime.

"Does the Senior Amban bring news from China?" he asked as soon as his visitor was seated.

"I have not come to talk of politics, but of my own affairs," replied Tuen Fang. "I followed your advice about the chief Khalon's niece and sent him a formal offer for her hand."

"And what did he reply?"

"He referred me to her parents."

"That is inconvenient," Tsering rejoined. "I hoped that he might have taken upon himself the responsibility for arranging a marriage which would be so advantageous for his family. But perhaps after all it will be best to deal direct with the father. Although banished from the capital Phala is still a powerful man. He would be flattered by the alliance, and it would be useful to get him on our side."

Tuen Fang was angered by this cool proposal, considering that Tsering was aware of the independent manner in which Phala had treated the Amban.

"I am obliged for your suggestion, which, however, is one which I shall not adopt," he answered. "As for Phala's power, I am not afraid of it. As I took no part in his banishment from Lhasa I have nothing to fear in that quarter."

The Regent fixed his small black eyes on Tuen Fang with a look of angry inquiry. What did he mean by these words? Did he intend to withdraw from their mutual compact? Tsering came to the conclusion that the Amban's wild defiance after a bout of opium smoking was preferable to his present state of cool determination.

"It is Rashwa's suggestion, not my own," the Regent replied. "How else can it be done?"

"That is the question which I came to ask you, but it

seems that you have no answer to it. I shall have to find a way for myself."

The Regent saw that the matter was getting serious. If Tuen Fang were foolish enough to try and carry Lotzung off by force in the open daylight a rising would undoubtedly occur, which would endanger not only the Amban but himself. He must be warned against taking such a course.

"Be careful what you do, for my countrymen are headstrong when a grievance once induces them to rise. Try and think of some pacific means of carrying out your wish, and I will do the same. Above all, let me know your plan. If I approve of it I will do my best to help you. If not, I will promise at any rate to put no obstacles in your way."

CHAPTER XXI

TUEN FANG returned to his palace congratulating himself on his recent interview with the Regent. A show of firmness had compelled Tsering to support him in his plans. It would of course be rash to attempt to carry Lotzung off by force from her uncle's house. Such an action would no doubt raise a storm of indignation which might very possibly end in a revolt. But there were other ways of obtaining possession of Lotzung than by mere force, and to these the Amban devoted a brain familiar from infancy to such devious methods. Though Lotzung could not be persuaded to enter his house of her own accord, it was possible that she might be decoyed to some place from which she could be conveyed to the Amban's residence without leaving any clue to her disappearance.

Nothing, however, could be done till more had been learnt of her daily habits, the stores at which she shopped, and the friends she went to see. For this purpose she must be closely watched, and the person whom Tuen Fang selected for the work was Jasi. The latter owed Rashwa a grudge for having persuaded his brother Khalons that the evidence which he wished to give against Philip was altogether unreliable. The Ladaki, therefore, set about his task with such perseverance that Lotzung was shadowed from the time she left the house till she returned to it again. Yet neither the young girl herself nor any of the household had reason to suspect that all her movements were thus closely watched.

Matters went on in this way for two or three weeks, without anything being discovered to forward the end which Tuen Fang had in view Lotzung would go out shopping in the morning, and for an occasional walk in the afternoon, but she kept to the main thoroughfares, and was always accompanied by Champa. The problem became a difficult one. If she would only visit some friends in the outskirts of the town, or if she went out after dark, the matter would be easier. But she did neither, for Jasi used to watch the house from sundown to midnight.

Tuen Fang began to think of desperate means, when the Ladaki made an important discovery. At ten o'clock one night, as he was dozing in a doorway opposite Rashwa's house, an unexplained impulse made him open his eyes just in time to see Lotzung slip out accompanied by her dog. She crossed the road and passed so close to him that her skirt almost brushed against his knee, though he himself was unnoticed by her. Walking quickly down the street, she took a turning to the right. Jasi was on his feet in an instant, hurrying after her. Here was his opportunity, and he must make the most of it.

The Ladaki followed his quarry at barely fifty paces distant, his boots of untanned hide making no sound upon the ill-paved road. As he went he planned his course of action. Hitherto during his night watches he had been accompanied by another of the Amban's servants to help him effect the capture if Lotzung should venture out after dusk. As she had never done so he had allowed his companion to go away this evening for the first time. Between them they could easily have seized the young girl in the deserted streets and carried her off to their master's house. Jasi was almost inclined to make the attempt by himself. If she were securely gagged and bound he could hide her in an empty cellar or in the doorway of a deserted house till he could obtain assistance from the Amban's household. The only obstacle to carrying out this programme was the presence of Champa.

This Tibetan mastiff was indeed sufficiently formidable to make any one wary of attacking his mistress. Jasi had for some time past carried poisoned meat with him. Here was an opportunity of administering it to some purpose. The Ladaki knew Lhasa well, and slipping down a by-road he regained the street along which Lotzung was walking at a point some little distance ahead of her. At this spot he dropped a piece of poisoned meat, and took shelter in a doorway to see if the bait was taken.

Lotzung soon approached, walking at a quick pace, with Champa trotting quietly at her side. He reached the spot where the bait lay, and to Jasi's chagrin had actually passed it, when he suddenly stopped, nosed the ground, and worked his way back again. On finding the meat he gulped it down and cantered after his mistress, with no doubt a twinge of conscience at having deserted her for even so short a space of time.

Jasi walked briskly after them, exulting in the success of his snare. The poison was powerful and the dog might be in his death throes at any moment. Eager to see the effect of the drug he crept up quite close behind the couple. In his hands he held a long, thick silken scarf. No one was to be seen in the street. As soon as Champa fell, what would be easier than to spring upon the girl from behind, throw the scarf over her mouth, and effectually gag her? Then, with a rope which he carried in the folds of his garment, he could bind her hand and foot and drag her into some sheltered nook while he ran to get assistance from the Amban's palace.

But the poison was already beginning to take effect. Champa would stop every now and again, shaking his head and making a guttural noise, as if a bone had stuck in his throat. Lotzung's attention was at length attracted, and she called the mastiff to her Jasi shrunk into the shadow of a house and watched the faithful animal struggle forward to have his shaggy head caressed by Lotzung's hand.

"What is the matter, Champa?" she said. "I have never seen you go on like this before. Has something stuck in your throat, or have you got a cough? Never mind, we shall soon reach the house."

Champa gave a little whine of pleasure at her touch and once more struggled to keep up with her. Why was he such a long time dying, Jasi asked himself. From Lotzung's words it was plain that she would soon reach her destination, when this unusually favourable opportunity would be lost for ever. Why not seize her now? Champa, although not dead, was too weak to offer any serious resistance. Jasi determined that if the animal did not collapse within the next hundred paces he would make the attempt.

Meanwhile Champa began to lag behind again. The poison seemed to have taken possession of his legs, for he dragged them after him with an effort. Surely it would be foolishness to wait any longer, the Ladaki thought. Someone might come down the street, or Lotzung might reach the house she intended to visit. Jasi summoned all his courage and crept up stealthily behind her. Soon he was on a level with Champa, who merely looked up at him out of the corner of his eye and tried to mend his pace. A few steps further, being within easy reach of his prey, he raised the scarf in the air, and was on the point of throwing it over Lotzung's head when the door of a courtyard, belonging to a house a little further on, opened and threw a feeble light across the street. Jasi shrank back, and Lotzung with her mastiff entered the courtyard. The Ladaki was too late after all.

Burning with vexation Jasi sat down in a doorway and considered what his next step should be. It would be useless for him to enter the house and try single-handed to carry Lotzung off. There must be other people in it, and even if they lacked the courage to oppose him, they could at any rate raise the alarm. Whilst thinking the matter over he caught sight of three figures coming down the street.

As they drew nearer it became evident that two of them were carrying a palanquin. Only very high officials were allowed to ride in palanquins. What could one of this class want in an out-of-the-way corner of the town at that hour of the night? Jasi concealed himself from view and waited.

The curtains of the palanquin proved to be drawn, so that he could catch no glimpse of its occupant. But his surprise was great when, after passing the spot at which he stood, it entered the door of the courtyard through which Lotzung had lately passed. Jasi followed stealthily, and took up his position in a dark corner of the yard, from which he could see the occupant descend at the entrance to the house. This to his astonishment proved to be a boy, whom he recognized at once as the Dalai Lama. There was no one to receive him, but this he seemed to have expected, and ran hastily up the stairs leading to the first floor. Jasi knew that Lotzung was the Dalai Lama's sister, and surmised that they wished to keep the interview secret, or they would not have met in this quarter of the town between ten and eleven o'clock at night.

The Grand Lama's attendants put the palanquin under shelter and then sat down at the foot of the steps to await their master's return. Jasi was anxious to slip out of the courtyard to give information to the Amban, but these men commanded a view of the only exit. Once more the Ladaki lamented having allowed his companion to go away. Both the Regent and Amban would like to be informed of this meeting. Yet how was it to be done with the Dalai Lama's attendants watching the courtyard door?

At length one of these three men stood up and, walking to the centre of the yard, looked up at the sky as if to judge what the weather was likely to be. He was smoking a wooden pipe, and as he drew in the smoke the glowing embers of the tobacco threw a ruddy glow upon his face and seemed to illumine the whole of the yard. He did not, however, catch sight of Jasi, and after another glance at the sky, he turned to rejoin the other two.

Here was Jasi's chance. While the man's back was turned, and he was partially obstructing the view of his two companions, the Ladaki made a dash for the door. He passed it without attracting the notice of the Dalai Lama's servants and reached the street in safety. Once clear of the building Jasi ran as hard as he could to the Amban's house. On gaining it he learnt that the Regent was with Tuen Fang. Knowing that his master would not like him to disclose before Tsering the nature of the work on which he had been employed, he sent in a note saying that he had some important private information to give him. Tuen Fang made his excuses and came out to see the Ladaki.

"I have just traced Lotzung to a house in a quiet portion of the town," said Jasi.

"Why did you not seize her on the way to it?" demanded his master angrily. "Now she is under shelter you can do nothing."

"I found she had arranged to meet her brother, the Dalai Lama, there."

"The Dalai Lama!" exclaimed Tuen Fang incredulously. "He never leaves the Potala."

"Yet he is undoubtedly with his sister now. I know him well by sight and saw him enter the house."

If Jasi's story were true Tuen Fang knew that an exceptional opportunity was afforded him of carrying out his cherished project.

"The Regent is with me to-night," he said; "I will tell him your tale."

On rejoining Tsering the Amban plunged into the matter at once.

"I am told that the Dalai Lama is now at a house in the outskirts of the city with his sister Lotzung."

Tsering realized from Tuen Fang's manner that the story

was probably true, and though much astonished at the news, retained his usual composure of expression.

"You can rely upon your information, I conclude?" he answered.

"I have no reason to doubt my informant," replied Tuen Fang.

"We must go to the house at once then," continued the Regent. "I will send the Dalai Lama back to the Potala; and as to his sister, well—she had better be lodged at the Senior Amban's residence, pending an inquiry. You understand me?"

Tuen Fang rubbed his hands with delight at the turn which events had taken.

"I understand, of course. The affair must be kept quite secret. Let us start without delay. I will tell the officer of my bodyguard to send two dozen troops with us."

"Two dozen soldiers to arrest two children!" exclaimed Tsering scornfully. "It would be ridiculous. Besides, that is not the way to keep the matter secret."

"My bodyguard would not dare to utter a word if once ordered to be silent. Still, as you object to the number, I will content myself with one dozen."

Tuen Fang was much too nervous to pass through the streets of Lhasa at night without an armed escort, and Tsering let him have his way. He told Jasi, however, to stop them at the corner of the street containing the house where the Dalai Lama and his sister had met, as they would walk the rest of the way without attendance. Tuen Fang verbally consented to this arrangement, though when the Regent had entered his palanquin he took the officer of the detachment aside and told him to bring his troops on to the house without fail when a sufficient interval of time had elapsed.

It was not very long before Jasi stopped the palanquins

as instructed, and their occupants got out and walked. The Ladaki, who led them, and who feared that the Dalai Lama and his sister might have left the house by this time, was much relieved to find the courtyard door still open and the Grand Lama's bearers waiting for their master at the bottom of the stairs. These poor men were terrified when they saw the Regent, and, falling on their knees, knocked their heads against the ground, crying, "Laso, Laso, be merciful, be merciful!" Tsering shot a withering glance at them from his keen black eyes, and waving them aside began to mount the steps. Tuen Fang, finding that he encountered no armed resistance, grew very brave, and, kicking one of them as he passed, followed in the Regent's wake. Jasi discreetly remained below.

On the first floor, which was dimly lighted by a single lamp, the Regent halted. From a room on the left of the passage two voices could be heard. He recognized one of them as the voice of the Dalai Lama, and he did not doubt that the other was his sister's. With a lowering countenance he strode to the door, threw it open, but came to a standstill on the threshold. For in addition to the Grand Lama, who remained composed in spite of the surprise, and to Lotzung, who uttered a smothered cry, a third person could be seen in the room. He was a powerful young man, who had snatched up a stool as the nearest weapon to his hand, and was prepared to aim a blow at any one who ventured to intrude. The Dalai Lama was the first to speak.

"Put down the stool, Khangsar," he said. "Do you not see it is the Regent?"

Philip observing that Tsering was unarmed and alone—for Tuen Fang had wisely kept himself out of view—laid aside his weapon, and the Regent said with an ironical smile:

"I am sorry to disturb this pleasant little party, but it is time that the Dalai Lama returned to the Potala."

The boy rose to his feet at once.

"I am ready, Tsering," he answered. "I know I did wrong in coming here without informing you of my intention, but I was very anxious to see my sister, and I was afraid that you would find some reason why I should not do so."

"A Dalai Lama has no relations, and should not concern himself with earthly ties."

The boy's eyes filled with tears. He had grown much thinner and more delicate since Philip had seen him last, and his will was no match for that of the autocratic Regent.

"At any rate my faults should not be visited on innocent people. I assure you that neither my sister nor this Eastern Mongol, Khangsar, are to blame, and you must promise me that they shall not be punished."

"Why should they be?" rejoined Tsering. "You may safely leave them in my hands."

"And the three bearers below?" continued the Pant-chen. "You will not have them flogged?"

"I will respect the Dalai Lama's wishes."

The poor boy's anxious face lightened.

"I thank you for your promise, Tsering. Good-bye, Lotzung; farewell, Khangsar. You have heard the Regent say that no harm shall be done to you."

He embraced his sister, who was weeping silently, and left the room. The Regent, however, did not quit his post at the door, and, when he thought sufficient time had elapsed for the Dalai Lama to be clear of the premises, he turned to Philip and said—

"Although, in accordance with my promise, I do not intend to punish you, you will have to accompany me to the Potala to be examined with regard to this matter."

Philip's first thought was of Lotzung.

"You will allow me first to conduct this young girl to her uncle's house?" he said.

"I will provide her with a proper escort for that purpose. Come, let us waste no more words."

Philip was being sorely tempted to thrust the Regent aside and carry Lotzung off, when the tramp of feet could be heard on the landing, and Tuen Fang made his appearance with a dozen Chinese soldiers. The cowardly Amban quailed before Philip's resolute look, and fell back a step or two as if he expected an immediate attack. The young man was, indeed, within an ace of delivering it, but prudence fortunately prevailed. He had no weapon on his person, and he could not hope to get Lotzung safely past a dozen armed men. Accordingly he said—

"I will bid you farewell, Lotzung. The Regent has promised to do us no harm, and the ruler of Tibet may be trusted to keep his word."

"I am not afraid for myself, dear Khangsar," answered Lotzung, her eyes still filled with tears. "They dare not treat me ill. But if they punish you merely for being found in the same room as my brother and myself, they will find that I have both an uncle and a father to come to your aid."

Philip was marched downstairs and out into the street with three armed soldiers in front and three behind him. He felt no alarm on his own account. Since the chief Khalon had found the means of shutting Jasi's mouth there was little fear of his being denounced as a peling, and, as Lotzung said, they could hardly punish him for being found with the Dalai Lama and his sister. It was for the Pantchen that the young Englishman felt the most concern. If he looked so much worse for the interruption to his visits to Philip's lodgings, what would he be like when they ceased altogether? It was fortunate that Lotzung, at any rate, was still free to work on behalf of her brother, so that he was not yet cut off from all outside help.

CHAPTER XXII

PHILIP'S concern for his two young friends would have been much greater if he had seen what occurred on his departure from his lodgings. The Regent, instead of providing Lotzung with the escort he had promised, exchanged a few words in an undertone with Tuen Fang, and then, descending the staircase, went off in his palanquin. Lotzung was left facing the Chinese Amban, who had sent his soldiers down below and stood alone in the doorway. The young girl was in no humour for talking to Tuen Fang, and so, drying her tears, she said—

"Please let me pass, I wish to go home."

But the Amban did not attempt to move, and with a smile of would-be gallantry replied—

"Surely there is no hurry. The hour is yet early. Let us have a little talk before you start."

He evidently meant to bar her exit from the room. What would she not have given to have had the trusty Champa with her now? But the poor animal had only just managed to reach the house, and though Philip, suspecting poison, had given him an antidote and put him under Mantso's care, he would not be able, even supposing he were still alive, to repeat the service he had done her on the occasion of her first meeting with Tuen Fang.

"I wish to return to my uncle's house at once," she answered. "If you do not let me go I will call for help."

But Tuen Fang did not want a disturbance of this character, and, withdrawing from the doorway, he said—

"Allow me at any rate to escort you downstairs."

Lotzung at once took advantage of the freedom offered

her, and ran lightly downstairs in front of him, wishing to escape from him as quickly as possible. On reaching the courtyard, however, she found the outer door guarded by the Amban's soldiers.

"Are you going to detain me here by force?" she asked Tuen Fang, who now came panting after her.

"I should not think of treating the chief Khalon's niece in such a manner," he replied. "The soldiers were stationed in the doorway to prevent the entrance of inquisitive persons. You shall go home in my palanquin, it is waiting ready for you."

But Lotzung began to suspect the Amban's designs, and said—

"I prefer to walk, thank you. I shall get there quite as quickly."

"Well, if you must go on foot," rejoined Tuen Fang, raising his voice, "why——"

The last word was hardly out of his mouth when Jasi, who had crept up unseen behind Lotzung, threw his khata over her head, and winding it round several times secured it firmly. The poor girl tried to scream, but her voice was stifled so effectually that she could not make herself heard. She was then bound hand and foot, lifted into the Amban's palanquin, and carried quietly but swiftly to his home. Tuen Fang followed on foot with the remainder of his soldiers, greatly pleased by his successful coup.

Meanwhile Mantso, who had gone out before the arrival of Tsering and the Senior Amban to supply an unexpected deficiency in Philip's larder, now returned just after Tuen Fang had left the building. Knowing nothing of what had occurred he ran upstairs to the kitchen and began to cook the supper. As soon as it was ready he gave the usual signal by tapping three times on the landing outside. Philip had been in the habit of taking the supper down himself, and not allowing his servant to enter the room occupied by the Dalai Lama and Lotzung, though Mantso usually contrived to catch sight of them either on their arrival or as they left.

When, however, there came no response to the signal, and he could not hear any voices in the room below, Mantso descended to the door of the apartment. All was silent, and he ventured to open it. No one was there, though in the light of its single lamp it was plain that the room had been recently occupied. Perhaps the Dalai Lama had been taken ill, and it had been thought best that he should return to the Potala at once. The landlord and his wife might be able to throw some light upon the matter, and Mantso descended to the ground-floor to ask them.

After knocking two or three times the door was opened cautiously and the landlord made his appearance in an evident state of alarm. On seeing Mantso, however, he seemed more at ease and asked what he wanted.

"I find that my master and his friends on the first floor have gone. Do you know when they left?"

"I know nothing about them," replied the man curtly, as if he were anxious to avoid the subject. "When the young girl took these rooms on the first floor she said that a high official of the state would occasionally visit them, and that my wife and myself were to keep out of the way when he did so."

"Then you can tell me nothing," continued Mantso.

"Nothing at all. My wife and I kept to these quarters all the evening. To judge from the sounds we heard there certainly seemed to be more visitors than usual; but we do not know who they were nor where they went."

There was nothing for Mantso to do but go upstairs again and await his master's return. He found Champa still alive, but in a kind of torpor and breathing heavily. After

Philip had administered the antidote the animal had been seized several times by a violent kind of fit, as though the poison and its antidote were struggling for the possession of the body. The fight was now over, and in the course of an hour or two it would be known with whom the victory rested.

Midnight came and Philip did not return. On former occasions, when he saw Lotzung home, he had not been absent at the most for more than half an hour. To-night he might have gone with the Dalai Lama as far as the Potala, and even entered the building itself. So far there was no occasion to be seriously alarmed, and Mantso settled down to a solitary vigil.

The monotony of this occupation soon caused the faithful Tibetan to fall asleep, and when he awoke it was already daylight. Going to Philip's room he found the door still open and the bed unoccupied. Mantso began at length to be alarmed. If nothing had gone wrong his master would surely have returned by this time, or at any rate have sent a message accounting for his absence. What was to be done?

The first place at which to make inquiries would be the Khalon's house. But what if Rashwa knew nothing of his niece's meeting with her brother at Philip's lodgings, and Philip himself were anxious to keep the matter secret from him? It would never do for Mantso to impart the information. Then what was he to do with Champa? The dog had survived the night, and, though still very weak, was evidently on the road to recovery. If he took the animal to the chief Khalon's house Rashwa would know that his niece must have been at Philip's lodgings some time the previous evening. After much deliberation Mantso resolved to go round to the chief Khalon's house without the dog and try to learn from Lotzung if she had any news of

Philip. She could say at the same time what she would like him to do with Champa.

The faithful Tibetan accordingly set out alone, and on nearing the chief Khalon's residence happened to meet one of his servants just coming from it.

"What news ?" he asked the man in a casual way, after exchanging the usual greetings.

"There is a great stir in the Khalon's house this morning," the other replied, conscious of possessing a fine piece of gossip, and not wishing to part with it too readily.

"What is the cause of the stir ?" asked Mantso.

"Well, you see, it is a family matter, and a discreet servant should not, perhaps, allow himself to babble of it."

"If it is something that the Khalon wishes to keep secret, I am the last man to want to pry into it. Farewell, brother," and Mantso made as if to move away.

This was not at all the effect which the Khalon's servant wished his words to produce, so he laid a detaining hand on Mantso's arm and said—

"Pray do not go away so hastily, we have hardly exchanged a dozen words. Besides, I was never told to keep secret the matter to which I referred. In fact, the Khalon might like you to know, in case you could be of service to him with regard to it."

"If I can be of any use to the Khalon, speak. Is he not my master's friend ?"

"Well, the truth is—" and here the man looked cautiously round him to make sure there were no eavesdroppers—" the Khalon's niece Lotzung cannot be found, and it seems that she has been out of the house all night."

This was indeed a piece of news for Mantso. Lotzung was missing as well as his master, unless the latter were at the Khalon's house. Mantso, not liking to ask the question direct, continued—

" Has no one come to the Khalon's house with news of her ? "

" No one. I have just been sent out to make inquiries everywhere. Her dog Champa is also missing, but this may be a means of tracing her. You do not know where she is, I suppose ? " the man concluded.

Mantso replied quite truthfully that he did not know, and, lest he should be asked some awkward questions about the dog, bade the Khalon's servant farewell and went his way. The disappearance of Lotzung made the matter still more inexplicable. Had his master and the young girl gone off together, or was the fact that they were missing at the same time a mere coincidence ? He had nothing to help him towards a solution of the question, and could only set to work to look for his master in every quarter of the town. This search he carried on throughout the day, returning to the lodgings every two or three hours to see if his master had come back.

Night came and the faithful servant returned home, disheartened by the failure of his efforts. He found Champa sufficiently recovered to be able to walk as far as the Khalon's house. Accordingly he put him on a lead, so as to avoid the risk of losing him, and made a detour lest the dog should be traced to Philip's lodgings. Having travelled about half the distance, Mantso felt a tug at the lead, and turned to see Champa trying to enter a large house, which proved to be the residence of the Senior Amban. The Tibetan could not account for the animal's behaviour till he remembered the first meeting between Lotzung and Tuen Fang, when Champa had growled so fiercely at the Chinaman. It was possible that the dog had scented him, and had his animosity revived against him. In any case he could not be allowed to enter the house, and Mantso pulled him away from the door, a not very difficult matter in the present weakened state of the animal. On nearing the chief Khalon's house the Tibetan let the dog loose and watched him find his way safely through the open doorway before returning homewards once more.

Meanwhile Philip was securely immured within the walls of the Potala. The first night he had spent in a comfortable apartment, with a lay monk detailed to wait upon him. The door of the apartment remained unlocked, but outside he saw half a dozen Tibetan soldiers on guard to prevent his escape. In spite of the situation in which he found himself the young man slept soundly, and it was daylight when the attendant called him, and served a light meal. The tea was excellent, and the bread better than he had yet tasted in Lhasa. If the Regent continued to treat him with such consideration Philip would not object to remain his guest for two or three weeks.

But at eleven o'clock a couple of lamas entered the room and said they had orders to conduct him to the Regent's presence. Philip followed them out of the room, and the soldiers on guard outside fell in behind them. After passing along several winding galleries and ascending two flights of steps, he was taken into an ante-room adjoining the Regent's private quarters. Here he was kept waiting half an hour, and wondered whether business really detained the Regent, or whether the delay was intended to give him a due sense of the Regent's importance. But at length a door at the further end of the ante-room opened, and a lama beckoned Philip to enter.

The chamber into which he was ushered was small, but tastefully furnished, though the young man did not have much time to notice such details. His attention was engrossed by the occupants of the room, for on the Regent's right sat Tuen Fang. Philip wondered if the Amban would know him, but there was no appearance of recognition in the apathetic glance with which Tuen Fang favoured him as he entered. A solitary secretary, seated in front of Tuen Fang, was the only other person in the room, for the lama who had introduced him had withdrawn. The Regent regarded him sternly with his keen black eyes and then began—

" You are an Eastern Mongol, and your name is Khangsar."

Philip bowed. Tsering spoke as if it were an established fact, and the young man was not anxious to deny it.

" I found you last night with the Dalai Lama and his sister in a small lodging in a remote quarter of the town. Tell me how you came to be in that house ? "

" I went there when I reached Lhasa some three months ago, being recommended to it because it was quiet and cheap."

" On what errand did you come to Lhasa ? "

" Being a merchant I came to see if I could do any trade with the capital of your country."

The Regent's expression underwent no change at this statement, but he looked at Philip in silence with his piercing eyes. The young man became angry under this keen scrutiny. Had Tsering any authentic information about his antecedents, or was he merely asking haphazard questions ?

" Was the room in which I found you one of those which you rented from the landlord ? "

" No, my two rooms were on the floor above."

" How was it you came to be in that room ? "

Philip saw that the examination was going to be a searching one, and that he would have to be careful.

" I went down to pay my respects to the Dalai Lama."

" Then you knew that he was there. Was it for the first time ? "

" No, it was not."

" You had seen him there before ? "

Philip assented.

" Perhaps you arranged the meetings between the Dalai Lama and his sister ? "

" No, Lotzung arranged them," answered Philip, knowing that Tsering could not punish the chief Khalon's niece for such an act.

On hearing Lotzung's name mentioned Tuen Fang was roused from his lethargy, and displayed more interest in the examination.

" What went on at these meetings ? " continued Tsering.

" Merely general conversation."

" They were not arranged to obtain religious advice or help from the Dalai Lama ? "

" As I did not arrange them I cannot tell their purpose."

" And nothing occurred beyond general conversation ? "

" We used to have something to eat and drink," replied Philip, thinking it best to be quite straightforward.

" You and Lotzung, I presume you mean, for, of course, the Dalai Lama did not partake of food."

" He needed it most," rejoined Philip. " You, being in his presence every day, did not perhaps notice any change, but we, who only saw him occasionally, came to the conclusion that he was starving."

Tsering, who had hitherto been so impassive, now lost his coolness and flushed at the remark.

" It is plain that you have forgotten, if indeed you ever knew, the precepts of Buddha, enjoining fasting at certain seasons of the year, of which the present season is one. The Dalai Lama must set an example to his followers in this respect. Who prepared the meals ? "

" My servant," answered Philip.

Tsering turned to Tuen Fang and said—

"Has not the man convicted himself?"

"Certainly, certainly!" replied the Amban, whose attention had again been wandering. "Let him be severely punished."

The Regent bent a stern look on Philip and said—

"You hear what the Amban says, though, as I promised the Dalai Lama, I will not punish you for your share in this affair. But there are other charges against you."

Tsering rang a small hand-bell on his table, and from a side door entered a man whom Philip recognized at once as Jasi. The chief Khalon had said that he knew how to deal with the Ladaki, and that he would give no further trouble. Had Rashwa promised more than he was able to perform? Philip saw that his situation was a serious one, but he resolved to show an unflinching front to his accuser.

"Look at this man," the Regent said to Jasi. "Do you recognize him?"

"I know him perfectly," replied Jasi. "When acting as a spy for the lamas of Eastern Tibet I engaged myself to him as mule driver."

"Where was that?"

"At Ta-chien-lu. I have recently heard, though I did not know it at the time, that he was the same man who interfered when His Excellency the Senior Amban was having a man flogged in the streets of Ta-chien-lu."

At these words Tuen Fang sat bolt upright and stared at Philip.

"But that man had not the dark complexion of the prisoner here."

"Complexions are not always real," said Jasi.

"Tell us what you know about him," continued Tsering.

"As soon as we reached Namcho I informed the lamas that the man with whom I had taken service was a peling.

They examined him and ordered him to return to Ta-chien-lu."

"He did not obey the order?"

"No, he turned off from the main road and stayed a couple of days with Phala, the Deba of the district."

"They were all well mated," observed the Amban, with a smile which only served to show his fangs.

"After leaving the Deba's castle he was married at the next village to the Deba's daughter Lotzung."

"What do you say?" cried Tuen Fang, almost jumping out of his seat.

"Although he married her he did not treat her as his wife, but merely as his servant," answered the Ladaki.

"That alone is sufficient reason for annulling the marriage," said the Regent. "Continue your story, Jasi."

"When I became guide, owing to an accident to the man who had been acting as such, I led them towards the monastery of Garthok, and then went on to warn the lamas. Unfortunately the peling managed to get past us, and we lost all trace of him through following a false trail."

"And so he got to Lhasa?"

"Shortly after my arrival here I caught sight of him in the streets and traced him to his lodgings. I then informed the Khalons about him, but the chief Khalon took his part, and I was warned to leave Lhasa. Instead of doing so I took service with His Excellency the Chinese Amban, and watched the movements of Lotzung and the peling till I discovered their meeting with the Dalai Lama last night."

"Have you heard enough to convince you of the prisoner's guilt," said Tsering, "or would you like to ask any questions?"

"I have no questions to ask," replied Tuen Fang. "It is only a matter of passing sentence."

The Regent then turned to Philip and said—

"You have listened to the evidence of this man. Have you anything to say in self-defence?"

"Only that by his own words he proved himself a traitor to his master, and therefore no credence can be placed upon his oath."

"He has been faithful to his real masters, the lamas, and that is what was required of him. It is clear that you persisted in your journey against the orders of the lamas, and that, though a peling, you have penetrated to our sacred city of Lhasa. In Ta-chien-lu you defied the Chinese representative, and here in my person you defy the temporal ruler of the country. You have richly deserved the sentence which I am now compelled to pass upon you, namely, that you suffer the extreme penalty of our law." Here the Regent rang his bell and said to the lama who appeared in answer to it—"Remove the prisoner."

"And let his sentence be speedily carried out!" said Tuen Fang, with a malicious laugh, "so that he may learn it is not wise to flout a mandarin of China."

CHAPTER XXIII

AS Tuen Fang rode home in his palanquin from the Potala his thoughts were busy with the scene at which he had lately assisted. He was glad to find that the man who had interfered with the execution of his orders in Ta-chien-lu had been found guilty of acting contrary to the laws of Tibet. The Chinese Amban never forgave an injury, and although he would not have taken the trouble to search for Philip merely to be revenged upon him, his resentment against him was revived in all its former force now that the peling had crossed his path once more. Tuen Fang could at last cry quits, with the certainty that his victim would not survive to cause him annoyance a second time.

The Chinese Amban possessed another source of satisfaction. If Jasi's story were true—and there was no reason to doubt it—in getting rid of the peling he was also getting rid of Lotzung's husband. As matters now stood, it did not much matter whether Lotzung had a husband or not, for none of her friends or relations knew that she was concealed in his house. The only witnesses of the abduction were half a dozen Chinese soldiers, and they knew better than to speak about it. A Chinese mandarin would think no more of cutting off a Chinaman's head for such a foolish act than an Englishman would think of giving his servant a month's notice. Still, if it should by chance be discovered that the Khalon's niece was in his house, he felt that it would be a less serious matter for him if she had no husband living.

Jasi's narrative also recalled to the Amban's memory the humiliation he had suffered at Phala's hands. Well, it might not be long before he had his revenge on the Deba as well. Apart from the fact that he had his daughter in his power—a matter which might not touch the Deba very deeply—they had Jasi's evidence that he aided and abetted the peling in eluding the lamas and entering inner Tibet. This was an act of treason against the Dalai Lama on the part of his subordinate at Namcho. If Phala ever got into the hands of the authorities at Lhasa they would be justified in putting him to death for it.

Full of these satisfactory reflections, Tuen Fang alighted at the entrance to his residence and made his way to some apartments which looked on to a central courtyard. Taking a key out of his pocket he opened the door of an ante-room, in which sat a Tibetan waiting-woman.

"Has the young girl eaten any breakfast?" he asked.

"She has partaken of a couple of dishes," replied the woman.

It was a good sign, reflected Tuen Fang, and showed that the Khalon's niece was not inclined to sulk or mope in her captivity. He passed through into the inner room with quite a sprightly air. Lotzung was seated on some cushions in a corner doing needlework.

"How is my dove this morning?" asked Tuen Fang, using the Chinese equivalent for Lotzung's name, and walking towards her with a mincing gait, reminiscent of the gallantry of his early days. Lotzung looked up at him, and could not restrain a smile of amusement. The healthy, joyous disposition of her Tibetan nature was proof against continued depression, and Tuen Fang certainly cut a most comical figure.

"I am glad to see you in such good spirits," the Amban continued, somewhat piqued by this reception. "It is a much better frame of mind than that in which I left you last night. But you have no doubt learnt by this time that you will not bring any one to your aid by screaming.

You are in the centre of my house, the walls are thick, and your voice will not reach the outside world."

"When are you going to let me return to my uncle's house?" she asked, looking up at him fearlessly with her clear, dark eyes. Confinement had as yet wrought no ill effect on her appearance. Her complexion had all the freshness and her hair the gloss of perfect health.

"Do you wish to fly away already, my little bird?" rejoined the Amban in wheedling tones. "You shall have whatever you want in my house—the finest of silks and the most costly jewellery. Why cannot my dove settle here and make her nest?"

"How long do you intend to detain me?" continued Lotzung, ignoring the inducements to stay which he was offering her.

"The matter does not rest with me," replied Tuen Fang. "The fact is, you are a state prisoner, and I am made responsible for your safe custody."

"What wrong have I done that I should be made a prisoner?" asked Lotzung.

"It is no work of mine, I assure you. I see no harm in your wishing to meet your brother, though a common lodging-house is not a fit place for the Dalai Lama; and the Regent, being responsible for him, was naturally very angry about it."

"Is the Regent imprisoning me for having arranged these meetings with my brother?"

"If it were only that I should have pleaded for you with him and obtained your release. But there is another point which makes the case more serious. A third person was found in your company last night."

"Khangsar, the Eastern Mongol? Was there any harm in his being in our company?"

"No; but in the examination of the man, which the Regent has just conducted, some very compromising evidence was given against him. It appears that he was ordered by the lamas of Namcho to return to Ta-chien-lu, but that he disobeyed the order."

"My father is Deba of the Namcho district," replied Lotzung proudly, "and he permitted Khangsar to proceed."

"If he did so he defied those in authority over him," answered Tuen Fang, angered by the recollection of his treatment at the Deba's hands. Then, remembering that it would not suit his purpose to give Lotzung reason for resentment, he continued: "But that is not all the story. Khangsar committed an unpardonable offence in entering Lhasa, for he is not an Eastern Mongol at all."

"Not an Eastern Mongol?" repeated Lotzung, her eyes wide open with astonishment. "What is he then?"

"He is a peling."

The information evidently took Lotzung by surprise, for there was a pause before she answered—

"Well, I am glad he is not an Eastern Mongol. I am a Tibetan, and I like the Mongols as little as—I like the Chinese."

Tuen Fang coloured beneath his yellow skin. He had always regarded the Chinese as the only civilized nation, and yet in the estimation of this Tibetan girl they were coupled with one of the most barbarous.

"You seem interested in this peling," the Amban remarked between his teeth. "Perhaps you are in love with him?"

"And if I am?" retorted Lotzung with flashing eyes. "Is it wrong to love one's husband?"

"Even if he is your husband," answered Tuen Fang with a sneer, "he has never treated you as anything more than his servant."

"And I would rather be his servant than any one else's wife! Yes, rather than even your Emperor's wife!"

Tuen Fang turned almost livid with rage.

"You may have been his servant, but you will never be his wife. He was condemned to death this morning."

Lotzung sprang to her feet, and confronting the Amban cried: "It is a lie! You are deceiving me. Confess you are deceiving me!"

In her agitation she advanced towards him, and he, cowed by the light in her eyes, retreated in the direction of the door by which he entered.

"Pray calm yourself. I did not sentence him. It was the Regent."

Lotzung realized that loss of self-control would not improve her cause, and, returning to her cushions again, resumed her needlework.

"If you speak the truth," she said in low but clear tones, as she bent over her work, "and if the peling is really put to death, the Regent will not live many days after it; nor will his friends survive the Regent's fall."

There was something terrifying in the cold assurance with which these words were spoken. Tuen Fang felt as if sentence of death were being passed upon him, and a cold sweat broke out upon his brow.

"You are evidently a little beside yourself," he answered in quavering tones, and with his hand on the latch of the door. "I will leave you for the present, and hope to find you more reasonable when I see you next"; with which words the Amban slipped out of the door, closing it hastily after him.

Tuen Fang's thoughts were far from agreeable as he sat alone in his room after this interview. The Khalon's niece evidently had a will of her own. So far from being in his power, it really seemed as if he were in hers. She did not betray the slightest alarm with regard to her position, and in their recent conversation the one who had been lacking in courage was himself. It was certainly unpleasant to hear the tones of conviction in which she said that Khangsar's death would be avenged, not only on the Regent, but on the Regent's friends. She had, of course, no ground for such a statement, which was only prompted by her desire to make the Regent afraid of allowing the execution to take place.

With regard to the detention of Lotzung in his house, the Amban came to the conclusion that he would best avoid suspicion by conforming to his daily habits, as if nothing unusual had occurred. He had lately been accustomed to take a walk at noon, and he now set forth with his retinue for this daily exercise. On reaching the main street, he found it in a state of commotion. Tibetan soliders were running in and out of the houses and making a great stir amongst their occupants. Tuen Fang spoke to one of the latter, who happened to be the owner of a store at which he dealt, and said—

" What is all this to-do about ? "

The man prostrated himself and answered—

" The chief Khalon has lost his niece, and is having a search made for her in every house in the town."

Tuen Fang felt uncomfortable. Although the Khalon would not dare to interfere with the Amban's residence, yet by a process of exhaustion the search might result in attaching suspicion to it. At this moment Rashwa himself came out from a house. The Amban decided to accost him.

" They tell me that you have lost your niece," he said.

Rashwa, who felt Lotzung's disappearance keenly, was in no humour for conversing with the Chinese Amban, and answered curtly—

" Yes, I have lost her, and I mean to find her ! "

" How unfortunate ! " exclaimed Tuen Fang, alarmed by the expression of set determination in the Khalon's face. " I am very sorry to hear it. Has she ever disappeared in this way from your house before ? "

" Never," replied Rashwa.

" Nor from her father's house ? "

The Khalon now remembered that she had left her father's house without announcing her intention, and he was irritated with Tuen Fang for reminding him of it.

"I have nothing to do with her conduct in her father's house," he rejoined. "I am only concerned with my present duty in connection with her. If I find that any one has carried her off by force he will regret the deed. I bid Your Excellency good day"; and with a ceremonious bow Rashwa resumed his search.

But Tuen Fang's suggestion kept recurring to the Khalon's mind as he performed his task. Lotzung had run away from her father's house without giving any hint of her design. Was she repeating her former exploit? Champa had not been found. If carried off by force, her captors would not have hampered themselves with her dog as well; whereas if she had gone of her own free will the animal would naturally have accompanied her. Rashwa had become attached to Lotzung, and did not like to think she had repaid his kindness by such conduct.

This possibility was present in the Khalon's mind all day, and he could not dismiss it as he reflected on the matter at home that evening. It was now that Champa returned. A servant, greatly excited, brought him into the room where his master sat. Rashwa saw at once that the animal had been ill-treated in some way, for his eyes were lustreless and his movements lacked his usual animation. But the dog's return made it seem more probable that Lotzung had been forcibly abducted. Rashwa longed to consult his friend Khangsar about the matter, for he had a high opinion of his judgment. But although he had sent round several times during the day to his lodgings, the Eastern Mongol had been out on each occasion.

Meanwhile Philip, in his solitary confinement at the Potala, was thinking of the friendly Khalon. Would he get to know of his imprisonment and impending fate, and if so, would he make an effort to save him ? The young Englishman saw that it was very unlikely that either Rashwa or his faithful servant Mantso would ever learn what had become of him. Mantso was out of the house at the time of his arrest, and would consequently know nothing of it. Lotzung could not explain matters to her uncle without disclosing the fact that she had met her brother at Philip's lodgings, a confession which would anger Rashwa, seeing that he did not allow her even to talk of the Dalai Lama. But supposing Lotzung should brave the Khalon's anger and tell him everything, matters would be no better. Rashwa could not charge the Regent with causing Philip's disappearance except by showing knowledge of the meetings held in Philip's rooms. This would implicate him in the affair, and give his enemies a chance of overthrowing him.

Thus the prospect before the young Englishman seemed almost hopeless. On leaving the Regent's presence he had been conducted to a smaller apartment than the one he had occupied before. It was scantily furnished, ill-lighted, and very cold. Since entering it he had seen no one, nor had he been given anything to eat or drink since his meal in the early morning. What did this mean ? Had his gaolers forgotten him, or was it usual to half starve prisoners condemned to death ? From the day he entered Tibet he knew he would have to face the risk of execution, and now that judgment had been pronounced against him he was not taken by surprise. It was the uncertainty of the nature of his fate which caused his mind uneasiness.

Philip was roused from these gloomy thoughts by the turning of the key and the entrance of a lama gaoler whom he had not seen before. The man was stout and jovial-looking, and Philip could not help liking his appearance in spite of the office which he held.

"How are you getting on?" inquired the lama pleasantly, peering into Philip's face with the light of the butter lamp he held.

"As well as can be expected when there is no one to talk to. You, however, have removed that inconvenience by your presence, and will not, I am sure, object to answer a few questions. In the first place, what is the date fixed for the execution?"

"There is no particular date," replied the priest obligingly.

"Then I may be taken out at any time and executed?"

"There will be no regular execution. Although you are a peling, you probably know that to take life is against the ordinances of our religion."

"But I am condemned to death. How then is the sentence to be carried out?"

"Prisoners condemned to death are left without food and water till they die!"

Philip experienced a feeling of revulsion against such a death, and remained silent. The jovial lama seemed touched, and went on—

"Of course, it is very seldom that such prisoners really die of starvation."

"Do you take pity and put them out of their misery?"

"Buddha forbid! I have never yet been guilty of taking a man's life, but I do not withhold from those who desire it the means of putting an end to their sufferings."

"You lend them a pistol or a dagger perhaps?"

"No; but I have sometimes supplied them with poison."

Philip had always held that self-destruction was a cowardly act, yet would it not be excusable when one was being deliberately starved to death?

"Within what time must I expire?"

"There is no fixed period, but the Regent will expect to hear of your death within a week or ten days at the utmost."

Philip pondered on the lama's answer, and then replied—

"I suppose you do not mind what kind of poison I take, as long as it has the desired effect within that period?"

"You are free to make your own choice of poisons."

"I have a chest full of drugs in my lodgings, and I know some one who is sufficiently acquainted with its contents to mix the poison I require. It would have to be taken in daily doses for nine days, and on the tenth I should expire without experiencing any suffering at all."

"There are many men in Lhasa," said the monk, "who would like to have that poison for use upon their enemies."

Philip wondered at this naive admission concerning the morals of his fellow-countrymen, but, making no comment on it, continued—

"Will you allow me to send a letter to my friend containing instructions how to prepare the poison?"

"Your letter shall be sent."

"I will tell him to mix a dose in a ball of tsamba every morning, and I will take it after my first meal. Then for the rest of the day I shall be able to eat what I like without interfering with the effects of the poison. I have a good sum of money in my pocket, and if I have only ten days to live why should they not be merry ones? You will join me, lama, and we will have the best of wine and food."

The lama's jovial face beamed with an expansive smile. His figure, which was inclined to corpulency, showed that he enjoyed good fare.

"It shall be as you say," he answered. "I like to brighten the last days of the prisoners entrusted to my care. Write your letter to your friend and I will have it delivered, taking care that the ball of tsamba shall reach you safely every morning."

Having gained permission to write this letter, the question next arose to whom should he address it? Philip's thoughts turned first of all to Rashwa. The chief Khalon, as leader of the party in opposition to the Regent, would like to know on what slender pretext he had been condemned to death. The young man was also anxious to have news of Lotzung, and to learn whether she had been punished in any way for arranging the meetings with her brother. But he remembered that Rashwa had never been informed of these meetings, and that even now Lotznug might have said nothing to her uncle about them. If he disclosed the matter to the chief Khalon he would be very angry with his niece for making appointments with her brother without his knowledge.

But there was another reason why Philip should not address his letter to Rashwa. Supposing his gaoler played him false, or the letter went astray, the Regent would possess evidence against the Khalon sufficient to bring about his downfall. The young man saw that it would be best to give up the idea of communicating directly with the chief Khalon. To whom, then, should he write? There was, of course, Mantso, but Mantso could not read, and would have to get a stranger to explain the contents of the letter for him, a dangerous resource.

Of Philip's few acquaintances in Lhasa there remained only Purdung. Purdung had always been afraid that his intimacy with the Eastern Mongol might bring down upon him the displeasure of the Lhasa authorities. Still, the letter could be written in such a way that, while it did not commit the Tibetan merchant, it would leave a way open for future correspondence. After much thought Philip took the pen and paper with which the lama had provided him and wrote as follows—

"A lama residing in the Potala where I am now imprisoned has promised to have this letter delivered to you.

For reasons which it is not necessary to explain I have been arrested and condemned to death. The Regent, in his merciful compassion, has granted me permission to meet my death by poison instead of the slow and painful process of starvation. I write to ask you if you will procure the poison for me. In my rooms, to which my servant Mantso will give you access, you will find a medicine chest. Open it with the key I send you. Take a wooden bowl and pour into it ten drops from the third bottle—counting from the left—in the back row, and twenty drops from the fifth bottle in the middle row. Add tsamba and water, and make into a ball of paste about as large as a fair-sized apple. Send this to me at six o'clock every morning for nine days, packed in the little china jar with a cover which you will find at the bottom of the medicine chest. The jar must be carefully cleaned every day. By obliging me in this matter you will confer a last act of kindness on your former acquaintance—Khangsar."

Philip, feeling convinced that this letter could not compromise Purdung, gave it to the lama to read, and he promised to send it that very night. When his gaoler had withdrawn the young man threw himself with a feeling of relief on the rugs which did duty for a bed. He had resolved to make a fight for existence. The supposed poison which he had asked Purdung to make was perfectly harmless, but its daily arrival and the returning of the china pot might be made the means of communicating with the outside world, if the Tibetan merchant had courage enough for the undertaking. His gaoler seemed inclined to be friendly, and over the wine and good fare, for which he meant to pay, he could perhaps succeed in gaining his confidence. At any rate, the young man had taken the best course he could think of under the circumstances, and now composed himself to sleep with an easy mind.

CHAPTER XXIV

PHILIP woke at an early hour the following morning, wondering whether his gaoler, whose name he found to be Kalsang, had caused his letter to be delivered to Purdung, and if so whether the merchant would comply with his request. About half-past five Kalsang brought in a light breakfast of excellent tea and cakes, for which the young man insisted on paying at once. They then sat down and partook of the meal together. As it drew near to six o'clock Philip asked Kalsang if he had sent off his letter to Purdung the previous evening. The lama replied that he had done so, his messenger informing him that he had delivered it into Purdung's hands himself.

"You remember that I asked him to send me the poison every morning by six o'clock. I wonder if it has yet arrived?"

"I had forgotten all about it," replied Kalsang, rising; "but I will go to the entrance gate to see if Purdung's messenger is waiting there."

The friendly lama hurried off at once, and Philip was left to his own reflections once more. He was prepared to find that Purdung had not complied with his request, preferring to have nothing to do with a man who was condemned to death. The fear of the authorities had always loomed large in the Tibetan merchant's mind. Half-past six, then seven o'clock arrived, but Kalsang did not reappear. Philip was beginning to give up all hope when his gaoler opened the door.

"Purdung has not responded to my letter then?" the

young man said, seeing that Kalsang carried nothing in his hands.

" On the contrary, his messenger was at the entrance when I got there. I should have been back before, but was detained by some friends who wished to speak to me. Here is the packet"; and Kalsang produced a small parcel wrapped up in a khata. Philip unrolled the khata and found within it the china pot he had described to Purdung. The pot contained a ball of tsamba. Purdung had done as he had been desired.

Seeing that Kalsang's eyes were fixed curiously upon him, the young Englishman began to eat the tsamba ball. He had demolished half of it, when his teeth closed upon a substance which resembled paper. Retaining his composure, the young man lodged the object in the hollow of his cheek, and then disposed of the rest of the tsamba ball. The lama seemed much interested.

" Do you feel any the worse for it ? " he asked.

" Not the slightest," replied Philip, as distinctly as he could with a ball of paper in his cheek. " As I told you, I shall not feel its effects till nine days have passed."

" It seems to have altered your voice," observed the lama.

" It is only a slight irritation in my throat, which will soon pass away," the young man rejoined.

Kalsang looked sceptical, but as some one knocked at the door to say he was wanted, he left the room without making any further remark. Philip lost no time in taking the paper from his mouth and unfolding it. It was of the best Tibetan papyrus, and so little the worse for having been first in a tsamba ball and then in Philip's mouth that the ink had not even run. The message it conveyed ran as follows: " I send you herewith the tsamba ball, which I hope may be as you desire it." With his usual caution

Purdung had left the letter unsigned. If discovered by the authorities, it compromised no one. But if undiscovered, it opened up a means of communication between Philip and the outside world as soon as the young man found a way of replying to it. But Philip had already matured a plan, and cut out with his knife six circles of paper to fit exactly the bottom of the china pot in which the ball of tsamba had been sent. On these circles he hurriedly wrote as follows :—

"Your letter safely received. You may continue to write to me by the same means as you employed this morning without any fear of detection. There is no more risk entailed by my mode of communication. The paper, when smeared with some of the butter remaining in the pot, looks much the same colour as the china. The reason I told you to clean the pot carefully was to make sure that the paper would not escape your notice. But to come to my point. The mixture I gave you directions to make is harmless, so that for the next few days I shall be able to make every effort to regain my liberty. Tell Rashwa that I have reason to believe the Regent guilty of compassing the Dalai Lama's death. Action should be taken at once if the chief Khalon wishes to save his nephew.

"And now with regard to my own affairs. Please tell my servant Mantso what has become of me, and let him carry to your house after dark my two rifles, pistols, ammunition, and medicine box. If I die within the next ten days I will present them to you, and Mantso shall have the rest of my property. If, on the other hand, there is a rising against the Regent, and I succeed in making my escape, I will come to you for the weapons to enable me to fight against the tyrant. Let me have your news, and say how Lotzung fares."

Philip had to write a cramped hand in order to get this letter into the six round pieces of paper which he had cut, but he succeeded in doing so. He then laid them at the bottom of the pot, one on the top of the other, and with a thin layer of butter between each of them. Finally, he rolled the pot up in a khata and put it on one side to be given to Purdung's messenger when he called for it after sunset.

Kalsang arrived with the evening meal at six o'clock. Philip, who had spent a restless day, asked the lama to provide the best of fare procurable, and Kalsang humoured his request. The meal was well cooked, and the wine which accompanied it very good. Kalsang, like the majority of his countrymen, was fond of wine, drinking freely of it on the rare occasions when it was placed at his disposal. Philip filled up the lama's cup twice as often as his own, with the result that when at the end of the meal he took charge of the china pot to deliver to Purdung's messenger he could not have noticed the round pieces of paper inside, even supposing he had taken the trouble to open it.

The following morning Kalsang was late in serving the breakfast, and when he at length made his appearance he seemed to have lost his usual geniality.

" Did you see Purdung's messenger last night ? " Philip asked at length.

" Yes he was there," replied Kalsang, avoiding Philip's eyes.

" Then he will be here again this morning with my tsamba ball."

" I will go and see."

The lama left Philip in an uncomfortable frame of mind. Had Kalsang discovered the note concealed in the china pot, and was he postponing the announcement of his discovery in order to collect further incriminating evidence ? Yet when he returned with the parcel brought by Purdung's messenger the ball of tsamba which the pot contained did not seem to have been tampered with.

Not wishing to be caught again with a piece of paper in his mouth, Philip said that he would allow a longer interval after his meal to elapse before taking the tsamba ball, so that the efficacy of the poison should not be impaired. Kalsang made no comment, and shortly afterwards left the room.

As soon as he was gone Philip took the tsamba ball and broke it open, but found no letter inside it. Had Purdung, when cleaning the china pot according to instructions, thrown away the round pieces of paper without noticing the writing on them, or had Kalsang taken possession of them ? This latter possibility became confirmed in the young man's mind as the day wore on by the lama's conduct. For not only did Kalsang cause the midday meal to be served by some one else, but he refused his prisoner's invitation to dine with him in the evening. Philip now felt convinced that all had been discovered, and that the lama would not even go through the farce of offering to return the china pot to Purdung. In this respect, however, the young Englishman was mistaken, for when Kalsang, after clearing away the dinner, was about to leave the room he asked for the pot. Philip handed it to him with the secret satisfaction that to-night, at any rate, it contained no evidence against him. The lama would at once discover this, and concluding that Philip's suspicions had been aroused would no doubt throw off the mask and denounce him openly to the Regent.

The following morning, however, Purdung's tsamba ball was delivered by Kalsang at the usual hour. Philip, feeling sure that there would be no message in it, began to eat it in the lama's presence. But he had barely demolished a quarter of it when he felt a piece of paper between his teeth. Perhaps Kalsang had inserted a letter as a trap for his prisoner. The young man felt inclined to examine it in his gaoler's presence, but on the remote chance that it might really come from Purdung he retained it in his cheek as before. Whilst doing so he became aware that Kalsang's eyes were fixed upon him.

"I want to have an explanation with you," the lama said.

"I am glad to hear it," Philip replied.

"You must have noticed a change in my manner towards you."

"I have observed it."

"The fact is," continued the lama in some embarrassment, "I drank more than was good for me the night before last, and I felt too ashamed to enjoy your society the following day."

The explanation sounded too good to be true.

"If that is all you wanted to say——"

"It is not all. We lamas are not supposed to drink wine, or, if we do, to take it very sparingly. For months together I touch no wine, and then when it is placed before me I cannot restrain my liking for it. I must not therefore join you at your meals unless you promise not to ask me to take wine."

Philip swallowed the last mouthful of tsamba ball with a gulp of relief, and regardless of the fact that the piece of paper made a visible protuberance in his cheek, replied—

"I give my promise, for I much wish to have your company. Is there nothing further that you have to say?"

Here Philip became conscious that the lama was looking at his cheek, and he hastily transferred the paper to the other side.

"Are you suffering from face-ache?" asked Kalsang. "I fancied that your right cheek seemed swollen."

"It is nothing," said Philip, keeping his left cheek carefully out of sight. "If I rest it will soon be all right."

"I will go and get you a lotion which we use for face-ache," rejoined the lama, and Philip, anxious to get rid of him on any excuse, said that he would be glad to have it.

When the door had closed behind Kalsang Philip took the paper from his mouth and read as follows :—

" I have done as you desire. The chief Khalon takes heed of what you say. Lotzung has disappeared."

The fear of the authorities still made Purdung's communications very brief. The first sentence Philip took to mean that the Tibetan merchant had removed the firearms, ammunition, and medicine chest to his own house, and had informed Mantso of his master's place of confinement. The second sentence pointed to his having communicated with Rashwa, but the third was not so easily explained. Perhaps Lotzung had been afraid of her uncle's anger if he found out about her secret meetings with her brother, and had gone to stay at the house of some friends in Lhasa till the matter had blown over, or she might have set out with some caravan for her father's house.

But there was another possible explanation of Lotzung's disappearance. Philip remembered Tuen Fang's presence at his lodgings on the night of his arrest. What had brought him there ? The doings of the young Dalai Lama chiefly concerned the Regent, and there was no occasion for the Chinese Ambassador to busy himself with them, even supposing the autocratic Tsering had been inclined to let him do so. The only other way to account for his presence was the fact of Lotzung being there. Philip had witnessed Tuen Fang's first meeting with the young girl and the admiration she excited in him. He also knew that the Amban had formally applied to her uncle for her hand, an application which had been practically refused by Rashwa's referring the matter to her father. It was possible that Tuen Fang, despairing of obtaining her by lawful means, had conspired with Tsering to carry her off by force. The young man resolved to tell Purdung his suspicions, and ask him to communicate them to Rashwa at once.

Accordingly, as soon as Kalsang had brought the lotion for the face-ache, and had withdrawn again, Philip sat down and wrote the following letter to Purdung :—

" Your secret communication reached me quite safely in the tsamba ball this morning. I conclude that fear of discovery made you keep me waiting a day for a reply to my second letter and caused your note to be so brief. Please write more fully. The lama who acts as my warder is very indulgent, and has no suspicion of the means we use for communication.

" I gather from your letter that you have taken possession of the articles I mentioned, and have told Mantso where I am. But what do you mean by saying Lotzung has disappeared ? If this is so, the Senior Amban may possibly know something of her present abode. Ask Rashwa to look into this matter, and also let me know if he is doing anything with regard to Tsering and the Dalai Lama."

That evening Kalsang dined with Philip once more, and the latter, according to his promise, refrained from asking his guest to partake of wine. Nevertheless the lama, although he conversed in a friendly way, seemed to have a load on his mind. Perhaps something he had seen or heard had aroused his suspicions after all. Philip, anxious to arrive at the truth, began—

" You do not yet seem quite yourself, Kalsang. It cannot be the matter of the wine, for I have obeyed your wishes with regard to it. Is there anything else which stands in the way of a complete understanding between us ? "

" Nothing," answered Kalsang. " The matter which occupied my thoughts was one on which I should speak to no one but a lama of the Potala, like myself. I have conversed with one or two of them about it, but their answers have not satisfied me."

"Why not take me into your confidence? I have only a few days more to live, and what you tell me will not go beyond the walls of the Potala."

The lama reflected for a while, and then resumed—

"The matter concerns the Dalai Lama."

Philip's curiosity was excited.

"Anything which relates to the Dalai Lama you may confide to me without fear. I am his devoted servant."

"Well then, the truth is, I am anxious about his health. I saw him to-day for the first time for a fortnight, and I noticed a great change."

This was the subject on which Philip much desired information, but as it was the cause of his confinement in the Potala he had not ventured to speak to Kalsang about it. Even now he thought it wiser to make sure of his ground before expressing his views on the subject to Kalsang. Accordingly he said—

"In what respect is he changed?"

"He is so much more pale and thin."

"It is the season of the fasts."

"Yes, but even a Dalai Lama must eat and drink something if he is to remain with us in his present incarnation."

"That is true," admitted Philip.

"Both the previous Dalai Lamas died at this time of the year," continued Kalsang. "I liked them well, but this one has taken possession of my heart. When I asked him how he was to-day he answered, 'I am well, Kalsang, quite well, though weak. We must all follow the ordinances of Buddha, myself especially, without complaining. Come near, Kalsang, and I will bless you before you go.' The sight of the transparent hand he stretched out to lay upon my head made the tears come to my eyes, and I left the apartment hurriedly lest my emotion should be seen."

Kalsang's story decided Philip to tell him all he knew.

"Have you heard why I was condemned to death?" he asked.

"I have heard nothing about the charges made against you. The Regent takes no one into his counsel."

"It was in connection with this matter of the Dalai Lama's health that my arrest took place. Do you know that he has a sister called Lotzung?"

"I did not know it, but I was aware that his father was banished from Lhasa for plotting against the Regent's life."

"That is the Regent's version of the story; but we need not discuss this matter now. What I wanted to say was that Lotzung, who is very fond of her brother, and came all the way from Namcho on purpose to see him again, arranged a meeting with him in the house in which I happened to be lodging. He fainted shortly after his arrival, and being called by Lotzung to help her tend him, I found that it was want of food that made him ill."

"You must have been right. Though during the fasts a Dalai Lama should abstain from meat and eggs, he ought to eat enough plain food to maintain his strength."

"The Regent would not allow it. We arranged several meetings, at which the poor boy ate heartily and began to improve in health. But Tsering suspected what was going on, put a stop to the audiences, and kept him confined to his room. He only came to see us once more, when the Regent, who got to know of it, made his appearance and sent him back to the Potala, while he arrested me and condemned me to death."

Kalsang seemed much distressed by the story. Tsering had been Abbot of the Monastery of Sera, to which he belonged, and the lama had always regarded him as a devout and holy man.

"Do you mean to say that he is deliberately planning the Dalai Lama's death ?"

"I do. As you know, the two previous Grand Lamas died young, and the Regent is preparing the same fate for this one. Look into the matter yourself, and if you find I am not speaking the truth I shall richly deserve the death to which I am condemned."

Kalsang sprang to his feet, his eyes aflame with anger.

"I will sift this matter to the bottom," he exclaimed. "I know the personal attendant of the Dalai Lama, and I will get the truth from him. If it should prove to be as you say I foresee mourning at the Potala, but it will not be for the Dalai Lama."

CHAPTER XXV

RASHWA sat alone in his private room with a long letter spread out before him. His brain was burning with the thoughts evoked by the communication, for it was from Khangsar, and contained information which seemed barely credible to him. Although it was only the evening following that in which the young Englishman had awakened Kalsang's suspicions with regard to Tsering's designs, the friendly lama had already found that they were justified, and from a devoted adherent had become one of the bitterest foes of the Regent. He at once communicated the change to Philip, and asked him if the poison he had taken was sufficient to prove fatal, as he wished to plan a means of escape, so that they might both go and stir up the enemies of the Regent against him. The young man confessed that so far he had taken no poison, and together they discussed the best course to pursue. The discussion ended in the long letter which Rashwa had just received.

So much of its contents were entirely new to him that it was small wonder that the chief Khalon could not at first realize the significance of the information it conveyed. He now heard for the first time of the frequent visits of the Dalai Lama and Lotzung to Khangsar's lodgings, how it had been found that his nephew was being slowly starved to death, and how he improved in health when supplied with sufficient food. Rashwa was told the manner in which the trio had been surprised by the Regent and Tuen Fang, how Khangsar had been taken to the Potala, and how Lotzung had in all probability been abducted by the

Senior Amban. Most important of all, he now learnt that Kalsang, one of the lamas in the Potala itself, confirmed Khangsar's account of the Dalai Lama, and was prepared not only to help the prisoner to escape, but to come out with him and assist the enemies of the Regent.

Rashwa could not control the whirl of thoughts excited by the information laid before him. Hitherto he had been powerless to act against the Regent. Possessing no proof of his treatment of the Dalai Lama, he could not hope to bring about a rising against him. Now, however, a lama of the Potala was prepared to give evidence in the matter, and one who knew the inner life of the palace would be an invaluable witness. Then Khangsar himself would be free, and, with the wonderful gun of which the Khalon had heard, would be of the greatest assistance. Finally, Lotzung could only be rescued from Tuen Fang by the overthrow of the man who connived at her abduction. Khangsar, it was true, could produce no proof that the Senior Amban had carried the young girl off, but the circumstantial evidence was strong against him. The Eastern Mongol's servant, Mantso, who had brought the letter from his master, and was waiting outside, might even be able to furnish some proof of the deed, and Rashwa had him brought into the room.

"You remember the night on which your master was taken to the Potala?" the chief Khalon began.

Mantso made a profound obeisance and said he remembered it very well.

"And you witnessed all that happened?"

"I witnessed nothing, for I had been sent out to make a purchase, and when I returned they had all three gone."

"So you did not see what became of Lotzung? Had you no suspicions with regard to it?"

"Not till Kalsang, who gave me that letter to take to

you, told me that the Chinese Amban was at the lodgings when my master was taken away. I then remembered something which happened the following day."

"What was that?"

"When I was bringing Champa back to your house I went somewhat out of my way and passed the Senior Amban's house. The dog stopped and sniffed at the door and tried to enter."

"Why did you not come and tell me this?" asked Rashwa sternly.

Mantso made an obeisance which was still more profound than the first.

"I am my master's servant," he answered. "It is not for me to talk unless he bids me."

Rashwa was pleased with this proof of Mantso's allegiance to his master, and telling him to call at dawn the following morning for an answer to the letter he had brought, he dismissed him from his presence. The chief Khalon no longer had any doubt as to where Lotzung was to be found. Action must be taken at once. A trusted messenger was dispatched to friends on whom he could rely, calling a meeting for midnight at a small house in an out-of-the-way street, where they had been in the habit of foregathering. The interval Rashwa devoted to drawing up a plan of action to submit to his associates.

Punctually at midnight the chief Khalon reached the house and entered the room reserved for the meeting. His appeal had met with ready response, and he found assembled nearly every one to whom a notice had been sent. They were all adherents of his own and enemies of Tsering. Purdung, though summoned, did not make his appearance, but sent a verbal message to Rashwa by one of his servants, regretting that indisposition prevented him from attending the meeting. As a matter of fact, the Tibetan merchant was in his usual health, and fear of being implicated in a conspiracy alone prevented him from being present.

Rashwa briefly explained to the gathering the reason for which he had called them together. He had obtained, he said, authentic information from an inmate of the Potala that the Regent was deliberately trying to bring about the Dalai Lama's death. They must act at once or it would be too late, and Tsering, with an infant reincarnation of the Dalai Lama, would enter on a fourth term of absolute power. Now was the time to rise against the tyrant, if they did not wish him to secure himself in his office for another twelve or fifteen years.

Every one agreed that something must be done, but when it came to deciding on a definite course of action the same unanimity did not prevail. Some said it was a little premature to have recourse to arms. The Dalai Lama might still live for several weeks, and the time could be usefully employed in rousing popular feeling against the Regent. If they took action at once, they would have arrayed against them not only the Regent's troops and the fighting monks of Sera, but the Chinese soldiers of Tuen Fang. Would it not be better to have Tsering put out of the way by poison ? No one, however, volunteered for this delicate task, and all seemed anxious to avoid doing anything which might be found out and for which they would be punished.

" We have no military leader on our side," said one of them to Rashwa. " Now, if your brother-in-law, the Deba of Namcho, joined us, it would be a different matter. He is skilled in the use of the matchlock, and he has gained experience in the local wars in which he has been engaged."

" It would take too long to send for Phala," replied the chief Khalon ; " but I know an Eastern Mongol who is quite as brave and possesses foreign firearms of deadly force and accuracy. Though lying in the Potala condemned to death by the Regent, a lama has promised to set him free, and we can arrange for a rising simultaneously. His name is Khangsar."

No one present except Rashwa knew him or had even heard of him, for both Purdung and the chief Khalon had their reasons for not making known their acquaintance with Philip. But Rashwa's statement made a great impression. At that time there were not half a dozen magazine rifles in the whole of Lhasa, and the ammunition for them had been expended in friendly shooting matches. A man who possessed two European rifles, with corresponding cartridges, was equal in efficiency of fire to a whole regiment of matchlocks. A sudden access of martial ardour seized the meeting, and the chief Khalon took advantage of it to arrange that the Potala should be attacked in the early hours of the following morning. This would allow at least twenty-four hours to warn the supporters of the chief Khalon to answer his call to arms, and would give Kalsang and Philip time enough to arrange for their escape.

When Kalsang received through Mantso next day a verbal message from Rashwa that he and Khangsar were to leave the Potala that night, as the attack was to be made the following morning, it came to him with something of a shock. The kind-hearted lama was not a fighting man, and though the treatment of the Dalai Lama had driven him into the ranks of the Regent's enemies, he had not anticipated having to take action against him within so short a space of time. Accordingly he entered Philip's room with a very long face, which made the young man think that something had gone wrong.

"I see you have bad news, Kalsang," he said. "Has the Regent intercepted any of our correspondence?"

"No; but Rashwa has sent a message saying that we

must leave the Potala to-night, as the rising takes place at dawn to-morrow."

"That is good news indeed," replied Philip with an expression of relief.

Kalsang regarded the young man with an air of surprise. "I do not understand how any one who hears that he has to fight on the following day can regard the news as good."

"Is it not a good thing that our suspense is at an end and all uncertainty removed?"

"Yes; but if the plot is discovered before we leave the Potala we shall lose our lives, while if we escape we shall still have to risk them fighting the Regent's forces."

Philip smiled good-humouredly.

"I can quite understand that as a teacher of the Buddhist religion you should recoil from taking life. But there will be no occasion for you to fight. Leave it to those whose business or whose pleasure it is to do so."

This view seemed a reasonable one, and Kalsang, with a lighter heart, discussed the details of their flight from the Potala. It was arranged that Philip should put on a lama's dress similar in all respects to the one which Kalsang wore. As to the hour for their escape, the lama decided that four o'clock in the morning was the most suitable. Although lamas were moving about the Potala at all hours of the night, there were fewer at that time than at any other. This would give them ample time to reach Rashwa's house before the dawn.

Philip spent a restless day, now confident in the success of the revolt, now utterly despairing of the issue. As for Kalsang, he became more anxious and depressed as time wore on, and Philip began to fear that he might fail him after all. At dinner the lama was reduced to such a doleful state, that if his prisoner had not broken his promise and persuaded him to take a little wine he might have lacked the courage for the venture. As it was, the young man succeeded in keeping the lama's resolution up to the necessary pitch by inducing him to spend the night in his apartment.

After what seemed to be an interminable vigil four o'clock arrived, and the two men stole quietly out of the room. Only one solider was on guard, and he lay snoring full length upon the ground, overcome by the liberal draughts of wine with which he had been plied. The lama, now definitely committed to the venture, summoned up all the resolution he could command and led the way. They passed along three or four corridors and down several terraces connected by ladders or steep stone steps. A few lamas met them, but the light was poor, and Philip attracted no attention.

In this way they drew near to the entrance to the Potala, and Kalsang was beginning to hope that they would get away unnoticed when a lama overtook them, and recognizing Kalsang said—

" Hail, Kalsang ! Whither are you going at this time of the morning ? "

" I am going to the temple of Jova," he said, inventing an excuse on the spur of the moment.

" That is my errand. Let us go together. And is your friend bound thither also ? Make him known to me, for I do not recognize his face."

" His name is Labran," answered Kalsang, mentioning the first that came into his head and cudgelling his brains for some means of getting rid of the man.

" He must be a fresh arrival at the Potala."

" Yes, he has only been here a few days."

They had now reached the gateway, and passed through without being questioned. Their companion, as well as Kalsang, was well known to the lama who acted as gatekeeper, and he thought there was no need to interrogate any one found in their society. When they were well clear of the Potala Kalsang said to their companion : " And now you are going straight to the temple ? "

" Are we not all going there ? " rejoined the man.

" Labran and myself have first to pay a visit to a friend who lives in a distant quarter of the town, so we must part here for the present."

Their companion seemed half inclined to go with them, but Kalsang bade him farewell in tones which expressed so plainly his desire to be rid of him that the man had no alternative but to go on by himself. As soon as a sufficient distance separated him from them Kalsang and Philip made off in the direction of the chief Khalon's house. This they reached at half-past four, having had no further interruption on the way. Mantso was awaiting them at the door, and was overjoyed to find that his master had really succeeded in making his escape. They were shown into the reception-room, where Rashwa soon came to welcome them. The chief Khalon was acquainted with Kalsang, and when the first greetings were over thanked him warmly for the part he had taken.

" You will not regret having joined us," he said. " We have received much more support than I expected, and in the next room there is a man come to help us, who is worth by himself a regiment of soldiers. Follow me, and I will present you to him."

The chief Khalon led the way into an adjoining compartment, where to their astonishment they found the Deba of Namcho. No one could be better calculated to attach the monk to Rashwa's cause. He won Kalsang's allegiance not only because he was the father of the Dalai Lama, but because he had been personally popular in Lhasa previous to his banishment from the capital. The lama made him a profound obeisance, saying how glad he was to welcome him back to the Holy City.

"You are very kind, my good Kalsang," said Phala, "and I can only hope that all my acquaintances will be as pleased to see me. I reached here but an hour ago on private business, only to find much more important public business on hand. And this is my kind friend Khangsar," he continued, turning to Philip. "I did not recognize you at first in lama's robes."

After the mutual news had been briefly exchanged Phala explained the plan of action he had recommended to the chief Khalon. The supporters of the movement were to collect in the side streets on either side of the main street by half-past five. Exactly at the half-hour a single blast of the horn would be the signal for them to pour into the main street, where the chief Khalon and himself would meet them. He then proposed to lead them direct to the Potala, surround it, and make the Regent prisoner. His followers, if once deprived of their leader, would not be likely to do much fighting on his behalf.

"But what steps will you take about your daughter, who, as you have no doubt heard, is in all probability a prisoner in the Senior Amban's house?" asked Philip, anxious to effect the young girl's rescue as soon as possible.

"We cannot risk the failure of our main enterprise," replied Phala, "by detaching a force to attack the Chinese Embassy. It will be time for us to deal with Tuen Fang when we have seized the Regent. There is no fear of his escaping us."

Philip saw that Phala was right, and that the release of Lotzung must be deferred till the action against Tsering had been brought to a successful issue. The young man then asked about his firearms, and was informed that Purdung had brought them round to Rashwa's house the previous evening. Phala also carried the rifle which Philip had given him, so that with the three pistols belonging to the latter they had in all six repeating weapons of modern manufacture.

But it was now time to leave the house. At the entrance a couple of saddle horses were waiting.

"Are you and the Khalon going to ride?" asked Kalsang of the Deba in surprise.

"Tibetan noblemen do not go into battle on foot," replied Phala quietly.

"But you will make a good mark for the enemy's bullets," protested the lama.

"And we shall be equally visible to our friends. That is why I told them to saddle my white horse. If you would like to ride too, Khangsar," he continued, turning to Philip, "I can soon provide you with a horse."

But Philip declined the offer, thinking that as a foreigner it would not be wise to take a too conspicuous part in an internal contest of this character. Accordingly he changed his priest's robes for ordinary attire, and then, shouldering one of his rifles, while Mantso carried the other, followed by two men with the ammunition, he was about to set out when Purdung made his appearance. The young man greeted him warmly, and thanked him for the part he had taken in enabling him to escape from the Potala, as well as for keeping his firearms in safe custody.

"Those are the rifles which protected us against the chukpas," remarked Purdung. "I should like to see them once more in use against our enemies."

"Do you, then, wish to come with us this morning?" asked Philip, for Purdung had never shown much desire for fighting.

"Why not?" answered the Tibetan merchant. "I shall be safe as long as I am near your guns."

Philip was amused by the confidence the merchant displayed in the efficacy of his weapons, and in return, to Purdung's great satisfaction, handed to him the rifle which Mantso was carrying. As they were moving off, Kalsang, who had been a silent spectator of the proceedings, now followed them, saying: "Why should I be left behind? Am I not an enemy of the Regent, and do I not wish to witness, as much as any one, the defeat of his troops?"

Purdung's example was infectious, and Philip's party thus reached the number of four. Shortly after they had taken up their position in a side street as arranged, the single blast of a horn was heard, and Rashwa's adherents began to pour into the main street, which soon became full of armed men. Everything was conducted in silence, and even when Phala on his white horse and Rashwa on a black one rode slowly down the street, the enthusiasm of their followers, on recognizing the Deba of Namcho and the chief Khalon, found expression only in whispered remarks and subdued exclamations of welcome.

On reaching the top of the street, near to which Philip and his party stood, Phala halted for a moment, pointed with his sword in the direction of the Potala, and moved on again without a word. Philip fell in behind the Deba and his brother-in-law. It did not take long to get clear of the city and reach the mountain on which the Potala is built. Here the force divided into two columns, one turning to the right and the other to the left, and following the walls of the building till they met on the further side. The investment of the palace was thus complete and the retreat of the Regent cut off. It only remained to enter and call upon him to surrender unconditionally. Phala undertook this task, accompanied by Philip's party and some twenty followers. The chief Khalon remained in command of the armed force outside.

CHAPTER XXVI

KALSANG, familiar with every corner of the Potala, led Phala and his followers in the direction of the Regent's quarters. They met with no more opposition within the walls than they had encountered outside them. Either the inmates of the Potala secretly sympathized with Tsering's enemies, or they had seen the armed force which Rashwa had collected and deemed it wise to support the stronger side. The various flights of steps would have been hard to take against determined foes, and two or three desperate men could have held the ladders against scores of assailants. But no one ventured to stop the intruders, nor even uttered a word of protest as they passed.

Thus it was not long before Phala and his party reached the Regent's quarters. A lay monk who was on guard outside the door stepped timidly aside as the Deba approached it. On being asked if the Regent was within, he replied cautiously that he had not seen him go out. Phala entered, and passing through a couple of ante-rooms came to the room where Tsering transacted all his business. It was unoccupied, but scrolls and official documents lay scattered on the floor, as if some one had hastily ransacked the drawers and cupboards, taking away only the most important papers. The Deba began to fear that Tsering had escaped him after all. Pushing on into the next apartment, which proved to be the Regent's bedroom, he found a lama in sole possession.

"Where is the Regent?" asked Phala curtly.

"He left here about a quarter of an hour ago," replied

the lama, "and went towards the Dalai Lama's apartments."

Once more Phala hurried off till he gained the portion of the palace occupied by the Dalai Lama. With this he was familiar, for he used to visit his son there in the days that preceded his banishment from Lhasa. He now passed hastily through the outer apartments till he reached the Grand Lama's bedroom. Waving aside the two priests on guard outside the door, he threw it open, but halted on the threshold. For the boy, with pale, drawn face and feeble frame, propped up by cushions, bore no resemblance to the rosy-cheeked lad he had last seen two years previously. The Grand Lama, however, recognized his father, and a wan smile lit up his face. Phala ran forward, and falling on his knees asked for the Dalai Lama's blessing. The boy stretched out a thin, almost transparent hand, placed it on his father's head, and pronounced the well-known formula. Then Phala remembered his errand and rose to his feet.

"I heard that the Regent was here. Whither has he gone?"

"He left me only a short time ago," replied the boy. "A message was delivered to him, and he went off hastily, saying that important business required his attention. But what brings you here at this early hour, and why have you returned from Namcho to Lhasa?"

"I too have important business," answered Phala.

"Business which concerns my good friend Khangsar?" continued the Dalai Lama, turning to Philip, who alone of the Deba's followers had entered the apartment. "I am glad to see that the Regent kept his promise and did not punish you for being found with me that night when we last met."

"I am alive and well," answered Philip, not wishing to

undeceive the boy on the question of the Regent's treatment of him. "But you, I see, have been fasting again, to the detriment of your health. And what is this ?" he went on, taking up a small silver cup full of an almost colourless liquid, which stood on a small table at the Grand Lama's bedside.

An involuntary shudder passed through the boy's pale frame as he glanced at the cup. "That is my medicine," he said; "the Regent gives it me every morning with his own hands. I am not sorry that he was called away to-day before I took it, for it always makes me feel unwell."

Philip dipped the tip of his little finger into the draught and tasted it. A single drop sufficed. Taking up the cup, he threw its contents out of the open window. Phala understood his action, and the colour mounted to his brow.

"Let us waste no more time," he said, "our business is pressing. Farewell, my son. It will not be long before we return."

They withdrew the same way as they had come, but before joining the others the Deba laid his hand on Philip's shoulder and said: "That cup that stood by the Lama's couch and which you emptied at the window, did it contain poison ?"

"It did," answered Philip.

A fierce light shone in the Deba's eyes.

"Come, let us track the fugitive to his hiding-place."

Kalsang's services were once more required, and under his guidance every apartment in the Potala was searched, but searched in vain. Phala in despair was on the point of going through the palace once more when a messenger brought a letter from Rashwa. The Deba glanced hastily at its contents and said to Philip—

"Rashwa sends word that the lamas of Sera are marching

in full force against the Potala. It is evident that Tsering has escaped and called his monks to arms. I am glad of it. I would sooner kill him fighting in the open than hunt him down and slay him when he was at my mercy. Let us join Rashwa without delay."

The small party followed their leader as he made his way to the western gate. Firing had already commenced when they reached it, and the ramparts were manned with Rashwa's followers. They found that the Khalon himself had taken up a position on the wall which commanded a view of the attacking forces and the surrounding country as far as the Monastery of Sera some three miles distant. An unbroken stream of dark-robed monks extended from the monastery gates to the Potala. As they came within a hundred and fifty to one hundred yards of the building they deployed to right and left of the gate. Then, taking advantage of such cover as a boulder or a solitary hut afforded, they opened fire.

This fire was almost harmless, as the range of match-locks does not exceed one hundred and twenty yards, and they cannot be aimed with any accuracy beyond sixty or seventy yards. The danger lay in the numbers of the enemy, supposing they had the courage to make an assault. Rashwa commanded barely five hundred followers. The Monastery of Sera could turn out five thousand armed men. They were massing in such numbers that an attack on the gate could be carried by mere weight. It was only a wooden structure and considerably out of repair. Sand-bags would have rendered it sufficiently secure, but on the barren rock on which the Potala was built not a single sack-ful of earth or sand could be collected. The only way in which it could be strengthened was with beams of wood, and Philip volunteered to do what he could with the material at their disposal.

Meanwhile it became evident that the enemy were going to concentrate their attack on the western gate. The bullets of their matchlocks, indeed, failed to penetrate the wood; but a gingal, or huge Chinese musket, with a range of three hundred yards, had been mounted on its rest, and its missiles, piercing the gate, wounded in quick succession three of the men who were helping Philip. The faithful Mantso, however, stuck to the work, and at length the gate was made as secure as possible with the scanty supply of beams which could be found for the purpose.

This had only just been done when a six-pound ball crashed through the structure, being followed almost instantaneously by the report of a piece of ordnance. Philip rushed up on the ramparts and found that a Chinese leather cannon had been mounted at a distance of five hundred yards. A few more such shots would make a breach in the gate through which the enemy could enter. The young man took a steady aim with his rifle, and shot dead one of the lamas who were loading the cannon. The fact that a bullet took effect at such a distance created astonishment amongst the enemy, but they nevertheless continued the loading and fired three more rounds. At the fourth discharge the leather cannon burst, killing three of the lamas who were serving it. Another cannon, however, had been mounted, and a third was being brought up. The enemy intended to make certain of success.

At this juncture a messenger came to say that the Sera monks were breaking into the eastern gate. This gate was protected by strong battlements, and on that account a smaller force had been left to guard it. Phala now realized the mistake that had been made, and gathering round him a body of men started off with Philip to retrieve it. On nearing the gate, however, the Deba found he was too late. A large battering ram had been employed, a breach had been effected, and the enemy were already pouring in. But a resolute stand might still save the situation, and the deadly volley which issued from the matchlocks of Phala's men, assisted by the continuous fire of the two repeating rifles, caused the Sera lamas to waver.

It was now that a man rode up to the gate, and, dismounting, called on the assailants to follow him. Phala recognized the Regent and covered him with his rifle; but Tsering only carried a sword, and it seemed a cowardly thing to shoot him down. The Deba therefore threw his rifle on the ground, and telling his men to cease firing, advanced with drawn sword to meet the Regent.

"It is you, Tsering, I see!" he exclaimed. "If you are as brave as you are unscrupulous tell your men to stand where they are, and let us settle the matter between ourselves."

"I accept your challenge, Phala," replied the Regent, drawing his sword. "When I have disposed of you it will be time enough for the monks of Sera to clear the Potala of the rabble you have brought with you!"

With these words he made a rush at Phala. Though some ten or twelve years older than his adversary, Tsering was still a powerful man, and had the advantage in both height and weight. There was little scientific swordsmanship on either side, and Philip saw that the conflict would not be a long one. The end came sooner even than he expected. A terrific blow which Tsering aimed at Phala's head was parried by the Deba and followed by a thrust which pierced the Regent's heart.

"So may all the enemies of my country perish!" exclaimed Phala. "Let those who wish to avenge his death advance!"

But the followers of the Regent, now that their patron had fallen, had no further relish for the struggle, and went off to spread the news amongst their fellows. The attack on the western gate soon ceased, and the lamas began to retire to the monastery. Philip's thoughts returned to Lotzung, and he asked Phala to spare him some men to search the Chinese Embassy for his daughter.

"Take as many as you wish," replied the Deba, "but you will have no fighting. I know Tuen Fang too well for that. My presence is still required at the Potala, but I do not think you will have any difficulty in recovering Lotzung from the Amban's residence."

The Chinese Embassy had been in a state of great commotion since the early hours of the morning. The secret of the rising had been so well kept that not even Jasi, Tuen Fang's Spy-in-Chief, knew anything of it. As soon, however, as the movement began the Ladaki heard of it, witnessed the gathering, and ran home to tell his master the chief characters who took part in it. He found the Amban in a heavy slumber, induced by having recourse the previous night to his opium pipe. His inability to make progress in his suit for Lotzung's hand had driven him to his usual solace when in trouble. No promises of either money or presents would induce the young girl to become his wife. When he threatened force, she answered that she would resist, and either kill her assailant or die by her own hands. It was evident that she had concealed upon her person some weapon which the Amban did not care to face. To console himself in his rebuff Tuen Fang took to his opium pipe, and the apartment was still heavy with the fumes when Jasi entered it.

Assisted by the Senior Amban's personal attendant, the Ladaki at length succeeded in bringing his master back to consciousness. In the usual reaction after this stimulant Tuen Fang's nervous force was at its lowest ebb, and his first sensation at being thus roughly roused was one of abject terror. Seeing, however, only Jasi and his personal attendant alarm gave place to anger, and he bade them be gone out of his presence, so that he might enjoy his sleep in peace.

"But I have important news for Your Excellency," said Jasi. "A revolt, headed by the chief Khalon, Rashwa, has taken place."

At the word "revolt" the Amban's previous fears returned, and he sat bolt upright on his couch.

"Revolt! Chief Khalon?" he echoed. "Are they coming here?"

"No, they are marching on the Potala."

Tuen Fang gave a sigh of relief and lay back on his cushions again.

"Has Rashwa a large following?" he asked.

"His brother-in-law Phala, the Deba of Namcho, has joined him."

The Deba's name sent a shiver of fear through the wretched Amban's frame.

"Who else is there with him?"

"Purdung the merchant, and Khangsar, the Eastern Mongol."

"Khangsar?" repeated Tuen Fang. "I thought he was condemned to death."

"The lama Kalsang, in whose company I saw him, no doubt helped him to escape."

"What if Rashwa takes the Potala and kills the Regent?" continued Tuen Fang, his fears returning. "They would then come here and attack my house."

"They may take the Potala, but they will not take the Regent, for I gave him warning to escape. I also sent word to the Monastery of Sera, so they will be ready to help the Regent."

"You are a clever fellow, Jasi," said Tuen Fang with an

approving smile, " and you shall be well rewarded. Go and call out the Chinese troops to guard the Residency, and then get me the latest news. There will be no more sleep for me this morning. I must get up at once."

Jasi gave the Amban's order to the officer commanding the guard at the Embassy and then went on to the Potala. Here he found the lamas of Sera already preparing for the attack. From a safe distance he watched their operations. When he saw the leather cannons battering the western gate he came to the conclusion that the monks would soon be victors. This belief became a certainty in his mind when the Regent entered the eastern gate, and without waiting to see any more he hurried back to the Senior Amban.

He found Tuen Fang consumed with anxiety. It appeared that the Chinese barracks were on the further side of the town, and the soldiers were afraid to venture out of them. The Amban had not only appropriated their pay, but had neglected to provide them with firearms, so that they could hardly be called a military force at all. Being driven to support themselves, they were most of them engaged in civilian occupations. Consequently no more men were available to protect the Residency than the half-dozen already there, and Tuen Fang was in the depth of despair.

Jasi's news, however, filled him with more confidence. As the Regent had defeated the revolutionists, both Rashwa and Phala would be executed, if not already killed in battle. The populace of Lhasa would have been taught a lesson, and Tsering and himself would now possess more absolute power than before. Better still, he was at liberty to do what he liked with Lotzung. The daughter of a rebel would have no claim to consideration. He debated whether he would make her his wife or his slave, but before doing either it would be necessary to take away from her the weapon which she evidently carried. The Amban thought for a while on the matter and then said to Jasi, who still stood before him, " How is Lotzung this morning ? "

" Her maid says that she is still complaining of being kept here."

" She will soon change her tone when she hears that her father and uncle have been killed, and that there is no one left to take her part. I will go and see her now."

Jasi made obeisance and turned to leave the room.

" Stay ! " said the Amban. " I have reason to believe that the girl conceals a weapon about her. It would be as well to take it away. You must wait outside the room while I am with her. I will provoke her to display her weapon, and when I cry, ' Hold, hold,' you must rush in and seize her."

" I will do as Your Excellency commands," replied Jasi, and withdrew.

Tuen Fang then summoned his personal attendant and had himself arrayed in a gorgeous costume. Satisfied at length with his appearance, and heavily perfumed, the Amban set out for Lotzung's chamber.

A man less absorbed in himself than Tuen Fang would have noticed the change that had come over the Khalon's niece during the last few days. The colour had faded from her cheeks, and her bearing lacked the vivacity for which it had always been distinguished. She was sitting at needlework with her back to the door as the Amban entered, and she neither looked up nor laid aside her work.

" How is my bird this morning ? " began Tuen Fang.

Lotzung took no notice of him.

" Has she yet no kind word nor tender look for me ? "

The young girl did not reply.

" I fear that my dove still frets at her confinement. But why should she ? Is it not better to be imprisoned in a house where every care is taken of her than to be thrust out into the streets and left to support herself ?"

Lotzung could not restrain a gesture of impatience. Tuen Fang observed it and was annoyed.

"Ah ! you may think it impossible now, but who would dare to befriend you if both your father and uncle had been put to death for conspiracy against the Regent ?"

"They would fight before they could be put to death," answered Lotzung proudly.

"If they fought they would soon be overcome. Perhaps you have not heard the sound of firing ?"

Lotzung had heard it, and wondered what it meant. She refrained, however, from expressing any curiosity, and Tuen Fang continued—

"This morning at dawn your uncle and father led a revolt against the Regent."

"My father is at Namcho," rejoined Lotzung, treating his story as a baseless rumour, though she was far from feeling the confidence which she assumed. The young girl had known for a long time the antipathy which her father and uncle entertained for Tsering, and the tale was not improbable.

"They took the Potala," continued Tuen Fang, ignoring her remark ; "but the monks of Sera retook it from them."

"What became of my father and uncle then ?" asked Lotzung incredulously.

"They were both killed."

The young girl started, but regained her self-possession almost immediately.

"I do not believe you," she answered in a low, clear voice, continuing her needlework.

Tuen Fang found the situation decidedly irritating. He had expected to frighten the young girl and make her think that her only hope rested in pleasing him, but he was met by a quiet statement of disbelief in his tale. Was there any one else to whom she looked for assistance? The Amban suddenly remembered Philip, and angered by the thought, exclaimed—

"Perhaps you fancy that the peling Khangsar will come to your aid, but that is impossible, for he was amongst the first to fall."

"If that is all you have to say I shall be glad to be alone again."

"No, it is not all I have to say," rejoined Tuen Fang, greatly incensed, though still retaining his composure. "You have now no friends left in the city. Your father and uncle have died traitors' deaths, and your lover Khangsar has met the fate which every peling deserves who enters Lhasa. You are entirely in my power, and I can make you my wife or my servant as I wish. But I am not vindictive, and you shall be my wife if"—here he advanced towards her with a mincing gait and a would-be gallant air—"if you will confirm the bargain with a kiss."

The old voluptuary bent forward with a leering smile as if to claim the kiss, but Lotzung sprang to her feet, and drawing a dagger from her bosom faced him with her back towards the door.

"Hold, hold!" cried Tuen Fang loudly, and in a moment both the young girl's wrists were seized from behind by Jasi, who had kept the door ajar so as to answer his master's summons without delay. Tuen Fang's yellow countenance—for the sight of the dagger had alarmed him—now relaxed into a smile at the successful issue of his strategy.

"You are caught now, my little spitfire," he said, gloating over his victim. "You may as well throw away the dagger, for it will only be taken from you by force. There is no one to come to your help, not even your beloved peling Khangsar."

Even as he spoke a shadow falling across the doorway attracted the Amban's eyes, and they became glazed with a look of abject terror. For there, pistol in hand, stood the peling whose name had but just that moment passed his lips.

CHAPTER XXVII

JASI, who had his back to the door, observed the Amban's fixed gaze, and turned his head to see what was the cause of it. One look sufficed him. Letting go of Lotzung, he rushed towards a door on the opposite side of the room.

"After him, Mantso, and bring him back alive or dead," said Philip to his servant.

But Mantso was forestalled. Lotzung's mastiff Champa, left to his own devices since the early morning, had been on watch at the gates of the Chinese Embassy, within which he knew his mistress was confined. When Philip entered he slipped in with him, and catching sight of Jasi struggling with Lotzung he uttered a vicious growl and dashed after him as he fled. The sound of his scuffling feet could be heard down a long passage and then up a wooden staircase to the first floor. Three piercing shrieks followed, and all was still. Lotzung, not able to understand what had happened, turned and caught sight of Philip. Running up to him for protection, she threw her arms round him and said—

"Ah, Khangsar! dear Khangsar! Is it really you? The Amban told me you were dead; instead, you have come to save me from him"; and her courage breaking down now that hope had come at last, she hid her face against his shoulder and sobbed aloud. Philip bent down and touched her forehead with his lips.

"Hush, Lotzung," he said, "why should you weep now? The man shall never trouble you again. Rest here while I see to him," and he led her to a seat. Then he turned to Tuen Fang, but before he could utter a word the cowardly Amban was grovelling at his feet.

"Deal with me as you will," he whined, "as long as you do not kill me! I have really done no harm. I was only playing with the child. Be merciful, and let me live!"

The sight of the wretched craven on his knees before him filled Philip with disgust. The man was too despicable to kill, and so far there was no proof that he deserved a death sentence. Besides, he was the ambassador of the Chinese Emperor, and his execution would put the chief Khalon's party in the wrong. Accordingly, Philip called in some of his followers and said—

"Take this man into the next room and keep him there till you receive instructions what to do with him."

They dragged the wretched Tuen Fang, whimpering like a beaten child, out of the room and locked him up in the next apartment. When Philip had put a guard at the door he went in search of Mantso, and met him accompanying four men who carried a body on a stretcher. Champa followed the bier with head erect and swishing tail, giving vent to the anger which was roused within him by emitting low growls of defiance at the corpse. Though the body was covered with a cloth, Philip had no doubt of its identity.

"It is the Ladaki," he said to Mantso. "How did he meet his death?"

"Champa caught him by the leg on the balcony of the first floor, and whilst struggling with the dog he fell over the railing to the ground and broke his neck."

"He will work no further harm then. Take his body to the public burying-place."

At this moment the Junior Amban made his appearance at the gate of the Residency. He was known to favour Rashwa's party, and was so confident that the revolutionists bore him no ill will that he had ridden through the city in his palanquin with only one attendant beyond his bearers. Though Philip was acquainted with him, having met him at the chief Khalon's house, he felt some embarrassment in being found in possession of Tuen Fang's house, with its master locked up in one of his own rooms. An indignity put upon the Senior Amban might be regarded by the Junior Amban as a slight upon himself.

" Is Tuen Fang within ? " asked the new-comer.

" He is within," replied Philip, " but hardly in a condition to attend to business at the present time."

" He must be under the influence of opium again, I conclude. But I must see him, whatever his condition may be. I have here a dispatch from Pekin, appointing me Senior Amban and ordering me to send Tuen Fang back to China under arrest."

Philip's relief was very considerable.

" I congratulate you on your appointment. As for Tuen Fang, he has got no more than he deserves. I found that he had carried off the chief Khalon's niece, and was keeping her a prisoner in this house. So I came to set her free, and at the same time I have put him under arrest pending an inquiry. What is he accused of ? "

" Maladministration in his previous province. As soon as he left, his proceedings became known at Pekin, and the dispatch which I hold is the result."

Philip led the Junior Amban to the room in which Tuen Fang was confined, and leaving him to settle his own affairs as he thought best went on to Lotzung. He found that the young girl had recovered her composure and was anxious to learn the news.

" Is it true that my uncle has revolted against the Regent, and that my father came up from Namcho in time to fight against him ? "

"Quite true," said Philip.

"And how have they fared?"

"The Regent has been killed, and the Junior Amban has orders to send Tuen Fang back to China under arrest."

"Then my poor brother will no longer be ill-treated, and I shall have nothing to fear from Tuen Fang? I have been very unhappy during the last few days, and was driven to despair just before you came and freed me. What can I do to show my gratitude?"

"I will tell you what you can do, Lotzung," said Philip, taking her hand. "You can promise to be my wife."

Lotzung's dark eyes opened wide with astonishment.

"But I was your wife once, and you made me promise that I should be your wife in name only till we reached Lhasa, and then I should cease to be so even in name."

"That was before I knew I loved you."

Lotzung's lips relaxed into a pretty smile.

"And do you love me now, Khangsar?"

"Very dearly, Lotzung."

"Then I will be your wife again," she answered.

"And what will be your reason this time?" asked Philip, moved by a spirit of mischief. "Last time it was simply because you wished to go to Lhasa to see your brother."

"Now it is because I wish to be with you."

"And why do you wish to be with me?"

"Ask Tuen Fang. He knows the reason."

"But you will not tell me?"

"Yes, if you wish me to tell you. It is because I love you!"

There was only one answer to this statement, and Philip gave it promptly. Then he remembered something and said—

"I have a confession to make, Lotzung. I have been deceiving you and every one else with regard to myself."

" You mean that you are not an Eastern Mongol."

" How did you know that ? " the young man asked, much surprised by this apparent act of thought-reading.

" Tuen Fang told me."

" Perhaps he also told you what I was ? "

" He said you were a peling."

" I am an Englishman. Will you still marry me ? "

" I do not know what an Englishman is, but I will be your wife if you will have me."

Philip would doubtless have ratified this statement also in the usual way if Mantso had not made his appearance. He had disposed of Jasi's body, and now awaited his master's orders.

" Get the mandarin's palanquin and take my wife to the chief Khalon's house."

Mantso grinned all over his good-natured countenance on hearing his master speak of Lotzung for the first time by that title, and went to get the palanquin. Philip having seen the young girl into it, set off for the Potala to hear how matters had progressed. He found the streets full of people, everybody turning out of doors as if to celebrate a public holiday. Trumpets and horns were being blown, and banners hung from every window. On the way he met Purdung, his face black with gunpowder and carrying Philip's rifle with a jaunty air.

" Ah, my dear friend Khangsar ! " he exclaimed on seeing Philip. " I have lived a day worth living. What a beautiful gun this is and how wonderfully it shoots. I have settled accounts with many of those rascally monks of Sera, and now I am content. They have asked for terms, and Rashwa has been proclaimed Regent."

" And what of Phala ? "

" He returns to the palace in which he lived before his banishment, and which is always reserved for the father of the Dalai Lama. Our good friend Kalsang has been appointed chamberlain at the Potala."

Now that everything had gone so well for the chief Khalon and his supporters there was no occasion for Philip to proceed any further. In fact, he judged it the wisest course to appear in public as little as possible during the present crisis. According to his own account of himself, he was not a Tibetan, but only an Eastern Mongol. A nation does not like foreigners to take part in their internal troubles, and Tibetans are particularly jealous of such interference on the part of Mongols. Besides, Tsering or Tuen Fang might have spread the report that he was a European. Supposing it got abroad that Rashwa had gained his victory through the help of a peling, his cause might be seriously imperilled by the fact. Accordingly the young man decided to return to his lodgings and wait till the city had settled down to its normal state.

On reaching home the landlord met him in the yard and greeted him with great effusiveness. During the last two or three weeks before Philip's arrest the man had kept carefully out of his way. No doubt he had his suspicions as to the identity of the boy and girl with whom the Eastern Mongol was on such familiar terms, and realized that there would be trouble if the Regent got to know of their visits to his house. But the Regent had been killed, and the party with which his lodger had been associated was triumphant. Consequently there was no attention too great to show his guest. He escorted Philip up to his room on the second floor, prostrating himself at each landing on the way. If Mantso had not made his appearance, the landlord, in his anxiety to ingratiate himself, might have bored the young Englishman with superfluous attentions for another hour.

The faithful Mantso soon prepared a meal, and as Philip

had eaten nothing since the previous evening he did full justice to it. Then, having had no sleep during the night, he threw himself on his bed and fell into a heavy, dreamless slumber. When he awoke, Mantso, who had evidently stationed himself just outside the door, answered his call without a moment's delay.

"Is it time for breakfast, Mantso ?" asked Philip, feeling hungry in spite of the good meal he had made before going to sleep.

"Time for dinner, Kushok," answered Mantso. "It only wants an hour to sunset."

"Then I will get up, eat my dinner, and go to bed again," said Philip. "I have not had enough sleep yet. Have you any news to tell me ?"

"Only that the chief Khalon's niece—I mean the Kushok's wife," replied Mantso, correcting himself slyly, "has sent twice to ask after you. I told the messenger that you were still asleep. The chief Khalon—that is, the Regent—also sent a message saying he wished to see you at his house when you had rested yourself."

Philip would like to have accepted the invitation, but he thought it wiser to refuse. Rashwa must have been hard at work all day, and needed the rest which Philip had already partly taken. Lotzung herself, too, would probably be tired, and so the young man decided not to go.

In spite of the long sleep he had enjoyed during the day Philip spent an excellent night, and regained consciousness with that delicious sense of recuperation which follows healthy slumber. But on opening his eyes his surprise was great to find Lotzung sitting at his bedside.

"Khangsar is not angry with me for coming ?" she inquired with a shade of anxiety in her eyes. "You did not go to my uncle's house last night, as he asked you, and this morning, when you did not appear two hours after dawn, I thought you might be ill, and could keep away no longer."

"You are a good little wife," said Philip, "and I am sorry that I have made you anxious. I did not know it was so late."

"Then you will get up at once, and I will cook your breakfast for you like I used to do on our journey to Lhasa."

Without waiting for Philip's consent to this proposal she ran out of the room to prepare the meal. It was ready by the time he was dressed, Lotzung insisting on serving it herself and waiting on him. At its conclusion a message came from the Regent, saying that he hoped to see Khangsar at his house, or if he was not well enough to go the Regent would come to his lodgings.

"We will go to your uncle's house together," Philip said to Lotzung.

"As Khangsar wishes," the young girl replied.

On reaching the house Lotzung slipped away to her own quarters, and Philip was shown into Rashwa's room. Here he found an informal council consisting of the Regent, Phala, and the three Khalons. They greeted him with much warmth, and Rashwa said—

"I am very glad to see that you sustained no injury in the fighting yesterday. We owe it to your quick-firing muskets and to your personal bravery that we were able to keep the enemy at bay till Tsering was killed. I have called together an informal council of state to put on record their appreciation of your services. But I feel that we owe you something more than thanks. We therefore offer you the appointment of a Khalon of this city."

Such an office was far from being the object of Philip's ambition. Besides, as a foreigner he saw that difficulties might arise if he were appointed. He therefore replied that he thanked them very much for the honour offered him, and regretted that he was unable to accept it.

" Is there any other position which you would prefer ? " asked Phala.

Philip reflected for a moment, and then answered with a smile—

" I should like the position of husband to your daughter. A temporary marriage has already been made, but I wish for a formal contract to which the parents give their consent."

" It shall be as you desire," rejoined Phala, " and I will give a dowry with the bride. As you may have heard, I am going to live in Lhasa, and will therefore bestow my castle at Namcho upon you as a wedding gift."

" And we will make you Deba of the district," added Rashwa.

Philip was too surprised by the offer to reply at once. He had seen enough of Lhasa, and he thought Namcho a very pleasant localty. He would have a fine house and the ruling of a large district, where as Deba he might do much for the prosperity of its inhabitants. But there was one difficulty. The council did not know he was a European, and they must be informed before he could accept the appointment.

" I shall esteem it a great honour to be Deba of Namcho, but I am not a Tibetan."

" There is no law against the office being held by an Eastern Mongol," said Rashwa.

" But I am not even an Eastern Mongol ; I am an Englishman."

This statement produced a silence in the council chamber. At length one of the Khalons said—

" What is an Englishman ? "

" He means that he is a peling," explained Rashwa, using

the title which is applied indifferently to all Europeans. "But whether he is a peling or no, he has done our country a great service. If he took the oath of allegiance to the Government, we could still appoint him Deba of the district."

Philip replied that he would readily take the oath, and that there was only one more point. He was not a Buddhist by religion, and he would like to have a priest of his own persuasion living in Namcho.

"That is a matter which the Dalai Lama alone can decide," said Rashwa. "He is in the next room. I will take you to him."

On being ushered into the Dalai Lama's presence Philip was pleased to see that he was already looking better. Although still extremely frail, there was a little more colour in his cheeks and a brighter look in his eyes than when Philip had seen him in the Potala the previous morning. The boy welcomed his visitor very heartily, and then Rashwa briefly submitted to him the point on which his decision was desired. He answered without a moment's hesitation—

"Khangsar has been of great assistance to our cause, and we cannot withhold our reward because he is not of our religion. Let the priest of his faith live in Namcho. The truth always prevails in the end. If Khangsar's religion should prove more inspired than ours—a possibility which we followers of Buddha cannot believe—it will succeed. On the other hand, if our faith is the only true one, Khangsar's priest will win no converts, and he will end in being converted himself."

"I am content to run that risk," said Philip. "Liberty for my religion is all I ask."

"There is still another matter," continued Rashwa. "Khangsar wishes to marry Lotzung. They would, I know, like you to perform the ceremony, taking advantage of your presence here for its performance."

The boy looked up at Khangsar with a smile.

"So you love my sister Lotzung?" he said. "I am glad of it, for I long ago divined that she loved you. Let her come here now."

Lotzung soon made her appearance, and a pretty colour came to her cheeks when the Dalai Lama told her that Khangsar had asked for her as his wife and wished to be formally married to her at once. He then bade them kneel before him, and after repeating the words of the Buddhist marriage service, put Lotzung's hand in Khangsar's and declared them truly married.

"We will have the wedding feast to-night," said Rashwa, "and I will place a suite of rooms in this house at the disposal of the newly married couple till Khangsar shall find it convenient to set out for Namcho."

It was a quiet wedding feast, for the time did not suffice for elaborate preparations. Only Rashwa's personal friends were present. Lotzung looked very bright and happy. "And so," said Philip laughingly to the young girl when he at length found an opportunity of speaking to her out of hearing of the others, "as you married me the first time to get to Lhasa, you are marrying me a second time to return to Namcho. Will you repudiate the contract when you get there?"

The young bride smiled prettily.

"You know that I am marrying you because I love you, and wish to follow you wherever you go, leaving all my relations and even my dear brother to be with you."

The following day Philip began to get together a caravan for his journey to Namcho. According to the usual Tibetan custom, where a Government official was concerned, the cost of the caravan was defrayed at the public expense, and Rashwa insisted that it should be in every way worthy of the office he held. Philip left Lhasa in a very different fashion to that in which he had entered it. Lotzung and himself were mounted on excellent horses, Mantso was well provided for, and a numerous train of mules and yaks carried the baggage. Esa, grown fat again with the indolent life of a town, and Phendi, his melancholy eyes gleaming with a pleased light at the prospect of joining his former master, had offered themselves as soon as they heard that Philip wanted muledrivers, and were taken permanently into his service. Champa, now quite recovered from Jasi's attempt to poison him, galloped up and down the line, barking his appreciation of the handsome caravan which had been provided for the husband of his mistress.

Only one incident on the journey to Namcho needs recording. At the top of one of the passes they came across the camp of a small detachment of Chinese soldiers. In front of one of the tents stood a coffin, which four of the men were using as a gaming table. Philip's curiosity being awakened, he approached them and said:- "Is there a corpse within that coffin?"

One of the men nodded.

"Who is it?" he continued.

"Tuen Fang, the late Senior Amban. We found him dead one morning when we went to call him."

"And now you are taking his body back to China. What was the cause of his death?"

"Who can tell? All we know is that he smoked opium so much at night-time that he could hardly sit his horse during the day."

Such was the end of the mandarin who had held so many high offices, and had consistently abused the trust reposed in him. Philip resumed his journey without telling Lotzung what he had heard. It was enough for him to know that they need now fear no attempt at revenge on the part of Tuen Fang.

On their last day's march, eight weeks after leaving Lhasa, while they were still some six miles from the castle, a horseman came galloping across the plain full speed towards them.

"That is Maru!" exclaimed Lotzung joyfully.

"You have good eyes, Lotzung, if you can distingiush your brother at that distance," answered Philip.

"I know his seat on horseback," replied Lotzung, and truly enough from the cloud of dust raised by his horse's feet the young boy at length emerged, pulled up his animal with practised suddenness on his haunches a few feet in front of them, and gave the pair a joyous greeting.

"I have been expecting you the last two days," he said, "and I thought you were never coming. You have travelled very slowly."

Philip explained that it was due to the size of the caravan, and then asked Maru for his news. He told them that his mother had been apprised of their coming by special messenger from Phala, and had been instructed to return to Lhasa as soon as the animals forming the caravan were sufficiently rested.

"I shall be glad to get to Lhasa," said Maru. "Father ought to have taken me with him when he went, and let me fight against the wicked Regent."

Although Maru was as full as ever of masculine superiority, he treated his sister with greater respect in her position as a married woman. A mile from the castle the retinue of the late Deba came out to escort their new master, and Philip entered his residence in full state. Phagmo had prepared a suite of rooms for them, and during the three days which elapsed before she set out with her son to Lhasa did all she could for the comfort of the bride and bridegroom.

Two months after the departure of Phagmo and her son Philip was in the courtyard one morning watching Lotzung feed her pigeons, as on the first occasion when he saw her there. He was admiring the pretty smile on her lips and the light in her dark eyes when the sound of approaching horsemen attracted her attention.

" I wonder who is coming, Khangsar ? " she exclaimed. Philip had definitely adopted the Mongol name which he had at first assumed for convenience.

" You will see in a minute," replied Philip, smiling at her curiosity.

The words had hardly left his lips when under the archway rode a grey-haired man who, though in Tibetan costume, was evidently not a Tibetan. At a short distance followed Philip's mounted retainers. On seeing Philip, the visitor jumped off his horse and came towards him with outstretched hands.

" My dear Harwood, how good of you to send an escort for me. A friend had just arrived at Ta-chien-lu to take my work, while I had leave of absence. I started the day after I got your letter, and have travelled as fast as my little caravan could take me ever since. All through your district I have been treated with the greatest kindness. But this must be your wife. Please make me known to her."

" This, Lotzung, is Mr. Ransome, a lama of the Church to which I belong. You will like him, in spite of his professing a different faith to your own."

Lotzung was at once attracted by the elderly lama, who looked at her with such kind eyes.

" I see that your wife is like her namesakes, the gentle creatures she was feeding when my arrival interrupted her. We are friends already, are we not ? "

Lotzung smilingly assented, and the traveller was taken into the castle, which was to be his home till a mission house could be built in Namcho. There is no occasion to follow Philip and his fortunes any further. Mr. Ransome persuaded the young couple to be married according to the ritual of the English Church, Lotzung readily consenting to any ties which bound her husband more closely to her. As to the struggle which ensued between the English priest and the lamas of Buddhism for spiritual ascendancy in the district, nothing more need be said than that, owing to the unfailing tact and good-nature of Mr. Ransome, it was carried on without rancour, and if he did not make many converts he won a number of friends even in the ranks of his religious opponents.

THE END